Introduction to
MODERN DANCE TECHNIQUES

JOSHUA LEGG

Cunningham, Dunham, Graham
Hawkins, Horton, Humphrey, Limón
Nikolais/Louis, Taylor

Princeton Book Company, Publishers
Hightstown, NJ
www.dancehorizons.com

Cover design, interior design and composition by Elizabeth Helmetsie

Library of Congress Cataloging-In-Publication Data
Legg, Joshua.
   Introduction to modern dance techniques / Joshua Legg.
     p. : ill. ; cm.
   "Cunningham, Dunham, Graham, Hawkins, Horton, Humphrey, Limón, Nikolais/Louis, Taylor."
   Includes bibliographical references.
   ISBN: 978-0-87127-325-3

   1. Modern dance—Study and teaching (Higher) 2. Modern dance—History.
I. Title. II. Title: Modern dance techniques

GV1783 .L45 2011
792.8/076
ISBN 978-0-87127-3253

Princeton Book Company, Publishers
614 Route 130
Hightstown, NJ 08520

www.dancehorizons.com

CONTENTS

There's something about the technique, the hand of these prime movers that we must not lose. People who understood how they placed the torso over the hips . . . how they encouraged the breathing . . . how they themselves inhabited a gesture . . .

—Bill T. Jones, choreographer, in *Limón: A Life Beyond Words*

This book is dedicated to my ancestors in dance

especially

Melissa Hayden
who taught me how to see dance
as it happens in the human body

ACKNOWLEDGEMENTS

S ometimes as an artist-academic, we have the opportunity to participate in a project that radically alters our understanding of our art form—that causes us to rethink both how we make art and how we teach the artistic process to our students. Developing this book has been such a project for me.

My publisher, Charles Woodford at Princeton Book Company, had the vision for a comparative look at modern dance techniques, and he has been a wonderful source of ideas and information. He and my editor, Connie Woodford, have been tremendously helpful in manifesting this project, and I appreciate their guidance, patience, and support.

The editorial teams at *Dance Teacher* and *Dance Spirit* magazines provided enormous encouragement and support during the time I was writing for them, and they prepared me for this project. Kat Holmes in particular helped me to shape our "Master Class Series"—the inspiration for this present work.

Tremendous appreciation goes to the dance artists who shared their insights into the work of the legendary dancemakers discussed in this book. Everyone I interviewed was generous in both time and spirit—agreeing to numerous (and sometimes lengthy) interviews, and they are the source of much of the information and class material presented here. In particular, it was an honor to have my own teachers Keith Lee (Horton), and Ting-Yu Chen (post-Judson) participate in this project. Kim Gibilisco's contributions made several aspects of the process possible, and I am grateful for her involvement. Ann Vachon and Renata Celichowska went above and beyond the call in their editorial contributions to Chapter 4. I am also indebted to Norton Owen as well for his help in identifying resources for Chapter 1, and the photos that appear throughout the book from the Jacob's Pillow archives.

Special thanks to Katherine Dunham and John Pratt's daughter, Marie-Christine Dunham Pratt, for her assistance in Chapter 3. In addition to her own invaluable insights, she provided much needed correction to biographical inaccuracies perpetuated by past authors, and helped me to avoid perpetuating my own.

During my three years teaching dance at Harvard University, I had the great fortune to work alongside Ruth Andrien, Christine Dakin, and Heather Watts while they served as visiting artists and lecturers. Their gifts as brilliant artists are matched by fierce intellects that pushed me to grow in extraordinary ways. Collectively, my experience with these women taught me the most important lesson of my career: there is no division between artist and intellectual. Those who achieve greatness in either area are, ultimately, both.

I am grateful to Harvard University's Committee on the Dramatic Arts, and the Office for the Arts, for providing me an extraordinary academic and artistic home. Elizabeth Bergmann, director of Harvard's dance program, is a visionary who has contributed much to contemporary dance as an educator and artist, and to my own dance experience. Jessica C. Flores and Susan Larson helped me to separate fact from fiction so that dance would always be the thing that mattered. Scott Lozier made it all make sense so often. Peter Richards stands out as the greatest of mentors for helping me come to understand the kind of artist I already was. Thanks also go to the Lamont Library staff for supporting my early research. Working with my students at Harvard (especially Molly Altenburg, Joanna Binney, Lauren Chin, Madelyn Ho, Larissa Koch, Julia Lindpaintner, and Claudia Schreier) was a particular honor. They never let me settle for the status quo, and that's made all the difference. Molly Altenburg was my editorial assistant early in this project and helped to shape part of its direction.

My dancer/writer comrades at Shenandoah University, Rosemary Green and Mary Robare, were always great sources of ideas and inspiration. Robyn Schroth was my first teaching mentor, and I'm still convinced that she is the guru of pedagogy and techniques of teaching dance. I am grateful to the Dance Division at Shenandoah—both faculty and students—for their interest and support as I worked on this book, presented lectures, and participated in other events around campus during my early writing process. My longtime colleague, Nicole Lichty, was a vital sounding board for much of this project. Thanks to Shenandoah faculty members Ting-Yu Chen and Elijah Gibson for serving as the models for technique photos in Chapters 2 and 3.

During this project, I was also fortunate to join the faculty of Theatre and Dance at Northwestern State University of Louisiana as a visiting assistant professor of dance. Thanks to Dr. Vicki Parrish for being a wonderful mentor, and the rest of the faculty for their support. Moreover, my students Kwame Lilly, Cody Olsen, Victoria Olivier, and Dominque Terrell asked those questions that inspire and move an artist/educator.

Last, thanks to my parents, for unwavering support of my life in art. They made it possible.

INTRODUCTION

··

The White House was the last place I had expected to meet Erick Hawkins, but there we were together, as he was making his way to his seat the day he received the National Medal of Arts from the President. He was clearly pleased that a dancer should be interning for the Clinton Administration, but I have to admit that I can't recall much of our brief conversation. I was too busy observing Hawkins' legendary gracefulness—a gracefulness he still possessed in the final weeks of his life. The turn of his head, even then, was extraordinary. The freedom—that trained and studied sense of "doing and not doing"—that had long been Hawkins' signature was apparent even in that simple journey across the White House lawn.

In the days following that chance meeting, I came to understand that dance training is not simply about artistic development. As I experienced my own training path from ballet to modern, and through varying degrees of contact with all the techniques and styles introduced in this book, I began to recognize that dance technique adapts our facilities to levels of communication and emotion that perhaps few nondancers ever experience. It trains us to feel and to express the deepest aspects of the self and of humanity—all through the conduit of dance movement.

That attention to who we are at the core, to the inner landscape of a person and how we interact with the world around us, plays a central role in this book because that attention drove the progenitors of these techniques and styles. From Martha Graham's illustrations of the darkness of the human psyche to Katherine Dunham's empowerment of the soul and Alwin Nikolais' examination of man as a component in the universal machine, each of these dancemakers taught us something about ourselves through their technique and choreography.

The Background of This Book

In 2006, I began writing a series of articles for *Dance Spirit* magazine to prepare students for their first master-class experience in the techniques and styles of Trisha Brown, Merce Cunningham, Katherine Dunham, Martha Graham, Lester Horton, and José Limón. As colleagues began to tell me how they were using the articles in their own technique and dance history courses, our conversations merged into discourses on pedagogy and teaching methodologies. In time, I noticed that my own teaching was evolving from the work I was doing outside the studio, and I finally found a deeper appreciation for dance training—it was no longer something I *had* to do and became something I actually *enjoy* doing as part of my involvement in the art form.

In recent years, two pivotal texts have been released that have made the job of teaching and discussing technique, pedagogy, and teaching methodologies much easier. Jan Erkert's *Harnessing the Wind: The Art of Teaching Modern Dance* brought methods for preparing students to become teachers into a new era, and provided sound ideas that can be used by any teacher regardless of whether we embrace a classic or eclectic approach to modern and postmodern training. *The Body Eclectic: Evolving Practices in Dance Training* by Melanie Bales and Rebecca Nettl-Fiol took a scholarly look at how we prepare for the action and/or art of dance in the postmodern era—an era they aptly renamed *post-Judson*.

What still seems to be lacking in the field of dance studies, however, is a scholarly examination of a broad spectrum of the classic modern techniques that also provides practical studio applications. While there are excellent texts on the individual techniques of Katherine Dunham, Doris Humphrey, and several others, many of them are increasingly out of print. Moreover, technique and pedagogy teachers have said that a single introductory source for these techniques and styles would be useful. That desire makes sense to me. As English faculties have long relied on comparative literature texts, it stands to reason that the dance field could benefit from a variety of comparative texts (and DVDs) on a range of relevant topics. This is particularly true as dancers and dance theorists have been talking about "dance as text" and "reading choreography"[1] for decades. A comparative dance source should help students to develop a critical, aesthetic literacy for not only what they "read" on stage or film, but also more importantly for what they experience within their own body, mind, and spirit as they themselves delve deeper into this art form.

Additionally, I have tried to place the generation of dance technique in the context of its historical era and cultural climate. We thus not only see the interconnectedness of choreography with American history, but also consider the development of technical training in the same light. In Chapter 3, for example, technical development is seen against the backdrop of Jim Crow laws, where physical expression of cultural attitude and awareness become a source of social liberation.

Structure and Usage of This Text

Designed with beginning modern dance students and their teachers in mind, *Introduction to Modern Dance Techniques* is an examination of the art form's foundations. Beginning with an exploration of dance training in the period between classical ballet and the establishment of what we now call classic modern dance, we will trace the development of some of the classic techniques and styles that have profoundly shaped modern dance training and choreography.

The book is divided into teaching units, with each chapter pairing compatible or contrasting training systems, and suggesting ways that students can prepare for an encounter with a particular technique.

Chapter 1 is an illustration of training methodologies in America and Europe that were prevalent in the era between the dominance of classical ballet and the rise of modernism.

Chapters 2–6 then break our nine focal tehniques and styles into teaching units. While this breakdown follows a largely (although not entirely) chronological framework, it also provides an interesting, organic series of pairings—some in stark contrast and others in compliment. In Chapter 2, there is the Apollonian-Dionysian set of opposites in Doris Humphrey and Martha Graham, while Chapter 3 is a comparison of quite compatible social philosophies driving the creative work of Katherine Dunham and Lester Horton. Erick Hawkins and José Limón might have been content with just accepting the legacy of their mentors, but we discover otherwise in Chapter 4. The dancemakers in Chapter 5—Merce Cunningham, and Alwin Nikolais and Murray Louis— long stretched the limits of modern dance ever forward. Then in Chapter 6, we see how Paul Taylor led us to ways of dancing beyond modernism.

After a brief discussion about each choreographer, the spotlight is turned to the technique itself with sample class materials based on the work of each artist. The book also includes ideas for experimentation so that students can begin developing an aesthetic sense for not only what is pleasing to their artistic eye, but also for what technical ideas are exciting while their own body is in motion. **Chapter 7** presents a brief consideration of how dance training is currently approached.

Each section also includes **Core Ideas**, a series of journaling and discussion topics students should consider prior to their first encounter in each training system. Some of these include brief observation assignments, completed outside the studio, to enhance the understanding of the core principles of the training modalities. There are also experiments to help students physically explore certain philosophical ideas through improvisation.

Technical Genesis includes biographical sketches on the choreographer with brief discussions of their choreographies and companies. Focus is then given to the evolution and core principles of each training system. With each methodology, I am presenting class material in a manner that respects the way the progenitors wanted their work represented. Some of these techniques were codified, others were not. In cases like Erick Hawkins (who did not want his system codified), movement experiments rather than a series of movement sequences are provided to assist the student in a physical exploration of certain ideas central to the technique.

Final Questions and Experiments address basic ideas that students can use to further their understanding of the material presented in the section.

Appendices A, B and C include considerations on efficient movement and cross-training, improvisation, somatic work, and ideas for ways to use this text in a variety of courses.

Far from being a comprehensive examination of the techniques that were created during this period in modern dance—Helen Tamiris and Anna Sokolow are absent, the Laban-Wigman-Holm lineage is discussed only with regard to the Nikolais/Louis tradition, and none of the training methodologies of the leftist dance movement are introduced.

This book is also not an in-depth exploration of those techniques and styles that are presented here. The criteria I used in making final decisions for which techniques and styles to include were fairly straightforward. The primary requirement was a matter of access. The systems here are living techniques, still practiced internationally in companies, professional schools, and universities; students or teachers can still easily connect with experts on each technique. In fact, by exploring the training philosophies and exercises in this book, students will gain a better sense of the movement aesthetics that resonate in their body. That, in turn, should serve as a springboard into deeper explorations of dance training.

Why Do We Study Technique?

....

Class Discussion Questions

1. How do you define what it means to be a dancer?

2. Why do we study dance technique? Is it a requirement that you want to be a professional dancer in order to study dance? Is it even necessary that you want to perform at all in order to train in dance?

3. In what ways do you think dance training is similar to training in sports, music, and acting?

4. How do we define technique, and what are the differences between technique and style?

....

There are no correct answers to the questions above. They are simply designed to motivate your thinking. Whether you are taking a dance course or just want to know more about the work of a particular choreographer, your answers to these questions will help you gain more from the ideas you are about to encounter.

As an example I will share my response to number two: why do we study dance technique? First, I don't believe that we have to desire a professional career in dance or even that we must desire performance opportunities in order to attend technique classes. As I often tell my students, the most important reason I know for studying technique is the thrill, the pure joy, of being an embodied spirit moving through time and space in some inspired form of motion. If there isn't joy, then the movement sequences are just mechanics, and we might as well go to the gym.

Here are some of my other answers; you may be in the process of developing your own: 1. to experience ideas about dance in the most practical way possible, 2. exposure to different techniques dispels the idea that there is only one generic modern dance technique, 3. to discover the kind of movement systems that resonate with us, pointing the way to further exploration, and 4. professional development—specifically, training in classic modern techniques and styles paves the way to performing the classic works created by these choreographers.

This brings up another question: *what is technique?* In his doctoral dissertation, my first Graham teacher, Barry Fischer, defined technique as

> a codified systematic series of movement exercises within the parameter of a particular style of dance. This is utilized by the dancers to develop their instrument (body) for strength and kinesthetic memory unique to the particular style of dance.[2]

In the context of examining a singular approach to movement like Graham's, that definition is quite effective. Considering other classic modern techniques like Humphrey and Limón, that definition seems less applicable (especially since not all techniques are codified). It also doesn't take into consideration that some systems also place an emphasis on creative training in addition to the expected physical development of the dancing body. Certainly, too, that definition doesn't extend to current training trends as "during the Judson period, questions about what constituted a dancing body, a dance vocabulary, or a dance style elicited many suggestions depending on who answered . . ."[3] Those questions and their responses naturally influence our viewpoint today. All of this together leads me to propose this definition:

• •

Technique
A technique is a system or method that trains the body-mind-spirit toward a series of ideas that may or may not have a performative end in sight. It is a path or developmental course designed for exploration, and ultimately, for mastery of the system's central ideas.

• •

What then is the difference between technique and style? *Style influences how choreographic or performance choices motivate (or activate) the technical foundation.* A perfect illustration is the choreographic bodies of Alwin Nikolais and Murray Louis. All their dancers were trained in the same technique, but both dance makers activated that training and vocabulary in vastly different ways. Looking at the work of a single choreographer, Martha Graham's *El Penitente* and *Letter to the World* premiered at the same Bennington College concert in 1940.[4] While she clearly utilized the same technical vocabulary, the works are quite distinct from one another owing to stylistic choices in choreography and performance.

How Are Techniques Created?

The techniques that are presented here were created in roughly two ways: they were either *generated* prior to starting the choreographic process, or they were *retrogenerated* by extrapolating ideas from existing choreography. Erick Hawkins, for example, had suffered two significant injuries in his career before establishing his own company. Those injuries led him to new philosophies and ways of moving before he really set to work creating a body of choreography. Martha Graham's process was (largely, although not entirely) the opposite: she began with making dances. Then, by deconstructing her own work, she retrogenerated (created in reverse) a process and a vocabulary for both systematically training dancers and making new dances based on components of existing work. Regardless of the originating process, these systems of movement—systems of training—reveal ideas that the individual artists were exploring about how the human body moves.

Philosophical ideas and principles of movement evolved out of research and experimentation. How those ideas, observations, and movement principles played out in the development of technique and style, in turn, helped to facilitate the emerging choreographic ideas and voices. Many of these artists were searching for a natural kind of movement and much of their work incorporated the latest scientific understandings of anatomy and kinesiology.

As much as dance training develops our flexibility, strength, coordination, and dexterity, it also establishes a body-mind-spirit connection that promotes a facile link to *metakinesis*: "the theory that the physical and the psychical are merely two aspects of a single underlying reality."[5] Without these modern training methodologies, modern dance as an art form would not have developed as it has. We might never have progressed from creating the well-intentioned barefoot versions of ballets and folk dances that marked the early period of the art form. The genesis of these modern training systems gave us radically new ways to prepare and execute movement.

That is critical in the making of a dancer because we don't learn to perform in a vacuum on stage. *We begin our performance training in our first technique lesson.* Stage experience is certainly crucial if artistic performance in front of an audience is the ultimate goal of the dancer, but the time on stage isn't where it begins. It is in the technique class that we gain the skills and craft our artistic direction—and where the body-mind-spirit connection is established. Scales, arpeggios, and theory are some of the fundamentals required in the artistic development of a musician who then becomes a composer. So, too, dance technique creates a dance artist who may move on to performance and/or choreographic prowess. The stage is then the artist's playground.

Division of Modern Approaches to Dance

In our technical exploration, recognizing the underlying historical periods will help to put the experience in context.

1880–1923 Early Modern. This period could also be called Modern Romanticism, "New Dance," and Expressionism. It was a time of great evolution and revolution in dance, and while it did not give us the first modern dance technique, it was certainly paramount in getting us close to that new way of preparing for dance.

1923–1946 Central Modern. The American Dance Frontier might be a more apt descriptor for this time in dance. Dancemakers in both ballet and modern, like Balanchine, Graham, and Humphrey, were looking for their own version of what American dance looked like, how we prepare for it, and how we create it. At the same time, workers and unionists paired with leftist dancers to fashion dance as a tool for radical, populist statement.

1946–1957 Late Modern. This era brought us clarity of abstraction and the rise of the avant-garde and postmodernism. Balanchine eschewed narrative and used classical ballet technique to create modernist dance (Agon), while Nikolais challenged our sense of "front" in dance by eliminating presentation. Cunningham introduced chance operations, and Taylor made us question what constitutes dance with 1957's *7 New Dances*—a work pared of any dance movement, sequenced by postures rather than steps, all accented by stillness.

Conclusion

Martha Graham said that it takes ten years to make a dancer. If that's true—then the same also holds true for dance teachers. Certainly both are extraordinary lifelong journeys where we are always evolving, being shaped and reshaped in all aspects of our being by this art form even as we try to shape it. It is so much like a forge, constantly expanding the ways we are able to express our humanity.

Joshua Legg
Winchester, Virginia
May 2011

Works Cited

Bales, M. & Nettl-Fiol, R. (Eds.) (2008). *The Body Eclectic: Evolving practices in dance training*. Urbana: University of Illinois Press.

Clark, V. A. & Johnson, S. E. (2005). *Kaiso! Writings by and about Katherine Dunham*. Madison: The University of Wisconsin Press.

de Mille, A. (1991). *Martha: The life and work of Martha Graham*. New York: Random House.

Fischer, B. (1986). *Graham's Dance Steps in the Street and selected early technique: Principles of reconstructing choreography from videotape*. Ann Arbor: University Microfilms International.

Martin, J. (1972). *The Modern Dance*. New York: Dance Horizons.

A note about voice in this text: Dance is at once a public and personal act, and while I have tried to maintain scholarly perspective and to limit what could be considered editorializing, weaving the first-person perspective/experience through various parts of the text has been impossible to avoid. Additionally, some of the classroom materials presented are my own and are based on more than twenty years of living inside certain training practices.   *JL*

The Expressionists

François Delsarte
Emile Jaques-Dalcroze
Isadora Duncan
Denishawn

The culture of the form and movement of the body is practiced today in two ways: by gymnastics and by dancing. Both should go together, for without gymnastics, without the healthy and methodical development of the body, the real dance is unattainable. . . . Into a body that has been harmoniously developed and brought to its highest degree of energy, the spirit of dancing enters. Movement and culture of his body form the aim of the gymnast; for the dancer they are only the means.

—Isadora Duncan, *The Art of the Dance*

In the decades following the American Civil War, tremendous global innovations were taking place in industry, the sciences, and healthcare concurrent with shifts in the humanities and the arts. The growing white middle and upper classes increasingly had (at least some) disposable income to afford leisure activities, as attention to physical fitness grew during the 1890s when "cycling, swimming, golf, and tennis were all at the height of fashion. For women, in particular, crushed by corsets and wearing mutton sleeves as big as balloons, a healthy, flexible body was beginning to look like a good thing."[1] It was in this atmosphere that a "new dance" was emerging as much from a rejection of social strictures as from dissatisfaction with ballet. Dance historian Jack Anderson also notes that "[t]he champions of physical education helped to prepare the way for modern

Ruth St. Denis and Ted Shawn in their first duet, Ourieda, a Romance of the Desert *(1914).*

dance, and gymnastic exercises often served as technical starting points for young women who longed to dance."[2] In fact, we know that by the 1880s, women's colleges were teaching some form of gymnastics set to music, and that in 1887 Dr. Dudley Sargent had incorporated "aesthetic dance" into the women's physical education classes at the Harvard Summer School.[3] We also know that by 1901, "dance was included in the convention programs of the American Physical Education Association [precursor to the current American Alliance for Health, Physical Education, Recreation and Dance]."[4] In his 1914 treatise *Aesthetic Dance*, Emil Rath noted:

> Music and rhythmic bodily movement are twin sisters of art, as they have come into existence simultaneously. . . . Dancing has, in fact, done much to aid the development of music by supplying novel movements as suggestions for new forms of musical composition . . . dance had to be contented for many years with ordinary musical accompaniment suitable to its characteristic movements. Yet today we see in the artistic work of Isadora Duncan, Maud Allen, and others the use of a form of dancing which strives to portray in movements what the music master expresses in his compositions—interpretative dancing.[5]

In this chapter, as we explore the early modern period, we will see the importance that leaders in this era placed on music and musicality in their physical training methods, and in their choreography. Music visualizations were paramount in both aesthetic and interpretive dance forms. In Chapter 2, we will see how pioneers like Martha Graham and Doris Humphrey came to place dance first in their works—how technique came to support movement rather than serve the music. (Even when Humphrey embraced musicality in her choreography, it was about the movement and the content, not an illustration of the music with her dancers' bodies.)

François Delsarte

Much of the movement training at the time (and in fact, the training that occurred well into the early twentieth century) was heavily influenced by the ideas of François Delsarte (1811–1871), the French voice teacher who developed an intricate theory of gesture and posture that he taught beginning in 1839. Because he died before compiling his thoughts in writing, several of his disciples passed on their interpretation of his teachings. When his system reached America, it became a "theory, a philosophy, and, ultimately, something of a cult."[6] The gymnastics that became central to much of the Delsarte training in America was artificially overlaid on his system, according to Genevieve Stebbins, author of *The Delsarte System of Expression*:

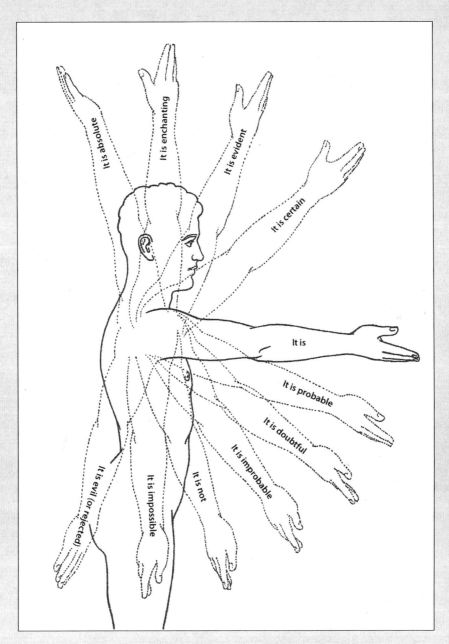

Note the scope of statements made at various points along the single arching gesture of the arm in this illustration from Ted Shawn's book Every Little Movement: A Book About François Delsarte *(1948).*

Attitude EX-ex	**Attitude NOR-ex**	**Attitude CON-ex**
Head raised and turned away from object or person	*Head raised but not turned in either direction*	*Head raised but turned towards object or person*
Pride or revulsion	*Exaltation, ecstasy*	*Abandon or vulgar familiarity*

Attitude EX-nor	**Attitude NOR-nor**	**Attitude CON-nor**
Head turned away from object or person	*Head facing the object or person*	*Head turned toward object or person*
Adverse criticism or a sensual examination	*Normal state*	*Favorable criticism or tenderness*

Attitude EX-con	**Attitude NOR-con**	**Attitude CON-con**
Head lowered away from object or person	*Head lowered but facing front*	*Head lowered but towards object or person*
Suspicion	*Reflection, meditation*	*Veneration or maternal tenderness*

The slightest tilt of the head or glance of the eyes has specific meaning in Delsarte's work. Illustration from Ted Shawn's book Every Little Movement: A Book About François Delsarte *(1948).*

Delsarte, as far as I know, did not elaborate any gymnastic system to develop perfectly body and soul. But he did teach a few gymnastic exercises; not as a means of physical culture, but to give his pupils perfect freedom of movement in gesture . . . [and through his principles] we have all the elements essential to evolve beauty of form, graceful motion, and artistic presentation.[7]

Beginning with the breath and radiating outward to every gesture, even to every movement of the eyes, the actions involved the rise of positive assertion and the fall of negative, which he called attitude. Oppositions, parallelisms, and successions comprised the Great Orders of Movement, and each movement related to the body's center by moving outward or inward toward it, or was balanced.[8] The other thing that is clear is that in whatever form(s) Delsarte's system was practiced in the United States, his ideas greatly influenced artistic development in the first decades of the twentieth century—Isadora Duncan, Ruth St. Denis, and Ted Shawn (in particular) embodied his system.

Emile Jaques-Dalcroze

Emile Jaques-Dalcroze (1865–1950), a composer whose works were beginning to receive popular production, became a professor of harmony at the Conservatoire in Geneva (1891), where he was also charged with teaching solfège. In those early teaching days, Dalcroze

noticed that the ears of my pupils were not able to appreciate the chords which they had to write, and I concluded that the flaw in the conventional method of training is that pupils are not given experience of chords at the beginning of their studies—when brain and body are developing along parallel lines, the one constantly communicating its impressions and sensations to the other—but that this experience is withheld until the time arrives to express the results in writing.[9]

As Dalcroze continued his early observations and was making changes to his teaching practices, he also had occasion to observe small children and the difficulty they had "following, while marching, a very slow movement in music, in halting or stepping out suddenly at command, in relaxing their limbs after an anxious moment, in taking their bearings and following each other's movements on being taught the gestures to accompany a song."[10] He came to see that musical rhythm was not simply a mental process/experience, but that it was physical in nature. This led him to determine that not only was ear and voice training important for children, but that the body required rhythmic training—students needed to be trained to move and think rhythmically. In *The Importance of Being Rhythmic*, Jo Pennington explained that there is a

> distinction between rhythm and meter—two words hopelessly confused in the average mind. They do not by any means have the same meaning though meter is part of rhythm. Meter is the measurement of regular intervals of time; rhythm deals with unequal intervals. . . . Rhythm may be defined as symmetry of movement and accent, whereas meter is measurement of movement and accent.[11]

Dalcroze noted that "by accustoming the body to regular symmetrical movements under the control of eye and muscular senses, a feeling for musical rhythm may be produced in an a-rhythmic pupil."[12]

In his quest to help a-rhythmic students acquire rhythm and then become capable of polyrhythm, he "began to organize total body responses to musical rhythms. The exercises began with walking, at first in two-, three-, and four-beat measures. Then came considerations of accent and arrangements of rhythmic figures within the measure, using the arms to delineate other rhythms"[13] and preceded musical studies in his system.

The system, *la rythmique*, is better known as eurythmics—a body-mind harmony allowing stabilized rhythmic motion of any single body part, or parts in concert. He found resonance in Delsarte's idea that "[t]o each spiritual function there responds a function of the body; to each big function of the body corresponds a spiritual act,"[14] and this drove much of Dalcroze's development of eurhythmics.

As early as 1906, Dalcroze was talking about *gymnastique rythmique* (rhythmic movement), and he eventually turned his attention to dance as a source of ideas for extending his range of exercises. In 1912, he stated in his essay *How to Revive Dancing*:

> My purpose is to determine within what limits the art of dancing may approach, in its conception and by purely human means, governed by physiological laws, the art, at present in full course of development, from which it very directly derives, namely, music.

and that

> [D]ancing is the art of expressing emotion by means of rhythmic bodily movements . . . once we admit that the art of dancing involves a fusion of rhythmic sounds and movement . . . we are forced to the conclusion that the state of decadence in which dancing has sunk in our time is due partly

to the exaggerated development of virtuosity at the expense of expression, and partly to the absolute negation of the principle of unity of corporal plastique and musical rhythm.[15]

Dalcroze was also not particularly a fan of ballet, or of Duncan's dance, as he found her choreography lacking in musical influence.

In *The Importance of Being Rhythmic*, Pennington provided a small sample program (the text from a lecture-demonstration) of Dalcroze Eurythmics:

Program of a Demonstration Lesson in Dalcroze Eurythmics[16]

- General response to music; expressing tempo and tone quality.
- Exercises of attention and inhibition.
  Marching, at command "hop" one step backward.
  Silent counting.
- Arm movements to indicate measure. From 2 to 12 beats in a measure.
- Note values.
  Quarter notes to quintuplets.
  Whole notes up to 8 beats.
  Syncopations.
- Conducting; changes of measure, pathetic accent, accelerando, ritardando.
- Phrasing.
- "Realization" of rhythms.
- "Realization" in canon, the pupils one measure after the piano.
- Independence of control.

A plastique exercise.

■ Rhythmic counterpoint; theme by piano, counterpoint (the unplayed note values) realized by pupils in quarter notes, eighth notes, and triplets.

NOTE: The music for all of the exercise is improvised. The word "hop" is used as a signal to the pupils to make some change in the exercise as previously directed. In this program, the word "realize" is used in the sense of expressing rhythms by movements of the body.

In his attention to dancing, Dalcroze desired practictioners to portray music through "interpretive movement," from which the term plastique arose—by which he meant expressive movement (see the Denishawn section below for a variation on a plastique). People around the world became interested in his approach to movement and music—although critics frequently insisted it was not dance—and as early as 1910, dancers were entering Dalcroze's school in Hellerau. Marie Rambert (eventual founder of London's Rambert Ballet, now Rambert Dance Company) was one such dancer, whom Dalcroze greatly respected, giving her teaching assignments at the school. She was so competent that Diaghilev asked her to help Nijinsky overcome the rhythmic challenges in Stravinsky's *Le Sacre du Printemps* (the realization of the rhythm was Nijinsky's goal in choreographing the work). Rambert assisted Nijinsky "in training the dancers and also performed with them. . . . The power of the music overshadowed the effect of the dance, but the movement according to Dalcroze principles was evident."[17] Other ballet companies like the Paris Opéra also began to train their dancers in Dalcroze, and those working with the "new dance" did as well. Although Rudolf von Laban did not collaborate with Dalcroze, Laban's own protégée, Mary Wigman, and in turn her protégée, Hanya Holm, both completed the teacher-training program at Hellerau. (For more about the German tradition of modern dance, see the Nikolais/Louis segment of Chapter 5.) Of course, Dalcroze's system was also taught at Denishawn (see Denishawn below).

Isadora Duncan

While Isadora Duncan (1877–1927) ultimately denied familiarity with Delsarte's principles, two of her biographers (Peter Kurth and Millicent Dillon) insist that similarities in her work to his system indicate that Duncan's assertion is not plausible. Of particular note were Duncan's statements about the connection between the body and the "inner man" as well as the nature of art that are nearly identical to Delsarte's. In an 1898 interview, "Duncan hailed Delsarte as 'the master of all principles of flexibility, and lightness of the body.'"[18]

That "lightness of body" would have been particularly interesting to Duncan for its inherent potential for new modes of movement. Prior to the turn of the century, Duncan had studied ballet and found it unnatural. The pointe shoes and corsets—the technique itself—seemed to her to deform the beautiful woman's body. She was "the first great romanticist, the first apostle of freedom and democracy in her art, the liberator from sterile conventions."[19] In terms of her work, Duncan is better remembered for her brilliant performances (barefoot and corsetless in robes or tunics with flesh revealed) and her ideas about children's education than for creating a movement vocabulary or teaching system that might be called a technique—or even for employing "virtuosity of any kind."[20] While she sought to allow the element of expressional movement to radiate from the solar plexus—the seat of the soul as she called it—and to relate movement directly to human emotion, dance critic and modern dance advocate John Martin asserted that she never achieved an independent dance form.[21]

Isadora in Iphigénia, pen and watercolor by José Clará

Duncan's training methods may not have been as thoroughly developed with a direct and comprehensive pedagogy as the training systems of the next modern generation, but she did have clear ideas about dance and how to prepare for it. "Freedom, flow and spontaneity are the keys to the quality of movement in the Duncan Dance. . . . Duncan, in shaping this art, took from the nature of universal peoples those movements common to all, such as walking, running, and skipping, to build a vocabulary for the basis of the new dance."[22] Like ballet and other modern dance forms, a Duncan class may include barre and center work, and combinations across the floor.[23] In *The Technique of Isadora Duncan*, however, Isadora's protégée, Irma Duncan, presented the following succession of exercises:[24]

> Lesson No. I Walking, No. II Running, No. III Skipping, No. IV Swing Step, No. V Jumping, No. VI Arm Movements, No. VII Lying Down and Rising, No. VIII Tanagra Figure, No. IX The Waltz, No. X Twirling, No. XI The Polka, No. XII Gymnastics

Example: In Lesson III[25], Skipping, Irma Duncan presented the first exercise as: Lift your right knee, as in Skipping Exercise No. 1 [Raise the right knee toward your chest. . . . Point toes down].

- When you have brought the right foot down, swing the left leg backward. At the same time, skip on the right foot.

- Then swing the left leg forward, raising the knee in front; at the same time, skip again on the right foot.

- Bring left foot down, swing right leg backward, skip at the same time on left foot, etc., around the room.

While there was not a prescient drive toward virtuosity in the athletic sense, gesture and gross motor function were progressively refined in her approach to training, along with artistic intention.

Denishawn

Where Duncan had embraced a simplicity of style (both in movement and in the understated tunics and robes she wore), the creators of Denishawn embraced splendor, opulence, and spectacle

in nearly everything they taught or performed—reflecting the era's artistic tendencies in the Hollywood/Los Angeles area where the school and company began in 1915. In fact, "in technical virtuosity and splendor of presentation, Denishawn was frequently compared to the Ballets Russes —proof to Isadora of 'the error that is born of imitation unsupported by original thought.'"[26] Ruth St. Denis (1878–1986) and her partner-turned-husband Ted Shawn (1891–1972) could not have had more divergent sources of artistic inspiration. Her choreography most often reflected

Ruth St. Denis and Ted Shawn in their first duet, Ourieda, a Romance of the Desert *(1914).*

interests in Eastern religions and Oriental art, while his (at least initially) stemmed from an early exposure to Western social dance forms. Despite its widely eclectic concerts, Denishawn was one of the most popular dance companies in the world and produced five of the most important artists to feed the growth of modern dance: Martha Graham, Louis Horst, Doris Humphrey, Pauline Lawrence, and Charles Weidman.

Between its founding in 1915 and the company's dissolution in 1931, Denishawn would encompass several schools around the country (including its final home in New York), and numerous teachers would come to call themselves Denishawn teachers. Like Duncan, St. Denis and Shawn never actually developed their own technique, but there was a training system that was ever refined by Shawn. "Although Ted was the prime mover and shaker, Ruth taught what could be taught from her 'Oriental Impressions.'"[27] Frequently in Los Angeles, Shawn invited a wide variety of guest artists to teach their specialties at the school—hula and Japanese sword dancing are just two examples.[28] Martha Graham recalled, decades after leaving Denishawn, that elements of cultural forms from Spain and India were fused with ballet (bare foot).[29] In 1948, years after Denishawn disbanded, Shawn noted[30] that the following components were fundamental in the training of a dancer's body:

> a) walking, b) jumping, c) swinging, d) falling and rising, e) unfolding and folding, f) torsion and twisting, g) bending, h) shaking/vibrating, i) successions, j) oppositions, k) parallelisms, l) stretching and limbering, m) indivisible units of movement [like an alphabet's structure], n) coordination, o) balance, and finally p) tension and relaxation.

Two other former Denishawn dancers, Jane Sherman and Barton Mumaw, have provided greater detail of their Denishawn training. Although Sherman recalled that "unlike 'toe-shoe' ballerinas, we seldom limbered up before a show,"[31] she and Mumaw later wrote that "the technique that sustained both institutions [Denishawn and Shawn's later company, Ted Shawn's Men Dancers] was highly disciplined"[32] and that "the three hours of morning class opened with stretching and barre work and proceeded to floor exercises, when students perfected their arabesques, attitudes, développés en tournant, grands jetés, and even fouettés before the mirror."[33] According to Sherman,

> next came a free, open exercise affectionately nicknamed "Arms and Body," done to the waltz of Tchaikovsky's *Sleeping Beauty*. A forerunner of the technical warm-ups now used in many modern dance schools, it started with feet placed far apart and pressed flat on the floor. With a slow swinging of the body into ever-increasing circles, came head, shoulder, and torso

rolls, the arms sweeping from the floor toward the ceiling. After a relaxed run around the circumference of the studio, we ended in a back fall.[34]

To give the dancers a break after the "Arms and Body" sequence, "we would then sit in a circle and practice hand stretches to force the fingers as far back as they could go, in imitation of Cambodian or Balinese flexibility."[35] Each student also performed the Denishawn pas de basque alone. "The Denishawn pas de basque was distinguished by arms held high and parallel overhead as the body made an extreme arch sideways toward the leading foot."[36]

"Class always closed with the teaching of another section of a dance, an important element of Denishawn technique based on the theory that one learns by doing."[37] Mumaw and Sherman noted that "Denishawn courses had also included *der moderne tanz* of Germany taught by [Mary] Wigman pupil Margharita Wallmann,"[38] although the extent of that experience or its longevity in the program is not clear. It is clear, however, that the training at Denishawn was progressive, becoming more difficult with each level.[39] Also, the pedagogy was clarified enough that Shawn produced instruction manuals that included both exercises and dances. "In fact, the first dance I did at Denishawn, a Gypsy number called *Maria-Mari*, was printed. Those booklets prepared a lot of ground that people didn't know anything about," Sherman said in an interview.[40] Shawn also "prepared choreographic notes of class dances for the teachers in the many Denishawn schools across the country who could not always come to New York to study directly with him."[41] Now, while this training methodology is not in itself an original system or vocabulary, it clearly paved the way for what would develop in the hands of former Denishawn dancers Graham and Humphrey later.

Of their guiding teaching and choreographic principles, Sherman noted that St. Denis and Shawn formulated a guide both for their pedagogy and their choreography:

> The art of the dance is too big to be encompassed by any one system. On the contrary, the dance includes all systems and schools of dance. Every way that any human being of any race or nationality, at any period of human history, has moved rhythmically to express himself, belongs to the dance. We endeavor to recognize and use all contributions of the part to the dance and will continue to use all new contributions in the future.[42]

St. Denis and Shawn both placed importance on the systems of Delsarte and Dalcroze.[43] In fact, St. Denis credited a performance by Stebbins as her inspiration to dance.[44] It is also important to note that Delsarte's system was so integral to Shawn's life's work that he wrote one of the most important texts on Delsarte available in English, *Every Little Movement*. One wonders if Graham's work *Lamentation* would have been possible had she not been exposed to the subtleties of gesture and the intricacies of detail inherent in the Delsarte system.

Meditation on the *Denishawn Floor Plastique*

The inspiration of this short etude is drawn from Jane Sherman's beautiful restoration of the floor plastique created by Ted Shawn in 1925. The intention here was not to recreate Shawn's or Sherman's work (although an attempt was made to maintain a clear relationship with their movement). The intention instead is to illustrate Dalcroze's interest in interpretive, expressive movement at the core of his idea of "plastique." (See the opening of the film *Denishawn: The Birth of Modern Dance* for Sherman's restoration of the *Denishawn Floor Plastique*.)

Music: Franz Schubert's *34 Valses Sentimentales*, Op. 50, D. 779: No. 5 in B flat

Start: On the downstage right diagonal, sit on the knees in "child's pose"—sitz bones are on the heels and the torso is curved forward so that the forehead is on the floor and the arms are extended backward with hands beside the heels.

Introduction:

2 sets of 3

[cts. 1–3] Roll up the spine until it is straight and you are sitting on your heels, extend the arms in front of you in a V (palms up) so the hands are in line with your shoulders.

[cts. 1–3] Continue reaching forward so that the energy of the reach causes your torso to float forward until you are "standing upright" on your knees (shoulders, hips, and knees are in alignment) and knees are about 3 inches apart.

[6 sets of 3] Arms round and fold into a balletic 1st position, and then port de bras with the R arm floating overhead as the L arm floats to 2nd position (head opening to the L). The R arm opens to 2nd, and both arms extend into a straightened 2nd position with palms facing the floor.

[3 sets of 3] The arms wave like a swan with the movement initiated from the shoulder and ripple outward toward the fingertips. Repeat 3 times.

[2 sets of 3] Port de bras the arms overhead to 5th position as you shift the body to face stage R—you'll need to shift your weight to the R knee for a moment as the L knee slides toward the stage R facing.

[4 sets of 3] Backbend into a nice arch and recover taking 2 threes to bend and 2 to recover.

[2 sets of 3] Unfurl the L arm from its place in 5th position by rotating the elbow down toward the floor so the palm faces you, and extend the arm onto an upward diagonal. Simultaneously, the R arm lowers and the R hand rotates until it is directly across from your eyes several inches away, as if shielding your eyes from the sun even as the L hand reaches for the sun.

[1 set of 3] You have reached so far forward that the L ft. is compelled to step out in front of you into a wide lunge.

[3 sets of 3] Round the torso forward over the L knee as your arms circle down and pull

	behind you into a curved shape with the palms facing stage R.
[1 set of 3]	Extend the spine forward on the diagonal and reach the arms forward along the same diagonal, palms facing upward.
[1 set of 3]	Draw the torso upright as the L leg slides in from the lunge until your legs

	are both at right angles, and the arms float overhead to 5th position.
[1 set of 3]	Spiral the torso to face the audience.
[3 sets of 3]	Port de bras arms open so the upper arm is parallel to the floor, the forearms perpendicular to the ceiling, and the palms flexed outward, making 90-degree angles at elbow and wrist.

A Period of Transition

Despite all the training material being developed in modern's romantic era, clear systematic methodology based on original ideas had not, as yet, emerged. The *zeitgeist* was, however, moving in the direction of recognizable, developmental, progressive techniques—an environment was being created through a mélange of work occurring in the growing professional and academic dance worlds. Just as Denishawn was consistently refining its training offerings, so, too, were dancers in colleges across the country. "From 1914 to 1932, a free and creative form of dance, a precursor to modern dance, began to take root in physical education departments of many colleges and universities,"[45] but while the dancing may have been "free and creative," the process was orderly and increasingly developmental. Curricula were emerging as early as 1918 when Gertrude Colby established the dance curriculum (though not yet offered as a degree) for the Teachers College at Columbia University.

The pivotal year in this combined process seems to have been 1923, a year of three significant shifts in the dance world. Martha Graham left Denishawn to pursue her own work, and Doris Humphrey returned to Denishawn after a two-year hiatus when she and Pauline Lawrence had been running their own company—decisions that, as will become clear in the next chapter, eventually led both artists to develop their techniques. Also in 1923 Margaret H'Doubler established the dance minor at the University of Wisconsin at Madison which would become the first undergraduate dance degree (and master's degree soon after that).[46] Pedagogies were being created and clarified, teaching methodologies employed, and dancers (professional and student alike) were beginning to seek a truly American vision of dance as an art form. The environment was ripe, and it was only a matter of time before the art of dance—and how we train for it—would change radically. In the next chapter, with the work of Graham and Humphrey, we will see how those radical changes took root and revolutionized the dance world by 1931.

Class at Denishawn Studio in Westlake Park, Los Angeles, c. 1918.

Final Class Discussion Questions

If you have participated in dance techniques in the past, what have been some of the highlights of your training experiences? What was the one thing that really stands out that did not work in your body? What one thing has worked really well for you so far? If you've never danced before, what brought you to a technique class? If you are new to dance training, consider other experiences like sports or social dancing: what really interested you about your body in motion?

Journal: Describe your relationship to rhythm, and what you've learned about the relationship of movement and rhythm in this chapter.

Works Cited

Anderson, J. (1997). *Art Without Boundaries: The world of modern dance.* Iowa City: University of Iowa Press.

Duncan, Irma. (1937). *The Technique of Isadora Duncan.* New York: Kamin Publishers.

Gallemore, S. (1978). Emergence of the Dance Division. In D. Fallon, (Ed.), Washington: American Alliance for Health, Physical Education, Recreation and Dance.

Gold, S. (1984). *A Selection of Isadora Duncan Dances: The Shubert selection.* La Jolla, CA : The Sutton Movement Writing Press.

Houseal, J. (2009, Spring). A Conversation with Jane Sherman. *Ballet Review,* pp. 14–22.

Jaques-Dalcroze, E. (1921). *Rhythm, Music and Education.* New York: G. P. Putnam's Sons.

Kurth, P. (2001). *Isadora: A sensational life.* Boston: Little, Brown and Company.

Levien, J. (1994). *Duncan Dance: A guide for young people ages six to sixteen.* Pennington, NJ: Princeton Book Company.

Lloyd, M. (1949). *The Borzoi Book of Modern Dance.* New York: Dance Horizons.

Martin, J. (1965). *Introduction to the Dance.* New York: Dance Horizons.

McPherson, E. (2008). *The Contributions of Martha Hill to American Dance and Dance Education, 1900–1995.* Lewiston, NY: The Edwin Mellen Press.

Mumaw, B. & Sherman, J. (1981). Ted Shawn, Teacher and Choreographer. *Dance Chronicle,* 4 (2), pp. 91–112.

Pennington, J. (1925). *The Importance of Being Rhythmic: A study of the principles of Dalcroze eurythmics applied to general education and to the arts of music, dancing and acting. Based on and adapted from "Rhythm, Music and Education," by Emile Jaques-Dalcroze.* New York: G. P. Putnam's Sons.

Rath, E. (1914). *Aesthetic Dancing.* New York: A. S. Barnes Company.

Rogosin, E. (1980). *The Dance Makers: Conversations with American choreographers.* New York: Walker and Company.

Shawn, T. (1948). *Fundamentals of a Dancer's Education.* Girard, KS: Haldeman-Julius Publications.

_____. (1954). *Every Little Movement: A book about François Delsarte.* New York: Dance Horizons.

Sherman, J. (1976). *Soaring: The diary of a Denishawn dancer in the Far East 1925–1926.* Middletown, CT: Wesleyan University Press.

_____. (1983). *Denishawn: The enduring influence.* Boston: Twayne Publishers.

_____. (Director). (1998). *Denishawn: Birth of modern dance* [Motion picture]. United States: Kultur International Films.

Sherman, J. & Mumaw, B. (1986). *Barton Mumaw, Dancer.* Hanover, NH: Wesleyan University Press.

Spector, I. (1990). *Rhythm and Life: The work of Emile Jaques-Dalcroze.* Stuyvesant, NY: Pendragon Press.

Stebbins, G. (1977). *Delsarte System of Expression.* New York: Dance Horizons.

CHAPTER 2

The Originators

Martha Graham
Doris Humphrey

A dancer may have a magnificent concept of significant form, may know fine movement when he sees
it, and may have vital things to express; but if he has
no muscular control, no strength, no elasticity, no
breath, he is absolutely helpless. You cannot play on
an instrument which you have not got.

—John Martin, *The Modern Dance*

Martin's statement is from a four-part lecture-demonstration series he organized at the New School for Social Research in New York (1931–1932) in order to foster a better understanding of the new dance form taking hold in America. He was acutely aware that many audience members (and many dancers themselves) were finding difficulty in penetrating the meaning of the new works beginning presented in New York. At the time, there was not yet a body of literature on the dance form, and "the only source of enlightenment [was] the actual performances of the dancers themselves."[1] Viewers at the time lacked a basis to examine modern dance because no two modernists worked with the same methodologies (either in terms of vocabulary or choreographic aesthetic).

By the time Martin organized the New School series, however, dancemakers were not only revolutionizing choreography, they were also defining movement vocabularies and training methodologies—and new pedagogical (systematic) training practices were rapidly emerging in America. In fact, when the Bennington School of the Dance opened its summer program in 1934, Martha Hill offered courses on fundamental techniques and on teaching methods (and

Doris Humphrey in her dance Passacaglia in C Minor, *c. 1938.*

related material). Enough technical material existed by that time for "a basic study of fundamental techniques of movement for the dance analyzed into its force, shape and time aspects; the elements of form and meaning in movement for the dance . . . teaching methods; terminology, [and systems] of dance notation."[2]

Much of this technical development can be linked directly to Martha Graham, Hanya Holm, Doris Humphrey and Charles Weidman (among others), all of whom were rejecting not only ballet, but also the naive interpretive dance of the early modern period. Graham, Humphrey, and Weidman had cut their artistic teeth as members of Denishawn, so they had been immersed in the training ideas developed by Ruth St. Denis and Ted Shawn (see Chapter 1). These artists, however, largely rejected their mentors' training ideas, save perhaps for the respect they each carried forward for performance preparation and impeccable standards. (And in the strictest sense, one can see in Graham's training system an element of yoga, which she did encounter in the Denishawn material.) For all intents and purposes, however, Graham and Humphrey each blazed their own trail in developing both their choreographic bodies, and in crafting their training methodologies.

1923 was a critical year for the Denishawn protégés, and for modern dance's evolution. Doris Humphrey had departed Denishawn in 1921 after the company suffered major financial troubles on the road. She and her colleague Pauline Lawrence spent two years managing their own small (yet successful) vaudeville touring company. While Humphrey and Lawrence toured, St. Denis and Shawn each had their own projects but eventually reestablished the larger Denishawn group, and Humphrey appeared as part of their 1923 New York Town Hall engagement. The short season there is likely the only time that Graham and Humphrey ever appeared on the same concert program (although they did not perform in the same dance at the same time). It was also as a result of this concert that Broadway producer John Murray Anderson asked Martha Graham to join his upcoming *Greenwich Village Follies*.[3] While Graham was likely attracted to the increased income the Follies offered, she had also grown weary of Denishawn's limited artistic challenges, and she seized the opportunity to move on to new work. In addition to the *Follies*, Graham was also hired to help direct the Department of Dance at the Eastman School of Dance and Dramatic Action in Rochester, New York, where she was able to begin exploring her own movement ideas.

At the same time, Humphrey returned to Denishawn with new responsibilities in addition to her performing and choreographic work. She became the company's ballet mistress, and joined the Denishawn Normal School in New York, where she taught dances to other teachers. Humphrey's next three years were awash in performing, teaching, rehearsing, and coaching at a pace that left little time for anything else.

While the establishment of new techniques was still a few years away, Graham and Humphrey each found formative opportunities in their respective Denishawn exits and entrances. In the years that followed, both women developed extraordinary ideas about movement and choreography. Questions about what constitutes natural, human movement—and how the human psyche motivates movement—drove their experimentations and discoveries. Although certain connections can be made in their techniques (the importance of breath in movement) and choreographies (motivated by psychological and philosophical factors), that is where the similarities largely end. As we will see, their philosophies were wildly divergent: Graham believed in awarenesses carried in *blood memory*, Humphrey that a dancer's point of view was relevant to his or her own times.

Even where breath is concerned, Graham and Humphrey each made their own discoveries about its potential in dance. Breath is certainly central to all dance—its regular cycles and rhythms allow the human body to function. How we use those cycles and rhythms, however, can greatly affect both the kind and quality of movement we create. So it is, therefore, that breath and the exploration of its use are central to this chapter because principle concepts in the techniques studied here require an understanding of the breath. Fall and recovery (Humphrey) and contraction and release (Graham) revolve around clear, intentional breath patterns. The content of much of the choreography discussed in this chapter is also influenced by psychoanalysis (the use of Freud's and Jung's ideas by Graham) and philosophy (Humphrey's appreciation of Nietzsche's works). The intellectual drive of both dancemakers in this section should not be seen, however, as overshadowing the deep emotional motivation in their works. They were both making intensely human, dramatic, accessible dances—even later more abstract works such as Graham's *Diversion of Angels* or Humphrey's *Passacaglia in C Minor* maintain solid relationships to the human being generating the movements.

The dynamic growth in modern dance between 1923 and 1931 was extraordinary. By the 1928–29 season, for example, two dance critics in New York (John Martin and Mary F. Watkins) had reviewed 129 performances in a single season. The new dance was taking root in New York City, if not in the rest of the country, and Graham and Humphrey were at the head of the charge. By then, they each had their own company and had become extremely articulate advocates for concert dance. In fact, they joined fellow dancemakers Charles Weidman and Helen Tamiris in creating the Dance Repertory Theatre (DRT) in 1929. DRT acted as a collective production company in order to afford its choreographers a season in a significant theater space that would otherwise have been nearly cost-prohibitive for the individual choreographers. While the group lasted only one more season (adding Agnes de Mille to its list of choreographers), it provided an important moment of stability to the burgeoning art form. Martin even then had enough clarity in his own vision of how modern dance should be addressed that he was able to present his 1931–32 lecture-demonstration series featuring Graham and Humphrey. This series was likely the first such public examination of modern dance in general—and specifically, two of the techniques that formed the hallmark of the central period in modern dance.

Core Ideas

••

Observations and Experiments

Journal I: Sit where you can observe people going about daily activities, such as shopping, sipping coffee, chatting with friends, and so forth. Watch how these individuals breathe, and how their breath affects their body. Look for the rise and fall of their shoulders and chest. Look for contractions in the lower abdomen as they laugh. Jot down notes about the rhythm of their breath and how the body moves in response. What are the qualities of their breath? Is the breath sharp and staccato or more like a thoughtful sigh? What happens in the body because of those qualities? Try to spot a long, rushing expression of exhilaration and see how that's different from a concussive contraction. Then, watch people in an active setting such as a gym or sports field. What qualitative differences do you notice in breath and movement?

Journal II: Find a series of spirals—a nautilus shell, a spiral staircase, a photo of a baseball pitcher (or watch someone playing baseball), a vine or fern unfolding, or a barber's pole in motion. Make note of how you perceive the energy flowing through or around the object. If the object is inanimate, what can you still deduce about movement from that image/object? From those things that are organic

and possibly in motion, what can you tell about oppositional energy?

Experiment I: In the studio, explore these words/ideas and see what kind of movement you can create: breath, fall and recovery, spiral, natural movement, gesture, contraction and release, isolation, rebound, dynamics, phrasing, rhythm, tension and relaxation, and delight and remorse. Then with a partner, try to pair one of your ideas with one of theirs that seem contradictory or oppositional. How can you evolve two opposed movement ideas into an organic movement phrase?

Experiment II: Symmetry and asymmetry are important design elements in choreography because they allow us to create something that is either balanced or unbalanced. This can add solid, stable energy to the work, or it can make something appear dynamic and risky, even if the dancers aren't necessarily in motion. How do you think symmetry and asymmetry play into technique? Try to create a movement sequence that you can teach to your fellow dancers that uses both symmetry and asymmetry, and tell them why you made the choices you did in preparing the exercise.

••

Technical Genesis

Martha Graham (1894–1991): Biographical Sketch

Dance in its varied forms and styles is directly affected by the country in which it manifests itself, but the physical principles of great dancing remain inherently the same. Although the manner of dancing may change so

Martha Graham, ca. 1959.

radically as to seem to affect these basic principles, the body, itself, which is the dancer's medium, is eternally subject to certain laws of rhythm definitely its own. Manner, however, is born of the climatic social and religious conditions of the land in which the dance finds itself.

—Martha Graham, *Martha Graham: The Early Years*

Martha Graham's experiences with the social and religious climate in America were broad-ranging in her lifetime and had tremendous influence on her artistic development. Critics in the early years of her choreographic career called her a dangerous revolutionary,[4] and referred to her and her dancers as fanatics (insinuating near-religious zealotry). For others, though, Graham was a pioneer who forged a uniquely American dance theater. Through her early dancemaking, she began to craft a new dance technique which historians have called "the beginning of American modern dance."[5] *New York Times* dance critic John Martin said that, for Graham, "in a singular degree the restraints of techn[ique] have meant freedom and a heightened expressionalism. The impact of her communication has been increased by being forced through the finely calibrated apertures of her method."[6]

Her method and vision were so highly calibrated, in fact, that between 1923 and 1991 Graham was able to choreograph more than 180 dances, and earned the Medal of Freedom Citation (October 14, 1976) from President Ford, who called her a national treasure. This was not enough, however, to secure her a 1983 grant from the National Endowment for the Arts (NEA). The NEA rejected the grant application, stating Graham had failed to demonstrate the long-term growth and stability of her company in the application—[7]this despite the fact her company was in its sixth decade. In his scholarly exploration of Graham's work, dance educator Barry Fischer found the NEA's decision ironic because the grant application had been for the "development of potential schools and companies that could further long-term institutional growth and stability."[8]

The dark, cold winters of Graham's childhood in Allegheny, Pennsylvania, were filled with the extreme Puritanism of her extended family and were in stark contrast to the world she encountered when her parents relocated to Santa Barbara, California, in 1908. The extreme differences between the two major experiences of her childhood repeatedly appear as polar opposites in Graham's work, as she mined a wealth of choreographic material from those dramatically different worlds.[9]

Graham first encountered dance in 1911 at a performance by Ruth St. Denis in Los Angeles, and it was in that moment that she knew she, too, would dance. "Despite what people have said about me and my upbringing, my parents never objected to my becoming a dancer. . . . I could do anything I wanted. I found myself inclined that way—the inclination to be beautiful and wild, maybe a creature of another world. I always have been myself in that sense."[10] After graduating from a junior college (the Cumnock School) in 1916, Graham enrolled in the Denishawn School, which Ruth St. Denis and Ted Shawn had established a year earlier. It was rough going at first, as St. Denis saw in Graham "a short, unmalleable lump," and she told Shawn that she could not teach Graham.[11] Since Shawn, however, was the school's business manager in addition to his teaching and artistic responsibilities, he did not want to lose a student and decided to instruct Graham himself. It was not long, however, before both Shawn and St. Denis saw Graham's potential, and she soon began demonstrating for classes. By the end of the summer, she had a small role in Denishawn's *A Dance Pageant of Egypt, Greece and India*, marking her first public appearance in a professional dance company.[12] For the next seven years, Graham performed, taught, and assisted with administrative duties at Denishawn, but by 1923, she had become aware of the limitations of the Denishawn repertory and resigned, seeking a different dance art.

That year, she moved to New York after securing a role in the *Greenwich Village Follies*—and she was also hired to help direct the Department of Dance at the Eastman School of Dance and Dramatic Action in Rochester. Eastman not only afforded relief from the lack of challenge in the vaudeville season, but at last provided the opportunity she had awaited: to develop her own material. From the start of this teaching experience, Graham was determined not to recreate the unchallenging and superficial material she had experienced at Denishawn and in the *Follies*. The time at the Eastman School was an opportunity to devise new pathways in dance, and "to test the very chemistries of her being, to fuse them, if possible into a new element of dance."[13]

On April 18, 1926, Martha Graham and her group presented their first New York concert at the 48th Street Theater. The group, consisting of Graham and three of her most successful students from Eastman, presented ten solos and seven pieces by the trio or Graham with the trio. Betty MacDonald, an original member of the group, said, "The greatness was there. I recognized something I had been yearning for, that I had been longing for, and this woman . . . changed dance forever."[14] The Martha Graham School of Contemporary Dance opened in 1926, and as Graham's choreography and philosophies developed, so did her dance technique (which she eventually codified). It was not, however, until Graham's first larger group work *Heretic* (1929) was presented that her style and philosophies became evident.

> Necessity made me a choreographer. I couldn't go on all the time just
> doing the kinds of spectacle-costume-dances I had learned at Denishawn.
> But I never set out to be a choreographer. I never heard the word until I
> got to New York. I just began to make up dances so I would have some-
> thing to dance. For good or bad, that's how I started.[15]

Where Graham rejected the choreographic ideas of St. Denis and Shawn, she found an unlikely mentor in her Denishawn colleague, the musician Louis Horst. She once said of the primary mentor of her entire career, "Louis Horst played for my first dance lesson [at Denishawn], and, with his faith and devotion, his ferocious standards, browbeat me into a kind of courage in the beginning."[16] If necessity played a role in Graham becoming a choreographer and securing her place in the history of dance (and American art in general), chance certainly played a similar part with regard to Horst's role in modern dance. His original plan may not have been a long-term stay at Denishawn, but then he met Graham in 1916, and "once Louis resolved that Martha Graham would be a major dance figure in America, he did everything in his power to make it happen."[17] He was constantly with her in the studio, giving feedback on movement ideas and creating music for her—he also accompanied all of her concerts in those early years. (Graham and Horst were also a couple for more than two decades, although they never married.)

Martha Graham with Erick Hawkins in the premiere of Appalachian Spring *at the Library of Congress, 1944.*

Horst met and challenged Graham's intensity, encouraging her forward. It was out of Graham's search for music, not his own need to compose, that he wrote music for her. The compositions Horst wrote for dances were not meant to stand solely as musical works, but rather to support the dance or give it boundaries. "The question is not how great a dance composer is; but what he does for the dance. The composer-accompanist must expect to sacrifice some of his identity as a musician when he writes or plays for the dance."[18] Eventually, the efforts of Graham and Horst paid off, and critics began to see Graham's choreography differently, calling her a diligent genius—it was said that she worked with a serious Protestant fear of God. "This may sound humorless. It was not, but masterpieces, whether humorous or tragic, do not come spontaneously. They are earned."[19] In 1938, Lincoln Kirstein (who had harshly criticized her three years earlier) wrote, "Graham finds the expression of her deeply American attitude in her own America. *American Document* is . . . the most important extended dance creation by a living American."[20]

In the late 1930s, Graham's work took on a new dimension as men began to join her company and she was able to tackle a broader range of content in her work. Erick Hawkins—whom Graham eventually married—was the first man to join her (appearing in *American Document*), followed by Merce Cunningham. Where her work had frequently addressed communal, religious, and social concerns—*Heretic* (1929), *Primitive Mysteries* (1931), *Panorama* (1935), *Chronicle* (1936), and *Deep Song* (1937)—she was able to deal with relationship themes like love, marriage, family, and the darkness of betrayal. Hawkins had studied the classics at Harvard University and fueled Graham's interest in mythology, which in turn helped her to explore the darkness inherent in the human psyche. Some of Graham's most successful works were made in the 1940s: *Letter to the World* (1940), *Deaths and Entrances* (1943), *Appalachian Spring* (1944), *Cave of the Heart* (1946), *Errand into the Maze* (1947), and *Night Journey* and *Diversion of Angles* (both 1948). Most of these still fill the company's repertory decades after their creation.[21]

By 1970, Graham had made the difficult decision to retire from the stage, but she continued to choreograph for her company until her death. In 1984, even after her extensive career, Graham said, "I am afraid—because of what I want to do, and will I have time? I don't think about what I have done; I only think of the things that I want to do, that I haven't done."[22]

During her career, Graham collaborated with exceptional composers such as Samuel Barber, Aaron Copland, Gian Carlo Menotti, Carlos Chavez, Hunter Johnson, and Paul Nordoff.[23] Pivotal modern artists like Alexander Calder and Isamu Noguchi designed decor for many of her dances, and the fashion designer Halston costumed many of her later works; Calvin Klein designed costumes for her final complete dance, *Maple Leaf Rag* (1990).

Numerous important choreographers danced as members of Graham's company, including besides Hawkins and Cunningham, Paul Taylor, Pearl Lang, Anna Sokolow, Jane Dudley, Sophie Maslow, Martha Hill, Donald McKayle, Dan Wagoner, and Gus Solomons jr.

Martha Graham: In the Studio

Near the end of her life, Martha Graham was asked how she chose dancers for particular roles, to which she said:

> I look for avidity, an eagerness for life, a blood memory in the sense that the dancer remembers and can call upon more of his or her life than has yet been lived. There has to be . . . a willingness to explore unknown feelings and daring to feel them and let them become a part of your being. It's scary. It's terrifying. But you do it because you have no choice.[24]

That intensity was reflected in her art almost from the beginning—in terms of her own performance, her choreography, and her technique. "The technique is a tool of communication, of expression," noted Janet Eilber, artistic director of the Martha Graham Dance Company. "It was born backwards, created out of the revolutionary dances Martha was making for the stage. She excerpted phrases out of those theatrical works in order to teach new students and company members. That's why the classes are emotive and theatrical. It's why the dancers must fill the movement with emotion."[25] We see this perspective magnified in Alice Helpern's *The Technique of*

Martha Graham—important for both Helpern's research and the rare technical photographs taken by Barbara Morgan. Helpern, director of programs at the Dance Notation Bureau, said, "More than a movement vocabulary, Graham's technique was a new way of training the dancer's body as an instrument of expression. . . . Graham intended that her method of body training should enhance intellectual and emotional growth as well as physical mastery."[26] Because the training is both about that physical development and internal exploration, we start to see it as ritual and the definition of technique I suggested in the Introduction begins to take focus. Therefore, caution against stereotype is important to avoid approaching shape as external, overlaid presentation, and to prevent drama from devolving into melodrama. The drama and shape originate from inside the dancer, are never ornamental, and are created as the emotion moves outward through the body.

"Martha was dissatisfied with the dance that came before her," Eilber stated. "So, she had to rediscover what the body does, and found a way of physicalizing the internal world and human issues. Also, she wanted to find a voice for America in dance. As part of her exploration, she found the connection between emotion and breath. This led her to explore the articulation of the torso and to the way she evolved natural human body language so that it became theatrical."[27] Graham used everyday gestures, amplifying them to allow the body to express the landscape of the heart and mind. The opening phrases of *Errand into the Maze* (1947), for example, are derived from quite human movements that expose how fear, confusion, and despair resonate through the body.[28] The fact that these movements are recognizable adds to the dramatic tension, setting the stage for what comes next. At the same time, however, there is an inherently animalistic quality in her choreography—and the technique facilitates that. Graham pointed out that an animal "is never clumsy unless it is domesticated. Movement never lies. In dancing, we try to discover our animal nature and, at the same time, to be completely human."[29] Spirals provided another connection in her work between the human body and the natural world around us. A "turn around the back" —a spiraling action around the spine—can take on the grace and beauty of a rose unfurling from its coiled center as it grows, or the fury of a tornado hell-bent on destruction.

The generation of the technique was not an overnight birthing process. It took countless hours of grueling trial and error—the kind of experimentation that begets any great invention: "Martha had to spin this new technique out of her own entrails: a way of moving the arms, a way of moving the legs with the torso, a way of breathing. She did not know how. No one had ever seen it. She just felt there must be a new approach."[30] Graham worked relentlessly to forge this new way of moving, making twenty-nine dances in 1926 alone—and sixteen the following year—with each step taking her closer and closer to her groundbreaking movement vocabulary. In those early years, the small audiences who attended her concerts went because they expected to have their minds jolted by incomprehensible movement—the primal contraction and release— driven by extremes of inhalation and exhalation, and by "raw emotion made apparent. This was what the Greeks could do. This is what Shakespeare did. This is what every artist attempts. But most, of course, cannot even conceive of it, and nearly all refuse to pay the terrible price in time and effort of finding it."[31] As early as her days teaching at Eastman, Graham was developing the primary principle of contraction and release in her work. She was "already working toward a way of moving in which the dance was in intimate contact with the floor/earth and with her own physical and emotional center."[32] So, the development of a floor barre at the beginning of class was key to the training. The use of the knee as a means of locomotion across the floor (or for spinning) and for hinge work was one of the unique elements to emerge from that floor work.[33] Graham also rejected the idea of teaching exercises separate from actual dances, as Denishawn had done. Instead, in Graham, "the entire class is a preparation for performance, and the technical work is choreographed in dance phrases."[34] Although a set series of material was eventually established, the technique was never rigid and unchanging. Evolving company membership and new choreographic ideas inspired adaptations to the training. In the 1930s, for example, Graham began to use turnout, pointed feet, and curved arms, all of which she had eschewed in the early years.[35]

The connecting factor between the inner landscape and the physical movement, as Eilber pointed out, is that Graham technique is driven by the power of the core work.[36] The breath, contraction, shifting in the hips, and spirals influence and drive the extremities. It is a rare moment in Graham's choreography when the limbs are not motivated by an impulse from the core, even if devoid of relationship to the pelvis or torso. It builds from the beginning floor work all the way through the final leaps at the end of a class. Eilber said, "This aligns with Martha's idea that choreography should be free of decoration. Each movement has to have purpose based in emotional ideas and driving physicality. When I teach a master class, I often suggest that students build an emotional catalogue, so they can become aware of what moves them emotionally. Those things can be stored for use later in their class and performance work."[37] She suggests finding photographs of people in various emotional states. Students can study these to see how the emotion informs the body language or gesture. "They can also use the photos to build movement phrases or short dances working with emotional movements suggested in the photos. Pictures of athletes are also great. Many sports have a great deal in common with Graham technique. Pictures of baseball pitchers, for example, often reveal incredible uses of both contraction and spiral at the same time. You see the pitcher clearly operating from the core, and there is coiling energy from the ground up that then powers their movement as they release the pitch."

Eilber also uses laughter as a means of helping students new to Graham explore the idea of contraction. It is impossible, after all, to laugh without contracting. "The use of joy creates the contraction because of the physical effort used to make the 'ha' sound. The students can even build a phrase based on long or short bursts of laughter. It could be bubbling, or rapid movements—it doesn't matter. Either way, it is a good, nonthreatening introduction to the contraction."[38] That, again, reinforces the natural, human source of Graham's technique. Graham herself said, "My dancing is not an attempt to interpret life. It is the affirmation of life through movement."[39]

Discovering Contraction

The material here is not intended to represent the codified Graham syllabus (which is under copyright). The primary home for the technique is the Martha Graham School of Contemporary Dance in New York, but over the last four decades or so, the training has been passed on at colleges and dance centers worldwide. Helpern pointed out that the technique "has gone through inevitable changes outside the confines of the Graham Center, for it has been adapted to new locales and settings."[40] In many places outside the Graham School, generic terms like "Graham-based technique" and "modern dance technique" are used to describe the training. So, rather than serve as straightforward exercises, this material is more experimental, although there is structure. These experiments are meditations on Graham's central principle of contraction and release.

Based on Eilber's suggestion above, explore the influence of laughter on the body. Try this lying flat on your back and then on your stomach; sitting up with your legs crossed; standing; and while running. Try chuckling first. The bubbling laughter Eilber mentioned can evolve into a deeper, rolling belly laugh. Looking at outrageously funny pictures or telling jokes can help with the spontaneity—the laughter needs to be real in order to be effective. Observe how laughter is initiated by a contraction in the abdomen, and how the different kinds of laughter require different qualities of contraction. Notice how the energy of the contraction moves through the rest of your body. It is important here to simply observe your body's natural responses, so try not to force anything. Let it develop organically. In time, you will probably become aware of the

muscles in your lower abdomen. Notice specifically the changes that occur in the pelvis and the lumbar spine as you move from short, staccato, rapid-fire, or bubbling laughs to larger, full-bellied laughter. The changes in the pelvis and lumbar spine will be slight, for the most part, as you explore laughter in this way, but try to note how these changes differ. For example, you may note in a deeper, slower, laugh that the abdomen hollows out more than with the faster, bubbling laugh, especially at the top of the pelvis. You may also find that the lumbar spine lengthens just slightly as well. Pay attention to everything that is happening.

As we move deeper into this contraction study, we'll add a structured, deliberate breath and a dynamic count.

Start: Lie flat on your back, arms at your sides and legs straight out in parallel. Elongate your lumbar spine so that it is in contact with the floor.

[cts. 1–8] Establish a long, slow exhale taking all 8 cts. to completely empty your breath. Focus on the lower abdomen at the pelvis to initiate the exhalation. Apply a sustained contraction there to help to expel the breath and hollow out the abdomen. As the abdomen pushes down toward the spine, you may feel an increased lengthening in the lumbar area, and the pelvic area may curve slightly. You may also feel a creasing in the hips and a slight bend in the knees. Try not to "make" anything happen. You are looking for the sensations of those changes rather than trying to make a shape. If there is a subtle response in the upper torso, that is all right; just try not to manufacture that response. As much as possible, focus this contraction in the pelvic area, allowing any slight lengthening of the lower spine to happen in response to the contraction in the pelvic area.

[cts. 1–8] Inhale deeply. As the belly fills during inhalation, the slight curve in the pelvic area returns to neutral, and the spine and knees respond in kind. Repeat this slow, sustained contraction 8 times.

Repeat the contraction and release in 4 cts. For the contraction, ct. 1 is percussive, and cts. 2-4 keep the contraction alive. The release is a sustained inhalation taking all 4 cts. As this experience becomes percussive, feel free to make the expulsion of breath audible. A HA! or HUH! sound helps to emphasize the energy of the contraction.

[ct. 1] Exhale/contract.

[cts. 2–4] Maintain the contraction.

[cts. 1–4] Inhale/release and return to neutral.

Repeat that 8 times.

Let's look more closely at the impact of the breath on the body. Be certain that throughout the sequence, the contraction remains focused in the pelvic region and the lower spine lengthens allowing a sloping curved shape to occur—similar to a C. Never drop into the contraction, but use a steady flow of energy as you exhale into the contraction. Try to remember how the lower back felt earlier as it lengthened along the floor in our contraction. Imagine that you are making contact with the wall behind you in the same way in order to encourage that lengthening in the lumbar area. This really helps in preventing a "dropping" sensation in the contraction.

Timing: 3/4 metre, 60 bpm

Start: In a seated position, R foot crossed over the L toes pointed and heels lifted (no sickling); arms in a natural low 2nd position with a breath of air keeping them open, middle fingertips lightly touch the floor; shoulders down in back, and the latissimus dorsi are engaged, as is the core. Contract the pelvis, with your focus out and on a downward diagonal in front of the body.

[ct. 1–3] On a slow inhale, roll up the spine, lengthening in both directions (focus rises with the breath—take care not to hyperextend in the lower back).

[cts. 4–6] Slowly return to contraction.

Repeat this at least 6 times.

[cts. 1–6] Extend legs forward as the torso moves into a high release (arched back) and then moves into a forward stretch over the legs; circle the arms back, to the sides, overhead, and then forward so that the hands move past the feet with legs in full extension.

[cts. 1–6] Contract to pull back into the original seated position. Straighten the spine.

In this series of images, Ting-Yu Chen (a faculty member in Shenandoah University's Dance Division) demonstrates the sequence of movement in "A last contraction experiment on the floor" (p. 33). Notice the clarity of her alignment (shoulders over hips, with a strong spine), the "C" shape created by the contraction, and that she remains connected to the floor even when her torso moves forward. On the release, her lower back lengthens but doesn't become "swayed."

A last contraction experiment on the floor

Timing: 4/4 metre, 95 bpm

Start: Sitting, extend arms and legs into 2nd, elbows slightly bent.

[cts. & 1, 2] Contract on &, on 1 hands cup[i] as they rotate toward mirror, the feet flex, head looks slightly on a diagonal toward ceiling following the contraction.

[cts. 3–4] Carry the contraction over slightly toward the floor, increasing the contraction with the arms straightening.

[cts. 5–6] Release from the pelvis, lengthening the spine on the diagonal as the legs reach out farther, extending the toes; arms release so that the fingers extend back out and the palms rotate back toward the floor, and return to your neutral starting place.

Repeat 4 times. When this is complete, stretch the legs out in front and round the back forward.

Come to standing, move to the barre.

Start: Both hands on the barre. Stand far enough away from the barre so that arms are not quite fully stretched; feet in a narrow parallel 2nd position. Find your sense of balance over your feet.

[cts. 1–8] Take a slow, sustained deep contraction. As the pelvis scoops under and the lower back opens (like an eye), you will feel your weight shift backwards—use the barre to support yourself a bit if you need to do so. As you did on the floor, think about drawing the spine toward the wall behind you to avoid a dropping sensation. Think back, not down as you hollow out. Your upper torso may start to respond a little more than it did while you were on the floor, but, again, try not to manufacture that response and don't let it creep into your shoulders.

[cts. 1–8] Inhale and return to a neutral standing position.

Repeat 8 times. Now let the contraction become more percussive.

[ct. 1] Contract HUH!

[cts. 2–4] Maintain the contraction.

[cts. 1–4] Inhale and return to neutral.

Repeat 8 times.

[ct. 1] Contract HUH!

[ct. 2] Maintain the contraction.

[cts. 1–2] Inhale and return to neutral.

Repeat 8 times.

Now that you've explored the concept of contraction and release a bit, think back over Eilber's comments earlier about the movement being connected to the inner landscape and emotions. Think about how emotion might motivate a contraction, how it would differ if you were seething or ecstatic. After you have gone through this set of experiments, you might use Eilber's idea of the emotional catalogue to inform the dimensionality of your contraction and release. Pick several different photos with contrasting emotional states and apply them to each of the sequences above. Notice how your movements change when you work from these internal motivators.

---

[i] One note about the "cupped hand" in Graham: in contemporary use, it is a reflection of dynamic energy in the body. As the energy runs through the arm, it radiates out from the palm, through the heel of the hand, pulling the hand backward into a slightly cupped shape. The fingers are not glued together or sharply angled. The movement does not have to be pronounced or stylized.

Doris Humphrey (1895–1958): Biographical Sketch

Modern dance has been accused of being remote and difficult. Our dance need not be a cult of unintelligibility, an esoteric enterprise with never a crack through which a gleam of humor can enter, an exercise in aloofness. By its very origins it is dedicated to an expression of life as a whole, today; it can and must involve itself closely with its audience in a mutual exploration of that complicated but fascinating territory.

—Doris Humphrey, *New Dance: Writings on Modern Dance*

Doris Humphrey recognized humans have a kinesthetic sense that allows us to understand movement "on its own terms."[41] As a result, she was able to evolve a training system derived from what comes most instinctively to the human body's daily motional experience, and a choreographic system that relied on what comes naturally to the human brain's ability to process patterns of both time and space. Order, balance and harmony are hallmarks of Humphrey's technique and choreography.

Like Graham, Humphrey was from a deeply religious family—both her grandfathers were Congregational ministers and had graduated from Andover Theological Seminary where they trained as missionaries. Unlike the heavy-handed Puritanism Graham encountered as a child, Congregationalists embraced education and music, and Humphrey's mother was an accomplished pianist who graduated from both Mount Holyoke and the Boston Conservatory of Music. Growing up in Oak Park, Illinois, Humphrey herself studied piano (although she later recalled dreading the experience as a small child),[42] and was allowed to participate in dance classes at school where her instruction included ballet, folk, ballroom and aesthetic dance. Just as high school graduation came in 1913, fate necessitated that Humphrey begin teaching dance classes (first in Oak Park, and then in other Chicago suburbs) to help support her family, and while it would be several years before she began performing professionally, her life in dance was sealed.

The teaching in Illinois was an important developmental element for Humphrey, but by 1916, she was feeling the weight of family responsibilities and the realization she was meant to perform. At this point, her former teacher, Mary Wood Hinman, sent her a brochure from the Denishawn School in Los Angeles. Hinman, who was herself a widely respected teacher, believed that Ruth St. Denis was "of tomorrow"[43] and that she had much to offer Humphrey. Humphrey's mother was not impressed at first by the idea of her daughter going to Los Angeles. After all, Humphrey's teaching was quite successful from the start and several dances she created were included in Mary Wood Hinman's *Folk and Gymnastic Dancing* instruction book. Her mother must have realized, though, that continued study with famous dancers would only help her daughter's own reputation —and that despite proximity to Chicago, advanced dance training was difficult to find. So at first,

Humphrey attended Denishawn's summer program with the idea that the experience would help her own teaching. In short order, however, Humphrey began performing and teaching for Denishawn.

While Graham and Humphrey became regular soloists with the company, there was no ranking system among the Denishawn dancers (except its namesake stars).[44] At the same time, however, Humphrey was the only choreographer other than St. Denis and Shawn to make works for the company. She made at least ten dances in the Denishawn repertory from 1920 to 1928 including the *Valse Caprice* (*Scarf Dance*) (1920), *Soaring* which she made with St. Denis (1920), *Sonata Tragica* (1923), *Hoop Dance* (1924), and *Whims* (1927)—all of which demonstrated her increasingly well-developed choreographic principles, but did not yet indicate her

Doris Humphrey c. 1935.

technical principles. It should be mentioned that *Sonata Tragica* was created with St. Denis after Humphrey and Pauline Lawrence returned to Denishawn following their own vaudeville tour. The piece was originally set to music by Edward MacDowell, but following its premiere, St. Denis observed that the work could be performed in silence while maintaining its artistic clarity, and thus became the first American dance on record to be performed in silence.[45]

Humphrey made the famous thirteen-month Oriental tour with Denishawn, and created several successful works while on the road including *Burmese Yein Pwe* (1926). Former Denishawn dancer Jane Sherman suggested that by the time the company returned to the States only to face an extended American tour a few months later, the seeds of Humphrey's ultimate dissatisfaction with the company's management may have already been planted.[46] In truth, Humphrey did not participate in the winter 1927 *Ziegfeld Follies* tour with St. Denis and Shawn. Instead, she, Charles Weidman, and Pauline Lawrence stayed in New York to run the Denishawn school there. By 1928, Humphrey and Weidman were experimenting with new movement ideas in classes, but largely continued teaching the core of the Denishawn system:

> The students were stimulated by our enthusiasm for some discoveries about movement, which had to do with ourselves as Americans—not Europeans or American Indians or East Indians, which most of the Denishawn work consisted of—but as young people of the twentieth century living in the United States. All this was quite nebulous as yet, but already vistas of a more genuine dance form could be glimpsed ahead.[47]

Writing in her autobiography, Humphrey recalled Shawn's displeasure when he learned that they had not been teaching pure Denishawn. Then the inevitable fracture occurred that August when Humphrey was summoned to a meeting concerning the Greater Denishawn school that St. Denis and Shawn had been planning for some time—a meeting that did not include Weidman and Lawrence who had been running the New York school with Humphrey. The building of Greater Denishawn had generated tremendous debt, and all members of Denishawn were expected to help raise funds to pay down the mortgage. Humphey refused, however, when it was announced that she and Weidman were expected to participate in the next *Follies* tour. She challenged the artistic integrity of the idea, and before the meeting was completed, she was voted out of the group. That night, she, Weidman, and Lawrence decided to find their own New York studio space and create their own company.

Humphrey had dreamt of being able to focus solely on making dances during the Oriental tour, but "as it is, I only do about one dance a year, and that's much too slow—life won't be long enough to get everything done at that rate."[48] She got her first taste of that while the Shawns were on the *Follies* tour. Now, she would have her wish on a permanent basis. From 1928 to 1944, Humphrey and Weidman ran one of the most significant companies of the central modern years. By 1931, her ideas about technique were emerging from her choreography, and she created major masterpieces during these years including *Water Study* (1928), *The Shakers* or *Dance of the Chosen* (1931), *New Dance* (1935), *With My Red Fires* (1936), and *Passacaglia in C Minor* (1938).

Much of Humphrey's repertory reflected her sense of balance and harmony as her rhythmic design was often made to "reflect the intricate manner in which the individual weaves his personal paths in counterpoint to the group, yet always in harmony with it."[49] Her observation and use of the way the body falls and recovers itself even in the simple act of walking reflected that same dynamic tension. A correlation can be drawn between her work and her interest in Nietzschean philosophy: humans should be able to channel passions creatively instead of suppressing them; the will to power that led from a moral code of "Thou shalt" to "I will," and that the human might transcend the self by embracing vitality, power, exuberance, and self-expression and would be capable of combining all those qualities in a harmonious way. Thus Nietzsche's ideas did not suggest racial or ethnic superiority any more than they could support fascism because both racism and fascism reject reason, logic, and will.[50] (Humphrey herself found it quite shocking when St. Denis and Shawn suggested that the school limit its Jewish enrollments in 1928.) She strove for an art that was humanizing, and harmonious—a fact clearly illustrated in her *Declaration* (see pages 38–39).

By the mid-1940s, Humphrey's health forced an end to her performing career. Her protégé, José Limón, founded his own company in 1946 and Humphrey served as his artistic director, making more than a dozen dances for him until her final illness. In addition, Humphrey served on the faculties of The Juilliard School, the Bennington School of Dance, and the American

Dance Festival at Connecticut College, and chaired the Dance Department at the 92nd Street YMHA in New York. Her groundbreaking choreography course at the Y led her to write *The Art of Making Dances*, the seminal textbook on classic modern dancemaking still used in college dance programs nationwide.

Doris Humphrey: In the Studio

Although Denishawn provided Humphrey the chance to choreograph, there wasn't space for her to begin making technical discoveries until near the end of her time with them. In fact, Humphrey wrote of her technical evolution:

> The aim had to wait until I was able to build a new technique. I feel that the old technique was foreign in every way to the world we live in and must be discarded. Therefore, the early dances had to be confined to experiments with form and movement. For me this consisted of rediscovering and reapplying the natural laws of movement to group composition.[51]

Humphrey spent a period of time after Denishawn searching for a deeper sense of what motivates the body. Former Humphrey dancer Nona Schurman commented:

> In exploring for new ways of moving, [Humphrey] spent hours in front of a mirror just observing how the body moves. . . . She discovered that if the human being is to progress through space he must first lose balance (in other words, fall) and then recapture his balance by taking a step. The human walk is just that—a series of falls and recoveries. On this principle she built her new technique.[52]

Therefore, Humphrey's pivotal observations of fall and recovery don't apply to her works made during the Denishawn years. Fall and recovery aren't found, for instance, in *Hoop Dance* (1924) but are clearly present in later dances like *Passacaglia in C Minor* (1938).

Schurman also stressed the importance of Humphrey's contributions to understanding the choreographic process and to teaching methods in composition. Generations of composition students have learned the basic craft of dancemaking from Humphreys' *The Art of Making Dances*, which laid out everything she had observed about choreography. It was she who "made distinctions among the elements of style, performance, technique and structure—distinctions which before had never been clearly made."[53] These are tools of the theater, not simply of modern dance.

Humphrey's understanding of musicality is so clear in her choreography, which itself is musical and complex. Her early musical training helped her understand structural elements, which is evident in both her choreography and her technique.

Additionally, Humphrey did not codify her technique in the way that Graham did. For example, while Graham's ideas were laid out in a syllabus, Humphrey did not go in that direction. Her technique is evolutionary, and because the material is founded on philosophy, it is also qualitative. This allows teachers to establish movement sequences based on Humphrey's own technique class exercises, or to draw ideas from her repertory that support the principles. So, there is a sense of flexibility and a degree of spontaneity to the technique.

Humphrey's *Declaration* and *Principles of Movement*

Before delving deeper into a studio experience, it is helpful to have an idea of what Humphrey had to say about her own work and developmental process. Unlike many other leaders of the early and central modern periods, Humphrey wrote a number of short essays or statements explaining her studies and findings in the studio and how that experimentation led to technical and artistic production. Below are two statements expressing her intellectual/artistic point of view, and the expectations she had for her own work.[ii]

Declaration

My dance is an art concerned with human values. It upholds only those values that make for harmony and opposes all forces inimical to those values. In part, its movement may be used for decoration, entertainment, emotional release or technical display; but primarily it is composed as an expression of American life as I see it today.

This new dance of action comes inevitably from the people who had to subdue a continent, to make a thousand paths through forest and plain, to conquer the mountains, and eventually to raise up towers of steel and glass. The American dance is born of this new world, new life and new vigor.

I believe that the dancer belongs to his time and place and that he can only express that which passes through or close to his experience. The one indispensable quality in a work of art is a consistent point of view related to the times. When this is lost, and when there is substituted for it an aptitude for putting together bits of this and that drawn from extraneous material and dead methods, there can be no integrity.

Since my dance is concerned with immediate human values, my basic technique lies in the natural movements of the body. One cannot express contemporary life without humanizing movement, as distinguished from the dehumanization of the ballet. The modern dancer must come down from

---

[ii]*Declaration and Principles of Movement* appeared in Humphrey's collected writings, *New Dances: writings on modern dance* (Dance Horizons, 2008). Reprinted by permission of the publisher.

the points to the bare foot in order to establish his human relation to gravity and reality.

I wish my dance to reflect some experience of my own in relationship to the outside world; to be based on reality illuminated by imagination; to be organic rather than synthetic; to call forth a definite reaction from my audience; and to make its contribution toward the drama of life.

Principles of Movement

Principles of Movement: I conceive movement, for the dancer's purpose, to be basically one of equilibrium. In fact, *my entire technique consists of the development of the process of falling away from and returning to equilibrium.* This is far more than a mere business of "keeping your balance," which is a muscular and structural problem. Falling and recovering is the very stuff of movement, the constant flux that is going on in every living body, in all its tiniest parts, all the time.

Nor is this all, for the process has a psychological meaning as well. I recognized these emotional overtones very early and instinctively responded very strongly to the exciting danger of the fall, and the repose and peace of the recovery. Only much later did I find in Nietzsche a word expression of the meaning of these movements which revealed to me the fundamental rightness of my feeling. His two basic *kinds* of men, the *Apollonian* and the *Dionysian*, forever opposed and existing both in one man and in groups of men, are the symbols of man's struggle for progress on one hand, and his desire for stability on the other hand. These are not only the basis of Greek tragedy, as Nietzsche pointed out, but of all dramatic movement, particularly dance. And dance movement should be fundamentally dramatic, that is to say, human, not decorative, geometric or mechanical.

The technique evolved out of this theory is amazingly rich in possibilities. Beginning with simple falls complete to the floor and recoveries to standing, many elements of movements reveal themselves in addition to the falling of the body in space. One of these is *rhythm*. In a series of falls and recoveries, accents occur which establish a rhythm, even a phrase, as the time-space is varied due to gravitational pull on the body.

Another element is *dynamism*, that is, changes in intensity.

A third element is design. Even the latter, usually considered to be linear, having nothing to do with movement, is a functional result of the body's compensatory changes.

If left to itself, the body will make a number of weight adjustments in the course of a fall; and each of these will describe a design in space. I call these compensatory movements *oppositions*, and they occur in partial falls as well as in complete ones. For example, one foot will step forward to save the body on its way down. At the same time, the arms will swing out. This is also true in walking, which is a partial fall. Each one of these elementary parts of movement is capable of more or less isolation and almost limitless variation.

Extension of movement into studies: In addition to the purely technical development in dance which these insights led to, there was, all the while, the growing discovery that these movements were satisfying, even exciting to do and to see—not pure abstractions in the sense that technique is an abstraction, but had content. Because they sprang so truly and psychologically from physical life, they were emotionally stirring even without a program. This characteristic led me to compose a number of dance studies and even dance compositions entirely without a dramatic idea. Indeed, I think sometimes that the composer's meaning can only be conveyed fully by movement.

In the future, when America is finally won over to modern dance, audiences will enjoy the drama of life in motion as they now enjoy the drama of life in abstract music. Sometimes, however, the dance composer wishes to say something that demands specific treatment as to time and place and people. Here I use the same technical equipment; but all the movements, themes, phrases—in short, all the material of the dramatic dance—are conditioned by the idea of being expressed. Whereas we begin technically with natural movements resulting from fall and recovery that tend always toward the ideal, these same movements will be changed and distorted on being subjected to drama, which frequently demands less than the ideal or struggle for it.

This is the real explanation of the angular patterns which have come to be the bywords of modern dance. The dancer cannot be concerned entirely with the graceful line nor even with the fine animal ease with which technical study can and does provide him, because he is a living being, played upon by life, bursting with opinions and compulsions to express them. Sometimes, not always, he is concerned with themes of strife, struggle, and oppression. These demand an acrid line, a steely quality not found in purely kinetic movement unconditioned by ideas.

In order to achieve this, Humphrey firmly believed that technical mastery of the body was required, and to that end, she drew upon "natural bodily movement" as the source of her dance.[54] To clarify here, Humphrey's sense of natural movement was not a pedestrian approach to movement such as the postmodernists embraced during the Judson era. Humphrey's idea of "natural" movement was based on observations of human anatomy and its relationships with the physical sciences. She said:

> Breath rhythm is the one principle of all movement, whether actuated by emotional ritual or physical or intellectual impetus. Breath rhythm in the time sense is a two-part phrase, the first longer than the second; in the space sense, a filling and expanding followed by a contraction; in the dynamic sense, a continuous movement growing in tension, followed by a letting go of tension which finishes with an accent. By combining these three elements of the breath rhythm consciously in various ways the whole of the dance may be evolved.[55]

Thus, "natural movement" is derived from what comes most instinctively to the human body's daily motional experience.

In her treatise on Humphrey's technique, *The Dance Technique of Doris Humphrey and Its Creative Potential*, former Humphrey dancer Ernestine Stodelle recalled that as late as 1930, "Doris's major concern was her ensemble choreography, not the creation of a basic technique."[56] According to Stodelle, it was in preparation for John Martin's *The Modern Dance* lectures in January 1931 that Humphrey honed her training methodology "to prove elementary points concerning balance, momentum, direction, and so on."[57] From this process, "Humphrey began to develop a series of studies in rhythm, in oppositional and successional movement, studies in the varying dynamics of falling, studies in walking, running, and leaping."[58]

As with the Graham material, this is not intended to represent a codification of Humphrey's work.[iii] Additionally, this material focuses on a selection of the center and floorwork, and does not introduce barre work or movement through space. *This way you can take your time with the material. Don't rush through it. The sequences are pared down to their simplest form so that you may spend time trying to establish movement based on the breath.* (For an in-depth look at the technique, see Stodelle's book and her video on the technique.) In exploring the observations and movement sequences below, keep Humphrey's comments about breath rhythm in mind every step along the way. Note that while metre and musical qualities are often suggested, counts are not given so that the dancer may explore how natural breath patterns influence the phrasing.

[iii] Adapted from Ernestine Stodelle's *The Dance Technique of Doris Humphrey and Its Creative Potential*. Used by permission of the publisher.

BREATH RHYTHM OBSERVATION PART 1

Begin standing in a comfortable but stable position, feet about hip distance apart, with a slight bend in the knees. Allow the pelvis to drop into a neutral place, and activate the core so that you are supported but not in contraction. Open the shoulders and chest, and close your eyes. Following the next exhalation, begin noticing the natural rhythm of your own breath. Don't try to control anything or "make it happen," simply allow the breath to flow. Notice your natural breathing pace, how deeply you breathe normally, the time it takes for your breath cycle, and if the first part of the phrase (inhalation) is longer than the second (exhalation).

BREATH RHYTHM OBSERVATION PART 2

As you continue breathing, notice what happens to space in your body. Humphrey talked about a sense of expansion and then contraction. Feel how this can be experienced in several ways. For example, during inhalation you can feel your lungs and rib cage expand outward, and then contract inward on the exhalation. You can also experience the sense of falling downward on the exhalation followed by a rising—a recovery—growing upward on the next inhale. Notice how shallow or deep your natural breath rhythm is and how it affects the sense of space in the movement.

BREATH RHYTHM OBSERVATION PART 3

Sense the dynamic quality in your breathing as it flows naturally: fluid and legato or punctuated and abrupt/staccato. Notice accents at the height of the inhalation and the depth of the exhalation, and what happens when you control the dynamics a bit by making a sharp inhale, like a gasping "Ah," and then a rushing "Ha" on the exhale.

BREATH RHYTHM OBSERVATION PART 4

Shift your feet slightly so they are a little closer together, decreasing your base of support. Still keeping your eyes closed and returning to your regular breath rhythm, notice any changes in your body, the kind of movement that occurs as a response to your breathing, perhaps swaying a bit side-to-side or front-to-back. Paying more attention to the swaying, sense the exhale creating a falling sensation in your body, with the energy perhaps moving down and backward. Feel the inhale taking you forward and up?

Take a moment and jot down anything that you found interesting as you focused on your body's own cycle.

SUCCESSIONAL STUDY

As you flow through this sequence, be sure that the breath guides the movement. Try it first in silence, then with music at a moderate and sustained pace.

  Timing: 4/4 metre, 52 bpm

    Start: Stand with feet in parallel, arms relaxed at the sides.

Ting-Yu's next inhale will begin the successional motion from the floor to standing.

The first exhalation sends the head and torso accelerating forward and the knees bend until the fingertips reach the floor. The weight of the head and the pelvis create a gentle oppositional stretch while four short, staccato breaths create a bounce forward and back.

On the next inhale begin recovery, followed by successional movement with the knees moving slightly downward as the hips shift forward and the torso unfurls into a back arch with the sternum facing the ceiling, head gently dropped back and arms released to the sides. Four staccato breaths generate four small bounces.

On the next inhale return the body to a full standing position, then exhale. An inhale causes an impulse in the knees sending breath upward along the R side, R elbow reaches upward and the torso increasingly curves to the L (head drops L).

R arm unfurls and the torso rises into a suspension as the breath (and fingertips) reach the zenith. Sharp exhalation drops the body to the R and the R leg catches the weight in a deep side lunge (allowing the knee to breathe into the lunge) where the heel can remain on the floor.

Staying low, using gravity to assist you, slowly pull the R leg back to parallel in the same overdrop position from the first forward movement.

On the next inhale begin recovery, followed by successional movement with the knees moving slightly downward as the hips shift forward and the torso unfurls into a back arch with the sternum facing the ceiling, head gently dropped back and arms released to the sides. Four staccato breaths generate four small bounces.

On the next inhale return the body to a full standing position, then exhale.

Repeat the sequence front and L. The entire sequence should be completed at least 4 times. See how the experience changes when you add music.

ISOLATIONS

Initiate each movement with an accented exhale and then let motion continue with a sustained breath flow.

> Timing: 4/4 metre, 50 bpm
>> Start: Stand in parallel, arms at the sides.

On an exhale, drop head forward and circle it R twice. Return to upright.

Exhale and move R shoulder forward, up, back, and down twice slowly. Return to neutral, riding the breath the entire time.

On an inhale, fingertips initiate 2 full arm circles. Suspend at the zenith and exhale as the arm continues back and down.

Repeat the arm circles double time.

Return to tempo, inhale as R heel lifts, pressing the foot forward over the ball.

Exhale and stretch heel back to the ground.

Repeat with R foot 4 times. Repeat entire sequence L 4 times.

BASIC SWING VARIATIONS

Swings are a wonderful example of fall, rebound, and suspension and can be executed in a wide variety of ways. In these introductory swings, try to coordinate your breath and the bending of your knees with the impulse of the swing.

Up and Forward, Down and Back

> Timing: 6/8 metre, 100–110 bpm. Each component of the pattern takes about three counts to complete with no pause in between.
> Start: Stand in parallel.

[cts. 1–3] Arms curve and lift backward, wrists rotated so that palms face forward.

[cts. 1–3] Torso swings down, curving forward.

[cts. 1–3] Arms move forward and rotate, elbows lifting in succession forward and torso moves upright until everything is unfurled upward in a suspension (with a slight back arch). Reverse the path on the drop.

Repeat at least 6 times.

Vertical Torso and Head Swings (half circle)

> Timing: 4/4 metre, 65 bpm. Counting is continuous.
> Start: Standing, feet slightly turned out and a little more that hip-width apart.

Exhale to cause the R knee to bend and the torso to fall to the R. As gravity (the weight of the head) brings the torso forward, the L knee bends. Inhale to extend the R knee as the torso is pulled sideways L, and then upward as the L knee straightens.

Repeat L, complete entire sequence 2 times. Then, add the arm: exhale to cause the R knee to bend and the torso to fall to the R.

The torso falls to the right.

As gravity (the weight of the head) brings the torso forward, the L knee bends. Inhale to extend the R knee as the torso is pulled sideways L, drawing the R arm across the body, curving overhead, arriving L with the torso.

As the L knee straightens, the R arm completes its circle down to the R side.

Repeat L. Repeat entire sequence 2 times.

Successional Breath Movement

Timing: 4/4 metre, 60 bpm
   Start: Sit on the floor, feet together, spine straight; hold the ankles.

Exhale slowly so that the torso falls forward in an overcurve. Recover with the inhalation. Exhale slowly and let the torso fall backward in a slight arch. Recover with the inhalation.

Repeat forward and back 4 times.

On the next *and* count, exhale sharply so that the torso falls forward for 8 bounces. Recover on the next inhale, taking all 8 cts. to roll up the spine.

Repeat in 4 and 2 cts.

Knee Stretch

The path of this motion is forward and upward.

Timing: 2/4 metre, 60 bpm
   Start: Seated as at the completion of Successional Breath Movement.

Rotate knees to face the ceiling, toes lightly touching floor. Extend arms to the side at shoulder level, palms facing out. Engage the core to support the spine, move the torso backward to a 45-degree angle. In fours,

[cts. 1–4] Inhale and extend R leg forward and upward to 45 degrees, lower on the exhale.

Repeat L, R, L. Repeat entire sequence on 2 cts. and then 1 ct. Extend both legs outward, hold for at least 16 cts.

Thigh Stretch

In this exercise, keep the muscles in the thighs and pelvic girdle active so that the posture is supported, and the weight isn't "dumped" into the knee.

Timing: 6/8 metre, 60 bpm
   Start: Sit on the shins/tops of the feet, with the sitz bones lightly touching the heels. Round the torso forward, sending the forehead to the floor, and place the hands beside the knees. Inhale and in succession roll the torso backward, sliding the hands along and behind the body. As the torso unfurls into a straight diagonal to the back, raise the pelvis to create a straight line along the spine with the knees, hips, shoulders, and head in alignment. (Sitz bones no longer touch heels; hands support some of the weight but don't sink into them because you'll have to move in a moment.)

Bounce gently 3 times in this position, then move hands forward along the body until they raise off of the floor and the arms extend in a straight line from the shoulders, palms facing inward. Hold for three counts, then release the hips as torso rounds forward in succession to return to the starting position.

Repeat at least 3 times.

Body Roll

Timing: 4/4 metre, 70 bpm. Tempo is moderate and sustained.
   Start: Sit with the legs extended together in front of you, torso rounded forward, head

toward the knees, hands resting on the floor beside you.

Inhale to begin unfurling the torso backward, pulling the hands out and behind you as the torso descends to the ground. After the head and shoulders have touched down, inhale again to lift the sternum so that the head falls backward, beginning an arch upward. During the ascent, the torso needs to carry its own weight; don't allow the weight to sink into the hands as they slide in and along the floor. Reach the height of the ascent on ct . 5.

Exhale to begin the descent forward again, returning to the starting place.

Repeat at least 4 times.

Diagonals with Transition

Timing: 4/4 metre, 45 bpm

Start: Legs extended as at the end of Body Roll, bring the entire body on a diagonal to face downstage R corner. Wrap the L leg behind you to a 60–70-degree angle with the foot close to the L gluteus, R leg completely extended, fingertips lightly touching the floor beside the hips. Torso is upright.

On the last two counts of the preparation, inhale and lift the arms in parallel, extended from the shoulder and reaching over the R leg. Exhale and round forward until the forehead reaches the R

Ting-Yu and her colleague Elijah Gibson demonstrate the beginning and midpoint of the first part of Diagonals with Transition.

knee, fingertips extended beyond the R foot. Inhale and recover backward to the starting position, arms release and fingertips trace a line beside the hips along the floor (thumb side up, little-finger side on the floor) until they are directed behind you, head begins to turn L. As the hands carry the weight backward, arch the torso slightly, head falls to the L. Torso finishes on the ground, arms in an extended V. R leg remains extended, L knee maintains floor contact the entire time.

Inhale to initiate a torso lift and return to starting position. (The arm preparation now becomes enveloped at the top of the next phrase.)

Repeat. On the third repetition, L arm remains forward as the body falls, so the slide is only on the R hand, head does not fall so that the gaze may remain on the L hand. The L arm remains where it is on the recovery.

Transition: Exhale and fold the R leg by drawing the R foot along the floor toward the pelvis. An overcurve brings the head and torso slightly to the R to sit on the R gluteus. As the arms move into parallel to the R, L knee folds in toward the body. Exhale to extend L leg across the body, arms reach on R diagonal.

Shift onto both sitz bones, move R knee upward so that the toes slightly touch the floor

Notice that the right legs have remained lengthened as the dancers have moved into the back diagonal, and that they have not allowed their legs to drift into rotation—their legs remain parallel. Also, both dancers have kept their cores engaged in order to protect their lower backs in this slight arch.

in front, L leg and both arms fan upward (arms toward the ceiling).

On the final counts of the phrase, turn R knee in as the arms open outward and L leg straightens toward the ground to original starting position on L side facing the downstage L corner.

Repeat entire sequence. Repeat transition again to finish on the R.

The Back Fall

In this sequence, you'll clearly see how the ideas you've been exploring are connected—elements from the Swings, Body Roll, and the Diagonal are here.

Timing: 6/8 metre, 70 bpm

Start: Stand in parallel, arms relaxed at the sides.

Preparation begins with a small impulse in the knees, curve torso over as elbows bend forward, inhale to cause the body to rise upward as it unfurls toward suspension on half-toe.

At the point where gravity pulls you forward, exhale to send R foot forward into a full lunge, torso curved over, hands catching the weight on either side of the R foot, L leg remains straight behind. Tuck L foot in behind R heel, slide hands backward (little-finger side down) as the torso rolls to the floor, ending the fall with much as you did the Body Roll (except L leg is rotated out, bent at the knee, foot roughly under R knee).

Recovery: Inhale to arch the torso, head drops back on the rise, hands slide back in toward the body and take weight. R leg bends as you continue forward to shift the weight upward and onto the R foot, bring L foot to meet the R as soon as possible. A small impulse in the knees curves the torso over as the elbows bend forward, inhale to cause the body to rise upward as it unfurls toward the suspension onto half-toe.

Repeat at least 4 times on both sides.

Final Questions

1. You've now experienced two dynamically different ideas about the impact of breath on movement. Consider your own observations about the impact of breath from the opening assignment in this chapter. How did what you observed compare with what you felt as you physically explored this chapter?

2. How has this experience changed the way that you view breath, and what are some ways you might want to further this exploration as a dancer? As a choreographer?

3. Was it easier for you to create movement with a staccato breath or with a sustained breath rhythm? What differences did you notice in those experiences when you moved in silence compared with those when you moved to music?

Works Cited

Armitage, M. (1978). *Martha Graham: The early years*. New York: DaCapo.

Barnes, C. (1991, July). Martha's dance immortal. *Dance Magazine*, p. 98.

Brown, J. M. (1979). *The Vision of Modern Dance*. Princeton, NJ: Princeton Book Company.

Cohen, S. J. (1992). *Dance as a Theatre Art: Source readings in dance history from 1581 to the present*. Princeton, NJ: Princeton Book Company.

_____. (1995). *Doris Humphrey: An artist first*. Pennington, NJ: Princeton Book Company.

de Mille, A. (1950, November). Atlantic Portrait: Martha Graham. *Atlantic Monthly*, pp. 26–31.

_____. (1991). *Martha: The life and work of Martha Graham*. New York: Random House.

Eilber, J. (2009, June 3). Janet Eilber on Martha Graham Technique. Interview by J. Legg.

Fischer, B. (1986). *Graham's Dance Steps in the Street and selected early technique: Principles of reconstructing choreography from videotape*. Ann Arbor, MI: University Microfilms International.

Graham, M. (1978). How I became a dancer. In M. N. Nadel & C. N. Miller, *The Dance Experience: Readings in dance appreciation* (pp. 237–239). New York: Universe Books.

_____. (1991). *Blood Memory: An autobiography*. New York: Doubleday.

Helpern, A. (1994). *The Technique of Martha Graham*. Dobbs Ferry, NY: Morgan and Morgan.

Horosko, M. (1991). *Martha Graham: The evolution of her dance theory and training 1926–1991*. Pennington, NJ: A Cappella Books.

Humphrey, D. (2008). *New Dance: Writings on modern dance*. Hightstown, NJ: Princeton Book Company.

Johnston, D. *A Brief History of Philosophy: From Socrates to Derrida*. New York: Continuum.

Kennedy Center for the Performing Arts (Producer). *Performing Arts Series: Martha Graham Dance Company*. [Motion picture]. Washington, DC: Kennedy Center for the Performing Arts.

Kennicott, J. (1991, July). Martha and Music. *Dance Magazine*, pp. 66–67.

Kriegsman, S. A. (1981). *Modern Dance in America: The Bennington years*. Boston: G. K. Hall & Co.

Kirstein, L. (1935, February 27). The Dance: Some American dancers. *The Nation*, pp. 258–259.

Martin, J. (1972). *The Modern Dance*. New York: Dance Horizons.

_____. (1975). *Introduction to the Dance*. New York: Dance Horizons.

McDonagh, D. (1973). *Martha Graham: A biography*. New York: Praeger.

Siegel, M. B. (1985). *The Shapes of Change: images of American dance*. Berkeley: University of California Press.

_____. (1993). *Days on Earth: The dance of Doris Humphrey*. Durham, NC: Duke University Press.

Sherman, J. (1994). Martha and Doris in Denishawn: A closer look. *Dance Chronicle*, 17 (2), pp. 179–193.

Schurman, N. (1970). "Looking at Doris's Works is Like Listening to Bach." In *Encores for Dance: Selected articles on dance iii 1968–1977*, (p. 63). Fallon, D. (Ed.). (1978). Washington: American Alliance for Health, Physical Education, Recreation and Dance.

Smith, W. (1944, January 10). Protestant dancer. *Time*, pp. 57-58.

Soares, J. M. (1992). *Louis Horst: Musician in a dancer's world*. Durham, NC: Duke University Press.

Sorell, W. (1984, December). The man of modern dance: Louis Horst. *Dance Magazine*, pp. 88–92.

Stodelle, E. (1978). *The Dance Technique of Doris Humphrey and Its Creative Potential*. Princeton, NJ: Princeton Book Company.

Terry, W. (1956). *The Dance in America*. New York: Harper and Brothers Publishers.

Tobias, T. (1984, March). A conversation with Martha Graham. *Dance Magazine*, pp. 62–67.

Tracy, R. (1996). *Goddess: Martha Graham's Dancers Remember*. New York: Limelight Editions.

CHAPTER 3

The Mavericks

Katherine Dunham

Lester Horton

In order to gain acceptance within a modern dance that was defined and dominated by whites, black artists needed to be able to obtain access to the vocabularies and techniques of the genre as well as avenues to patronage . . . the process was hardly straightforward, considering the problematic nature of race in America. White critics struggled . . . to define a "Negro" high-art dance . . . and struggled again to decide how a black person might be a modern dancer rather than a "Negro" one.

—Gay Morris, *A Game for Dancers*

I t is difficult for Americans coming of age today to comprehend the force and weight of the legal segregation and deep-seated discriminatory social attitudes levied against persons of color in the last century. We have to consider that the advent of modernism coincided with the age of the Ku Klux Klan in order to develop a sense of the tremendous obstacles black dance artists faced. Legalized and de facto segregation not only limited travel, public accommodations, and educational opportunities for persons of color in America, but also had an impact on seating arrangements in many theaters nationwide. For example, even when Katherine Dunham's company was allowed to play a particular theater while on tour, she often had to fight with the manager to establish an integrated seating arrangement—a situation of great importance for several reasons, including the

Esther Brown, Alvin Ailey, and Joyce Trisler in Lester Horton's Combata de Amor, *ca. 1953.*

Year	Civil Rights / Historical Events	Dance Events
1876		
1896	Plessey v. Furguson	
1900		Loie Fuller performs at Paris Exposition
1908	Springfield Race Riots	
1909	NAACP founded	Isadora Duncan opens Paris dance school
1915		Denishawn opens
1924		Edna Guy begins dancing at Denishawn
1925		Hemsley Winfield forms first group/Charles Williams begins dancing
1926		Martha Graham's first concert
1928		Humphrey-Weidman founded
1930		Katherine Dunham founds Ballet Negre
1931		Asadata Dafora presents 1st work/ Randolph Sawyer in Gluck-Sandor's Petrouchka
1932		Lester Horton founds dance company
1934		School of American Ballet opens
1935		George Balanchine founds American Ballet
1943		Pearl Primus holds first concert
1948		Ballet Society becomes NYCB
1951		Donald McKayle choreographs *Games*
1954	Brown v. Board	
1955	Rosa Parks/Montgomery bus boycott	Arthur Mitchell joins NYCB
1956	NAACP banned in Louisianna	
1957		Balanchine's *Agon*
1958	Year of the Bombings	Alvin Ailey founds company/Eleo Pomare dances 1st time
1960	Woolworth sit-in	Ailey's *Revelations*
1961		Gus Solomons, jr. begins dancing
1962	Ole Miss integration	
1963	March on Washington	
1964	Civil Rights Act signed	
1965	Malcolm X assassinated. Watts Riots	
1966	Black Panther Party founded	
1967	Loving v. Virginia	
1968	Martin Luther King, Jr. assassinated. Chicago riots during DNC Convention	
1969		Arthus Mitchell opens Dance Theatre of Harlem
1970		Garth Fagan founds company
1973		Bill T. Jones/Arnie Zane Co.
1982		Alsonso King's Lines Ballet
1984		Urban Bush Women
1985		Bebe Miller founds company
1992		Rennie Harris Puremovement
1994		Dwight Rhoden/Desmond Richards/Complexions Dance Company
2001		Robert Battle/Battleworks
2008	Barak Obama elected 44th President	

period of Jim Crow Laws with legalized and de facto segregation

idea that "watching Dunham's dances, critics and audiences engaged in the dynamics of cross-viewing, the possibility for spectators to catch glimpses of perspectives conditioned by subjectives and social identities that differed from their own."[1]

These circumstance and the fumblings of the white dance critics Morris refers to are anathema to the dance world in which I grew up. My generation of artists, and those that follow, experience art in general, and dance specifically, in a much different light from prior generations that grew up during the near-century of Jim Crow laws. That is not to say that the specter of racism is vanquished. Contrary to discourse around the 2008 election of Barack Obama, we do not live (and do not make art) in a postracial society.[2] Still, those of us who came of age in the hip-hop generation have never known a legally segregated America, which means that dance companies and audiences have for the most part been integrated since we first saw a human body in motion. How does one fathom, then, that white critics actually felt they had a right to decide between an identifier "Negro" against "modern" when describing a dancer? How does it affect our present view of the body of John Martin's dance criticism when we read his 1931 coverage of the Gluck-Sandor Dance Center's *Petrouchka*, in which Randolph Sawyer (the show's only black dancer) performed the Blackamoor. Martin was bemused by how Sawyer's "native talents. . . . equip[ped] him to do a type of dance quite out of the range of his colleagues."[3] Then, too, there is Martin's 1940 derision of black dancers trying to work inside European concert forms as using "the gloss of an alien racial culture that deceives no one," and that in Katherine Dunham's company he found the incorporation of academic ballet technique "distressing."[4] Additionally, many white dance critics talked about the black dancer as exotic and erotic. In the review of Dunham's company mentioned above, Martin even went so far as to conclude his critique with "P.S.—Better not take grandma," revealing the naïve and primitive racial attitudes that pervaded much of the era's dance writing.

Although some of this sentiment continued at least into the 1960s, there are, of course, a few notable exceptions to the pervasive naiveté or outright racism that dominated dance criticism at the time: Margret Lloyd's work stands in contrast to Martin's for her ability to see quality as the criterion of merit, rather than expectation built upon a folksy stereotype. Lloyd never seemed bemused or derisive in writing about black dance artists. Rather, she seemed to find their work increasingly on a caliber with their white peers. Marian Hannah Winter, in her 1947 essay *Juba and American Minstrelsy*, provided a vital first piece of scholarly documentation charting the roots of an African American dance experience, and gave us insight into the development of widespread racial stereotyping in both social and concert contexts. Generally though, as is often the case with public memory, mainstream critical attitudes are a significant determiner of historical visibility. As a result of the politics of exclusion and denial, the work of majorities is often seen as the

The timeline Jim Crow Laws and American Concert Dance illustrates dance development set against a variety of significant events in the struggle for racial equality in the United States.

worthwhile contribution—socially or artistically—over the work of minorities. In dance history, that played out for decades as near-invisibility for black dance artists and their contributions to concert aesthetics. Even into the 1990s, significant dance history writers made the marginalizing of the black dance artist *de rigueur (exclusion),* or they completely omitted the existence of these artists altogether (denial).

Solidarity Isn't Integration

By the late 1920s, there were white choreographers working both in leftist and modern dance who cast black dancers. While leftist dancemakers were supporting black artists in their own right by the 1930s, it is important to note that for revolutionary dance presenters the color that mattered was not black, but red. Researchers Ellen Graff, a former professor at Barnard College, and Mark Franko, Chair of Theater Arts at the University of California–Santa Cruz, provide excellent scholarship illustrating that racial unity was a major concern for the Communist dancers of the era. Graff noted:

> A key issue engaging the Communist press and igniting radical fires during the 1930s was racial discrimination and violence against Negroes. Head-lines in the *Daily Worker* reported lynchings and terrorism in the South and pointed to the need for black-and-white solidarity in the class struggle. . . . In like manner, [J.C.] Eden's poem [*Black Fists, White Fists*] . . . linked the equality of the races to their mutual experience as workers.[5]

What becomes evident upon further reading, however, is that few of the most significant works choreographed in "racial solidarity" actually included black dancers. Helen Tamiris, who was among the most important leaders in developing modern dance, and Jane Dudley made two of the best-known solidarity pieces—*How Long Brethren?* and *Harmonica Breakdown,* respectively—where white dancers intended to empathize with their black comrades. Yet, no black dancers appeared in these works (it should be noted, however, that a black gospel choir was used for the Tamiris work. For more on Tamiris, see Chapter 4.) So, to a certain extent, what dance criticism was saying can also be seen in some of the work of dance itself in the central modern period—even in work that was supposed to be in solidarity. Susan Manning, a dance historian at Northwestern University, noted that "both leftist [dance] and modern dance[i] relied on assumptions about the generalizing power of white bodies that created a critical conundrum for black dancing bodies."[6] Even if, as Franko asserted, Tamiris's work—considered in the context of the era—was in accord with black

---

[i] Manning's distinction between leftist dance and modern dance refers to the sociopolitical motivation of those involved. Leftist dancers were often union members and their work reflected labor concerns and frequently socialist or communist ideals as well. Modern dancers may have had individual political associations or occasionally made politically-motivated work, but the thrust of their dancing was not intended as political speech.

artists working inside left-wing dance and should be viewed as "cultural cross-dressing,"[7] the work of Popular Front artists was driven by class struggle and not by a desire to describe the unique experiences of black dance artists and of what we now identify as the African Diaspora.

Mainstream choreographers often took a similar approach. Charles Weidman's *Lynchtown* (1936) was an examination of abstracted mob mentality boiled to a frenzy that culminated in a lynching. The work, made on an all-white cast, could have taken place anywhere, but the connotations would have been clear to an American audience during the era. And, while Doris Humphrey choreographed Hall Johnson's Broadway musical, *Run, Little Chillun* (1933) for an all-black cast, dance companies did not begin to integrate until Martha Graham hired Mary Hinkson in 1951. Examining the body of work in both mainstream and leftist dance, then, ignores the work black dance artists were creating, their interests, or their contributions to the burgeoning art form.

This was certainly in stark contrast to the work of the Harlem Renaissance taking place at same time, where black writers and intellectuals illustrated that their contemporary perspective wasn't simply one of a postslavery experience. They expressed, instead, a complex experience with direct lineage extending back to Africa. Among the first dance artists to truly address this challenge head-on was Katherine Dunham, whose work, Manning observed, can be read as the performance of diaspora.[8] Aside from Dunham and Pearl Primus, little is known about the training practices of other prominent black dancemakers of this period. As a result, artists like Helmsley Winfield, Edna Guy, Randolph Sawyer, Ollie Burgoyne, Charles Williams and Asadata Dafora do not fit directly into this present study, but did make a range of important contributions to modern dance during the era. [See John Perpener's *African-American Concert Dance: The Harlem Renaissance and Beyond* for more on these artists.]

Brenda Dixon Gottschild, professor emerita at Temple University, has illuminated the aesthetics African diasporic artists contributed to American dance (among other modalities of culture and communication). She referred to these as *Africanist aesthetics*. In this context, Africanist concerns concepts, practices, attitudes, or forms that have roots/origins in Africa and the African Diaspora. Gottschild also identified five traits inherent in this aesthetic: embracing the conflict (an aesthetic of contrariety), polycentrism/polyrhythm, high-affect juxtaposition, ephebism (youthfulness), and the aesthetic of the cool.[9] While each of these traits is important, polycentrism/polyrhythm will figure into this present study prominently. In polycentrism, simultaneous movements originate from multiple centers in the body. Polyrhythm is the employment of more than one rhythm occurring at the same time. As we will see in Katherine Dunham's work in this chapter, moving from multiple centers in the body then allows a dancer to simultaneously perform layers of rhythm. She noted that irony, multiple meanings, and innuendo are

> three interrelated attributes of the Africanist aesthetic that have been worked, reworked, and brought into high relief because of the need of

diasporan African peoples to simultaneously conceal and reveal, disguise and display themselves in alien, if not hostile, New World environments.[10]

Along the way, white choreographers and music composers have also incorporated Africanist aesthetics into their work. Gottschild pointed out the influence of Africanist principles on Igor Stravinsky and George Balanchine. For instance, in Stravinsky, we see the use of radical rhythms and chromatic scores not common in European music composition. In Balanchine, "…the underlying speed, vitality, energy, coolness, and athletic intensity that are fundamental to his Americanization of ballet" have a direct correlation to these aesthetics.[11] Additionally, the presence of these aesthetics is not limited to historical works. Instead, their infusion into and influence on contemporary artistic and cultural processes globally is an ongoing, evolutionary occurrence in literature, theatre, dance, music, and film (not to mention philosophy, politics, and religion). Furthermore, Halifu Osumare, a faculty member in African American and African Studies at University of California–Davis, observed that

> The Africanist aesthetic in the Americas continues to reflect similar musical, dance, and oral practices that resemble those in West and Central Africa, the source of the Atlantic slave trade. Though this aesthetic in the United States is no longer African per se, it still retains enough resonances in the performer's attitude, artistic methodology, and relationship to audience to make apparent its cultural connections to African expressive practices.[12]

Osumare's primary mechanism for this aesthetic transmission is global hip-hop culture—an observation that certainly resonates for me as my own first dance experience was with b-boy (break boy) as a young teenager in the early 1980s. The transmission of those aesthetics continued in my formal dance training when I encountered Balanchine's ballet style, and in the techniques of the two main artists in this chapter, Katherine Dunham and Lester Horton.

It is fitting on a number of levels that Dunham and Horton should be paired together here. While Dunham enjoyed success in Hollywood and on Broadway, she and Horton both spent much of their careers as outsiders to the modern dance world. Although both are critically acknowledged as pioneers in the art form, their contributions often receive less than adequate coverage in dance history courses (or books). On the surface, there is the locus of their work outside New York City. The vast majority of Horton's work was made in Los Angeles, away from the eyes of New York audiences and perhaps more importantly, away from the eyes of the major dance critics of the time. Clive Barnes (former dance critic for *The New York Times*) wrote in a special piece on Horton for the *Los Angeles Herald Examiner* more than a decade after the choreographer's death that "The neglect of Horton is easily understood. For a modern dancer he committed the unforgivable crime of working on the wrong coast, choosing Los Angeles as his center rather than New York."[13] Dunham, on the other hand, carved a place for herself in New York—even locating her school for a time in Isadora Duncan's old studio—and achieved critical acclaim for her work there. Unlike her contemporaries Graham and Limón, Dunham had artistic, intellectual, and social interests that could not be met by concentrating her work almost exclusively in that city. Even after she stopped performing, she continued making significant contributions to society and culture—particularly through her work as an activist and educator.

As will become clear, however, dance itself was not the only important concern that Dunham and Horton shared. The choreography these mavericks created obliterated the dance world's racial barriers in the 1930s and 1940s. They provided homes—training grounds—for black dancers who would emerge as some of the most significant dance artists of the twentieth century. Their companies and choreographies gave a sociocultural voice to what eventually evolved into the Civil Rights movement. The fact that Dunham herself was black, and that both she and Horton employed black dancers, severely limited their touring capacities within the United States owing to Jim Crow laws, which further hampered them from receiving the same attention as their contemporaries.

The final reason why this pairing is so appropriate, of course, is that their techniques are so complementary —in terms of both their raw, powerful physicality and the utilization of what may be modern dance's most complex musicality. The kinesthetic ideas and stylistic choices of both dancemakers inspired jazz choreographers in the second half of the twentieth century, and jazz students regularly encounter many of the following ideas without ever knowing the source of their training.

Core Ideas

....

Observations and Experiments

Journal I: Listen to music with polyrhythm (several different rhythms performed simultaneously). It is strongly suggested that you work with live musicians for this experience, as they can highlight the primary or secondary rhythms to make it easier for beginning dancers to distinguish the different layers. If a recording is necessary, consider this: polyrhythm appears in traditional cultural music forms the world over (particularly in African forms), and in Western classical and twentieth-century art music as well. Try a piece that is percussion-based and one that is orchestrated. The third movement of Beethoven's *String Quartet No. 6 in B flat, Op. 8*, for example, is a scherzo (in 3/4 time), but its cross-rhythm makes it feel like a 6/8. The swinging jazz standard *Afro Blue* is a more contemporary example (listen to John Coltrane's 1963 live recording from Birdland as other recordings may be in a different metre). Both of these examples employ a specific form of poly-rhythm called cross-rhythm, and feature a 2 played against a 3. Try to find other options.

Once you have your music, close your eyes and

see which musical pulse you feel most strongly in your body and notice where your sense of the beat is clearest: in your feet, stomach, or chest. See if you can count the beats and make sense of the layered rhythms.

Write a few notes in your journal about the experience, describing if it was hard to find a single beat to follow, to distinguish the dominant rhythm, and to leave that dominant rhythm and explore the subordinate rhythm(s).

Journal II: As you walk around campus, city, or town, pay attention to the geometrical shapes you encounter. Consider the shapes in architecture, nature, and the people you pass as well. Make special note of horizontals and laterals—those shapes that are either parallel or perpendicular to the ground.

Make sketches of the shapes that most interest you. Jot down a few observations about how these shapes relate to one another. Think of what might happen if you tried to recreate that shape in your body or to establish a similar relationship between your body and the ground, and what impact gravity might have in that exploration.

Experiment I: In the studio, explore these ideas and see what kind of movement you can create: hip isolations, undulations, pelvic contractions, coccyx (tailbone) balance, and flat back. See if you can create a short phrase without using music that incorporates a couple of those movements, and then try to move one part of your body in a rhythm that is different from the rhythm in the rest of your body. Make a few notes about that experience, stating if it was difficult to come up with two rhythms without music to follow.

Experiment II: Think of what a fusion of ballet and modern dance might look like. Try building a movement phrase that incorporates familiar ballet vocabulary with these ideas: pelvic contractions, freedom in the pelvis, off center, and parallel vs. turnout (working with one leg turned out against the other in parallel). Notice if you were able to move in some unusual or unique ways, and if it was exciting or frustrating to struggle with gravity in a new way.

· ·

Technical Genesis

Katherine Dunham (1909–2006): Biographical Sketch

And though I have not smelled the smell of burning flesh, and have never seen a black body swaying from a Southern tree, I have felt these things in spirit, and finally through the creative artist comes the need of the person to show this thing to the world, hoping that by so exposing the ill the conscience of the many will protest and save further destruction and humiliation. This is not all of America, it is not all of the South, but it is a living present part.

— Katherine Dunham, *Southland* program note

Katherine Dunham in Tropics.

As a high school sophomore in Joliet, Illinois, Dunham joined the Terpsichorean Club, "where her natural love of dancing was fired to ambition."[14] Her dance studies early on included ballet and modern (which incorporated the ideas of Jaques-Dalcroze and Laban), as well as East Indian, Javanese, and Balinese forms. Dunham studied with Ludmilla Speranzeva, Bentley Stone, Harald Kreutzberg, and Mark Turbyfill, and she eventually began her performing career dancing for ballet great Ruth Page. As a student at the University of Chicago, she entered Dr. Robert Redfield's ethnology class that led her to major in ethnology and later to pursue graduate work in anthropology. In an interview, Dunham once said, "My great interest in dance had been a subconscious feeling that it was more than a physical exercise; that it was somehow closely related to the people who danced, and naturally I was tremendously excited over the confirmation of this theory which I found in ethnology."[15] In 1935, she received a Rosenwald fellowship to study traditional Caribbean dance forms, of which she later said, "My desire was to see first-hand the primitive dance in its everyday relationship to the people; and anthropology, which leads one to origins and the simple basic fundamentals of art which is made complex and esoteric by civilization."[16]

In addition to her cultural examinations abroad, she was also developing a career in concert dance. In 1930, she had created her first dance company in Chicago, Ballet Nègre—one of the first African American dance companies—and founded the Negro Dance Group in 1933 as a training ground for young black dancers. It was in that same year that Ruth Page invited Dunham to perform in her ballet *La Guiablesse*. When the Chicago Opera asked Page to present the work in their regular season, she was already committed to other work, and asked Dunham to restage the piece and take over the lead role. Of the project Page said, "I told the opera people that there was a very intelligent and attractive dancer named Katherine Dunham. If they wanted the ballet she could rehearse it and dance the lead. They agreed, and Katherine was put in charge. . . . Again it was a success, and Katherine had an experience of directing a large group, some of whom, like Talley Beatty and Archie Savage, became part of her permanent group that would later tour the world."[17] It can be speculated that because *La Guiablesse* was based on a West Indian legend, Dunham must have felt her own intellectual and artistic interests piqued during the experience—perhaps reinforcing her growing desire to present Afro-Caribbean dance forms based on scholarly inquiry so that more integral stage representations of these peoples might be created.

Dunham's first field exploration allowed her to examine the dance forms of Jamaica, Martinique, Trinidad, and Haiti. She emerged from these cultural studies with not only ideas about the social implications of the dance forms she encountered, but also a deep awareness of the physical attributes that separated these cultural forms from those of other parts of the world. By adding her observations on the Afro-Caribbean use of the pelvis as well as isolations and undulations of the torso to the more European-American ideas about concert dance, Dunham created an entirely unique dance technique and vision of not only what modern dance might be, but also how it might affect racial and cultural understandings worldwide.

> The techniques that I knew, and saw, and experienced were not saying the things I wanted to say. I simply could not, with purely classical ballet, say what I wanted to say. I could do a story, of course—as you know, so much of ballet is narrative—but to capture the meaning in the culture and the life of the people, I felt that I had to take something directly from the people and develop that.[18]

Dunham also made significant contributions to scholarship in her field. In her career, she produced several books, including *Journey to Accompong*, *Las danzas de Haiti* (with a preface by Claude Levi-Strauss), *Island Possessed*, *A Touch of Innocence*, and *Kasamance*, as well as a wide variety of magazine articles, short stories, and poems. She presented scholarly lectures at universities and other forums worldwide, including the Royal Anthropological Society in London (1948).

When Dunham returned to Chicago from her first Caribbean project, she "reassembled her group of dancers and started putting her findings into practical use."[19] In 1937, she made her first New York appearance on a program called "A Negro Dance Evening" working alongside Edna Guy, Alison Burroughs, Clarence Yates, and Asadata Dafora—all artists who were illustrating dance from an Africanist perspective by presenting works based on traditional dances from their home in Africa (Dafora) or by creating an artistic response to the current black experience in the Americas.[20] Marie-Christine Dunham-Pratt, Katherine Dunham's daughter, points out that "My mother's work, of course, was different than the work a lot of the other choreographers were doing. Even though the Caribbean dances had roots in Africa, there was a French influence on the movement, so the movement would have looked very different from what others brought from Africa."[21] Dunham's work was also different from choreographers such as Pearl Primus who, after observing traditional dance in Africa, often placed literal translations of what she witnessed on the stage as a "dance documentary" of sorts. For Dunham, though, the material she gathered in the field served as a foundation for broader creative development in her work.

Dunham returned to New York with sixteen of her dancers in 1940 to present a concert at the 92nd Street YM-YWHA. This concert was so successful that the production moved to the Windsor Theatre for a thirteen-week run.[22] She would soon go on to collaborate with George Balanchine on the Broadway production *Cabin the Sky* (in which she and her company also performed for a year), and eventually choreographed and starred in a large number of Broadway and Hollywood productions. Perhaps her most popular film appearance (and choreography) was in the film *Stormy Weather*. Dunham's company, the Katherine Dunham Dance Company, had visited fifty-seven countries by the time she stopped touring.

A moment from Dunham's L'Ag'ya.

In all, Dunham choreographed more than 150 works for stage and film, and she was the first black choreographer for the Metropolitan Opera (the opera *Aida*). As mentioned above, the works she made for her own company regularly reflected concerns of the African Diaspora—in some instances, these were theatrical adaptations of Caribbean rituals or stories, stories familiar to the African American landscape, or work she made in reaction to the African American experience. Works like *L'Ag'ya* retold Caribbean stories—in this case, the tale of love, hatred, and zombies— and incorporated movement derived from the Martinique fighting dance, *l'ag'ya*, in part of the choreography.

Other pieces such as *Shango* are theatrical stagings of the Vaudun rituals Dunham observed as an anthropologist. It should be noted here that Dunham was not making satirical works in this vein. On the contrary, she herself was a Vaudun initiate and was also introduced to its Cuban relative, Santería.[23] *Rites de Passage* was performed as a substantive component of the Dunham Company's 1944 *Tropical Revue* tour and after the tour's opening night in Boston that January, the local censor required that the *Rites* section be removed from subsequent performances despite its being less erotic and animalistic than other sections of the *Revue*. By the time that the tour opened for an extended New York engagement, the press and public became acclimated to the so-called tropical atmosphere, and accepted the undulating rhythms, not as a sign of moral undulant fever, but as sincere native expression. African movement is pelvic movement, natural and unselfconscious. It becomes erotic on the stages of civilization, where the translator is faced with the onerous task of moderating it to meet a different set of tastes and standards, without too drastically sacrificing its essence.[24]

By 1946 critics had come to an understanding of what Dunham was doing. *The New York Times* dance critic, John Martin, noted in his review of Dunham's November season at the Belasco Theatre that *Shango* "manages to make a legitimately theatrical spectacle out of a primitive religious ritual."[25]

Dunham's 1951 dance, *Southland*, was a different story. Made as the nation was heading deep into McCarthyism, the work began with Dunham speaking (in Spanish) the lines quoted at the start of this section, "Though I have not smelled the smell of burning flesh, . . ." voicing outrage over lynchings that locked the American South in terror for nearly a century and over the hatred at the root of that terrorism. Dunham had to premiere the work in Chile because, "Unlike the sixties, in the late forties and fifties artistic expression could provoke suspicion and outright repression. It was a time when dissent itself seemed illegitimate, subversive, un-American."[26] Even there, though, she experienced American-mandated censorship. The American Ambassador to Chile, Claude G. Bowers, had published *The Tragic Era: The Revolution after Lincoln* in 1929, providing his justification for the Ku Klux Klan's existence. After opening night, the production of Southland was shut down, and the company had to leave the country a few days later. Three short years later, the U.S. State Department began "sending representative American artists abroad as cultural diplomats. . . . Dunham was continually denied both support and subsidy and never chosen to represent the United States officially. . . . In 1954, the José Limón Dance Company was chosen as the first State Department–sponsored dance touring company to perform in South America."[27] So, in addition to obvious challenges Dunham faced because of her own racial identity, governmental opposition to her willingness to speak against violent repression may have been a significant factor in why her work is less well known than that of her contemporaries.

While many of Dunham's influences are clear at this point, it is also important to note the role her husband played in shaping her artistic presentations. John Pratt was a successful costume and stage set designer and had already worked with major dance artists like George Balanchine and Agnes de Mille when he and Dunham met. For Dunham, Pratt was clearly a welcome colleague, as he served as one of the rare individuals in her life capable of providing her with valuable creative feedback that she could then put to active use in her work.[28] Pratt's designs also played a significant role in her performances— "Dunham recognized the critical importance of Pratt's designs to her stage presence"[29]—and his designs were highly respected as being "brilliantly theatricalized from authentic sources,"[30] as he would sometimes use a traditional hat or other item that Dunham had obtained in the field as inspiration for his designs.

Some of the important artists who danced for Dunham's company include Eartha Kitt, Ruth Beckford, Glory Van Scott, Julie Robinson, Charles Moore, Talley Beatty, Vanoye Aikins, and Archie Savage. Other artists such as Marlon Brando studied at Dunham's school in New York.

In addition to her bodies of choreography, performance, and scholarship, Dunham also devoted tremendous energy (and her own income) toward arts and intercultural education. Stemming from her first school in mid-1930s Chicago, she established a school in New York in 1944 (located for a time in Isadora Duncan's former Caravan Hall studio).[31] The Katherine Dunham School of Arts and Research (where José Limón taught in 1946–1947) offered certification in dance, drama, and cultural studies at the instructor, artist, field research worker, and master teacher levels.[32]

Decades after her retirement from the stage and screen, Dunham is still remembered as a vivacious performer, capable of both high camp and high art, who was at once effervescent and the quintessential professional artist. Dunham's commitment to racial and cultural understanding was infused into all of her work and is perhaps, ultimately, the reason her work remains so significant. Dr. Albirda Rose, director of the Dunham Certification Board, commented:

> Most people think of Ms. Dunham's company as being African American
> . . . but the reality is she built a multinational, multilingual company. Most
> of her [original] dancers spoke several languages. In fact, that's one of my
> first memories of being with her and her dancers and students. As soon
> as I walked into her home the first time, I heard conversations through
> the house in three or four different languages. She wove that into her
> work. When she danced or choreographed, she took down those cultural
> barriers.[33]

By the late 1960s, "Katherine Dunham was still at the height of her creative powers. . . (When) she found a [new] context for her mission of 'culturalization,' as she termed it, in the ravaged city of East Saint Louis, Illinois, by joining with black social and political movements of the time."[34] Dunham biographer Joyce Aschenbrenner points to Dunham's status as a civil rights veteran as early as the 1940s as the foundation for her commitment to East Saint Louis, and to her experiences in Haiti as preparation for the work she would take on there—work that would become known as the Performing Arts Training Center (PATC). Dunham established the PATC in East Saint Louis as an extension of Southern Illinois University's idea that universities should have a role in serving the communities where they are located and, in this case, that meant helping to address root causes of gang violence. Dunham said, "In our capsule of arts training here in East

Saint Louis, we have seen art serve as one of the methods of arousing awareness, of stimulating life to be thinking, observant, comparative, not automatic; of surpassing alienation, and of serving as a rational alternative to violence and genocide."[35]

Dunham's humanitarian work reached farther still, though, and her daughter recalled, "My mother ran a clinic at her home in Haiti, Habitation Leclerc. Her doctor in America, Max Jacobson, was able to arrange for medical supplies to be sent to the clinic so that local residents would have access to medical care. I remember that my mother even had to perform a minor surgery once for a local boy."[36] Because of her respected place in both Haiti and the United States, Dunham became a link between the two governments—particularly during and after the 1990 election when Jean-Bertrande Aristide became president of Haiti, and then was ousted by a coup. As a result of a brutal crackdown on the uprising supporting Aristide, some 16,000 Haitians fled the country by sea and were detained at Guantanamo Bay by the United States. At that point, Dunham was at her home in East Saint Louis, where she began a hunger strike lasting forty-seven days as a humanitarian protest over the treatment of the Haitian refugees. Aristide himself visited Dunham in East Saint Louis and finally persuaded her to end the hunger strike. (Dunham was eighty-two years old at the time.) The meeting with Aristide is included in Mark Silverman's film *Forty-seven Days of Fasting*, which documented Dunham's internationally renowned activism in the situation.[37] Ultimately, it was that profound sense of human responsibility that shaped so much of Dunham's work and life—a sense of responsibility that is core to her technique.

Katherine Dunham: In the Studio

Philosophy

"So much of Ms. Dunham's work," Rose stated in a 2008 interview, "was related to three ideas: intercultural communication, socialization through the arts, and form and function."[38]

> Between 1937 and 1945, Dunham established a research-to-performance method to which her first dance company was exposed. She would use this method of scholarly inquiry as a means to recreate the memory of regional dances among her dancers and a variety of audiences in North America and abroad.[39]

Decades before "fusion" forms became popular in concert dance, Dunham built a training system that integrated the traditional material she observed in cultural context (both in the Caribbean and in urban areas in the United States) with ballet and other forms she had studied while still a young dancer. "We work with the same length and line as in ballet," Rose said. "We work with turnout."[40]

Katherine Dunham teaching, 2004.

The technique presents a mental manifestation of Miss Dunham's years of observing, studying, assimilating, creating, understanding, and living. Dunham technique uses all the physical elements of dance: space, time, force, quality, isolation, locomotor, and non-locomotor movements.[41]

The materials are rooted in primitive rhythms in dance and were always accompanied by live drummers. Dunham's work had a focused usage of polyrhythm, and classes still often use more than one drummer at a time. That means that in one exercise, multiple rhythms might be overlaid so that a 5/8 or 7/8 plays against a 4/8, which may also mean that a dancer's individual body parts are working in counter-rhythms at the same time.

While Dunham technique is physically demanding and builds strong, flexible, musical dancers, those are not the system's only goals—developing an understanding of one's own culture and others is a major focus as well. To that end, Dunham designed three theoretical models that must be grasped in order to master the technique: (1) Form and Function provides an understanding of dances and singular dance movements within cultural patterns; (2) Intercultural Communication helps to gain an understanding and acceptance of others through dance and dance theater; (3) Socialization Through the Arts prepares students as artists and communicators, and encourages their civil participation and responsibility. And, in order for teachers to effectively communicate these foundations of the technique, they must experience them in their own dance experience and the everyday lives.[42] These three theories together reinforced the idea that the technique is a way of life—not just a training system.

The technique is also based on three philosophical principles of self-knowledge, detachment, and discrimination:

> Self-knowledge encourages the dancers to look within and helps us learn the art of personal survival as artists and as people. When Ms. Dunham talked of detachment, she was talking of a stripping away of ego so that we can be completely involved and feeling—so that we are totally invested. And with discrimination, she was trying to show us when and how to make changes.[43]

Because Dunham technique is a codified system, classes generally follow a common structure. At the same time, individual teachers will likely have a daily lesson plan, and students are encouraged to come to the studio with a daily objective to further ensure their total involvement in the class. *Drumming is recommended for accompaniment. If piano is used, it should still be played percussively.*

AT THE BARRE

Breath Work

Dancers should keep in mind that "the three most important things to bring to a Dunham class are an open mind, body, and spirit."[44] Breath and body-mind-spirit work have gained popularity in contemporary approaches to dance training in the last few decades, but have long played a role in Dunham technique. Dunham recognized that breath, the source of life, plays a fundamental role in movement so she came to see the breath work as a means for the dancer to attune their attention to their own breath rhythms.

Timing: Tempi below are suggestions. The actual tempi in the classroom are at the teacher's discretion. 4/4 metre, 90 bpm

Start: Facing the barre, stand in parallel and activate (but don't actually contract) the core so that the spine is supported and you are prepared to move if required. Place the hands on the small of the back, and focus on the wall ahead of you just below eye level. Breath is taken in through the nose and exhaled through the mouth, emitting

a throaty sound similar to the yogic breath (for those familiar with yoga). Imagine a circular flow of energy through the body at all times. The breath is deep and fills the abdominals; shoulders and rib cage are still.

[cts. 1–4] Inhale, filling the belly.
[cts. 5–8] Exhale through the mouth.
[cts. 1–4] Inhale.
[cts. 5–8] Exhale.
     [2/4 metre, 90 bpm]
[cts. 1–2] Inhale.
[cts. 2–2] Exhale.
[cts. 1–2] Inhale.
[cts. 2–2] Exhale.
[cts. 1–2] Inhale.
[cts. 2–2] Exhale.
[cts. 1–2] Inhale.
[cts. 2–2] Exhale.

[ct. 1] Inhale. [ct. 2] Exhale. [ct. 1] Inhale. [ct. 2] Exhale. [ct. 1] Inhale. [ct. 2] Exhale.

    [ct. 1] Inhale. [ct. 2] Exhale.

This breath work can be done again with a demi-plié and the Dunham Presentation of the Arms.

Dunham Presentation of the Arms, Plié and Relevé

From this point forward, the student should always be aware of placement, and when standing straight, each bone should be stacked in a clear, neutral manner. The student should also continue to be aware of the breath throughout class. It is also at this point that connections to ballet will be made.

Timing: 4/4 metre, 95 bmp

Start: Stand parallel facing the barre, exhale to

[ii] The Dunham class materials are based on Dr. Albirda Rose's book *Dunham Technique: "A Way of Life."* Used with her permission.

activate the core, and quickly ensure proper alignment. Hands gently touch the front of the hip socket, elbows are bent and are directed to the side.

[cts. 1–4] Arms raise to center of body.

[cts. 5–8] Hold arms in center of body, keeping them alive, palms flat (toward floor).

[cts. 1–4] Arms continue upward.

[cts. 5–8] Hold arms, hands slightly in front of face (toward wall in front of you).

[cts. 1–4] Arms return center.

[cts. 5–8] Hold center.

[cts. 1–4] Arms return to starting position.

[cts. 5–8] Hold at starting position.

Repeat the entire phrase.
Center the mind, steady the breath, and focus on the music to build a relationship with the musician for the day's class.

[cts. 1–2] Demi-plié.

[cts. 3–4] Straighten.

Repeat for a total of 4 demi-pliés.

[cts. 1–2] Relevé.

[cts. 3–4] Roll down into demi-plié, straighten legs.

[cts. 1–2] Demi-plié.

[cts. 3–4] Straighten.

[cts. 1–2] Relevé.

[cts. 3–4] Roll down to straight leg.

Repeat the 12-count phrase for a total of 4 times, or 48 counts altogether. After the final roll down, relevé again, and find your balance. Finish.

Pelvic Placement

Alignment is the focus here.

Timing: 2/4 metre, 100 bpm

[cts. 1–2] Plié.

[cts. 1–2] Straighten.

[cts. 1–2] Relevé.

[cts. 1–2] Lower.

Repeat for a total of 4 pliés and relevés.

[cts. 1–2] Plié.

[cts. 1–2] Hold in plié, pelvis neutral.

[cts. 1–2] Contract pelvis forward.

[cts. 1–2] Return to neutral.

[cts. 1–2] Pelvis contracts back.

[cts. 1–2] Return to neutraL.

Repeat enough times that students grow comfortable with moving the pelvis into and out of alignment. The entire sequence may then be repeated at a faster tempo, and the metre may be changed at the teacher's discretion.

[cts. 1–8] Contract the pelvis, arms fall to the sides, heels lift, and the knees bend as you move deeper into a hinge.

Keep this alive for as long as the instructor directs.

Press-ins at the Barre

This sequence warms up the back and aids in building upper-body strength.

Timing: 4/4 metre, 80 bpm

Start: Face the barre in parallel, feet shoulder-width apart, hands lightly touching the barre, fingertips facing each other. This movement will look like a vertical push-up of sorts.

[cts. 1–8] Arms bend and the center of gravity moves toward the barre.

[cts. 1–8] Core is actively engaged as you press back out to standing.

Repeat at least 10 times.

Flat Back and Beginning Fall and Recovery

This sequence flows directly from the end of the Press-ins. The series lengthens the hamstrings and warms up and strengthens the lower back.

Timing: 4/4 metre, 90 bpm

Start: Feet are shoulder-distance apart. Stand far enough back from the barre to allow room for the torso and arms to fully extend from a forward bend at the waist.

Preparation:

[cts. 6–8] Arms present forward, palms flat.

[cts. 1–8] Core is activated, extend torso from the waist until back is flat, hands rest lightly on the barre, legs are straight.

[cts. 1–8] Core strength supports the lower back as torso returns to upright position. Repeat this twice on 8s, four times on 4s, and 8 times on 1 ct. After the final return to standing, extend forward again, keeping the flat back alive for 8 cts.

[cts.1–2] Contract pelvis.

[cts. 3–4] Release to neutral flat back (no hyperextensions!).

[cts. 5–6] Contract pelvis.

[cts. 7–8] Release to neutral flat back.

[cts. 1–8] Repeat the phrase.

[cts. 1–4] Pelvic contraction continues the curve into the upper back.

[cts. 5–8] Return to neutral flat back.

Repeat the full contraction phrase at least twice. Return to standing for 4 cts., checking your alignment.

Ting-Yu Chen demonstrates the Flat Back—notice her head is in line with her spine, and she isn't pressing into her shoulders.

Return to flat back for 4 cts.

[ct. 1] Release the barre and allow the torso to fall forward, hands touching floor.

[ct. 2] Recover to flat back, arms at sides.

[ct. 3] Fall forward.

[ct. 4] Recover to flat back.

[cts. 5–8] Repeat.

[cts. 1–4] Contract pelvis and roll into the fully curved upper back.

[cts. 5–8] Release to flat back.

[cts. 1–8] Repeat.

[cts. 1–8] Slowly roll up to standing and finish, arms at sides, palms flat.

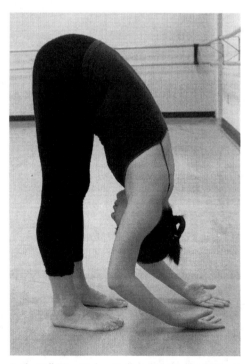

In the Fall, Ting-Yu hasn't allowed her hips to shift backward. She maintains a long spine, and keeps her head neutral on the spine (she isn't tucking).

Foot Isolations

In Dunham, footwork is done facing into the center of the room, back to the barre with the hands resting gently on the barre. This placement of the hands slightly behind you requires you pay special attention to your alignment, and means that the core must be active the entire time. Keep breathing.

Timing: 4/4 metre, 110 bpm

[ct. 1] From parallel, brush R foot forward, point.

[ct. 2] Flex.

[ct. 3] Point.

[ct. 4] Brush in to close.

Repeat R and L 4 times.

[cts. 1–2] Relevé.

[cts. 3–4] Lower.

[cts. 5–8] Rotate hips open into turned-out 1st position.

[ct. 1] Brush R foot forward.

[ct. 2] Close.

Repeat brushes R and L 4 times.

[cts. 1–2] Relevé.

[cts. 3–4] Roll down.

[cts. 5–6] Grand plié.

[cts. 7–8] Straighten.

[ct. 1] Brush R foot to the side.

[ct. 2] Close.

Repeat R and L 4 times.

[cts. 1–2] Relevé.

[cts. 3–4] Roll down.

[cts. 5–6] Grand plié.

[cts. 7–8] Straighten.

[cts. 1–2] Relevé.

[cts. 3–8] Lift hands off the barre, bring them through the center (palms flat) and raise the arms overhead as in the Dunham

Presentation earlier. Keep this alive en relevé at least 16 cts.

Leg Swings

Throughout this sequence, pay close attention to the hips, ensuring that they face forward at all times. For this beginner movement, the attitude to the front should bring the thigh into alignment with the hip socket, so avoid crossing over toward the center of the body.

Timing: 4/4 metre, 100 bpm

Start: Back to the barre, hands gently touching the barre, feet paralleL

Preparation: activate the core and open to 1st position turned out, tendu the R foot to 2nd.

[ct. 1] Brush to front attitude through 1st position.
[ct. 2] Lower leg and brush to 2nd.
[ct. 3] Lower leg, raising it to front attitude and circling open to 2nd.
[ct. 4] Step to the R.

Repeat 4 times R and L. Repeat entire phrase 2 times adding a plié as the foot brushes through 1st. Repeat again 4 times maintaining the plié on the brush and adding a relevé at the top of the attitude. Instead of stepping R following the last circle, carry the leg to front attitude again while in relevé. Release the barre and carry arms to Dunham Presentation in 2nd. Extend the leg, flex the foot, and lower to close. Raise the L leg and repeat balance. Close 1st position parallel, arms finish in Dunham Presentation low.

Leg Extensions

Timing: 4/4 metre, 145 bpm

Start: In parallel, back to the barre, hands lightly touching the barre.

[cts. 1–4] R foot brushes back in a slight arc and the knee lifts, foot parallel with the L knee, extend the leg forward.
[ct. 5] The leg is straight at 90 degrees.
[ct. 6] Flex the foot.
[cts. 7–8] Leg extends downward to close.

Repeat 8 times R and L.

[cts. 1–4] Relevé.
[cts. 5–6] Lower.
[cts. 7-8] Turn out.

Repeat entire sequence 4 times R and L from 1st position turned out. Return to parallel, arms at the sides (palms flat). [Instructors may want to vary the metre of this sequence. It could be done in a 5 or 7 so that the students begin to experience unfamiliar musical patterns.]

Progressions (Across the Floor)

For the purposes of this text, the remainder of sequences focus on movements across the floor that, for the most part, emphasize isolating various body parts while traveling. This coordination is a key element in Dunham technique. The combinations are purposefully simple so that the dancer may attend to alignment, breath, coordination, and the Cultural Context.

Dunham Walk

Commitment to alignment, placement, and the circular flow of energy should be reaffirmed as you begin across the floor. There should be a constant flow of energy driving you smoothly through the studio. In Cultural Context, this walk is performed to the Ibo rhythm (see below for more on Progressions in Cultural Context). You should glide across the surface of the floor in this walk.

Timing: 4/4 metre, 80 bpm, counted as &-a-1-2.
Start: In parallel, arms at the sides, palms facing the thighs.

[ct. &] R foot peels off the floor.
[ct. a] Foot moves forward, knee bends.
[ct. 1] Step into 4th position relevé.
[ct. 2] Plié 4th position parallel.
[ct. &] L foot peels off the floor.
[ct. a] Foot moves forward, knee bends.
[ct. 1] Step into 4th position relevé.
[ct. 2] Plié 4th position parallel.

Repeat this pattern across the floor. Once the coordination of steps is secure, the instructor may add the Dunham Presentation of the Arms (perhaps going from low to high), and the tempo may be faster.

Rocking Step (Rocking Horse)

Keep the core activated throughout this phrase, and always step from one foot to the next, rather than jump. You will still be dancing in the Ibo rhythm.

Timing: 4/4 metre, 110 bpm
Start: 4th position parallel, R foot forward, weight back on the L. Shift weight forward on R in plié

[cts. &–a] L foot brushes forward to parallel attitude, L arm in second, R arm bent, hands in fists
[ct. 1] Shift weight forward to L foot, R leg comes to attitude, arms change.
[ct. 2] Transfer forward to L foot, R leg to attitude, arms change.
[ct. 3] Transfer weight to L foot, arms change.
[cts. &–4] Brush R foot through to attitude front, slight chug forward on L, arms change.

Repeat entire phrase moving across the floor.

The forward and back portions of the Rocking Horse Step.

Traveling Isolations

This series pairs simple foot patterns with isolations of the head, shoulders, torso, and hips.

Timing: *Metre and rhythm can vary.* After working the feet and isolations together at the same tempo, the feet can move in one metrical pattern against a different pattern for the isolation in order to introduce polyrhythm. Always be certain alignment is correct, and core is activated.

Variation 1

[cts. 1–4] Head circles R as the feet take four steps forward.

[cts. 5–8] Head "pecks" forward and back.

[cts. 1–8] Repeat L.

Continue the pattern across the floor. Come back across the floor, face the mirror, and repeat the head circle as you step sideways (step, together, step, together).

Variation 2

Facing across the studio again

[cts. 1–4] Step R, L, R, L, raise the shoulders in opposition to the foot you step on (R foot/L shoulder), pivot to your L on the last step.

[cts. 5–8] Step, together, step, together with the shoulders in opposition to the foot, pivot R on last step.

Repeat the phrase pivoting R and then L when appropriate.

Variation 3

Repeat the foot pattern above, and add a quiver in the shoulder, where the shoulder moves forward in opposition to the leading foot and the other shoulder moves backward (twist the shoulders but keep the hips still). The shoulder quiver can also be done with a descending plié as you move forward.

Variation 4

Walking forward, circle the chest R for 4 cts and then L for 4 cts. Arms are in Dunham low for this phrase.

Variation 5

With the arms in Dunham Presentation 2nd position, undulate the torso against the walk (take two steps to complete each undulation). This undulation begins with a pelvic contraction as in the Flat Back sequence at the barre, and should be repeated with the descending plié.

CULTURAL CONTEXT

Progressions in Cultural Context are a "direct influence of Miss Dunham's work as an anthropologist and her belief in synchronization. Her work in Haiti gives the basic information and concepts for Progressions in Cultural Context."[45] Each of these styles relates to particular Vaudun Loa (deities) and each has its own associated rhythmic pattern. In some cases, like *Damballa* and *Zepaules*, the dance is an illustration of the Loa. In cases like *Yanvalou* (see below) and *Mahi*, the dance honors the deity. Damballa, the Snake Loa, is represented by the undulating movements and is interwoven throughout the technique. The spine must maintain fluidity regardless of the tempo or level changes that may be paired with the movement. Papa Legba, Loa of opportunities and known as the Gate Keeper, is represented in Zepaules, or the shoulder isolations emphasizing the downward motion in the isolation. This is one movement where the upper and lower body would remain in the same rhythmic space, and steps would be small and tight.

Yanvalou honors Damballa and Erzule (the Loa of the Elements and Love) and one of her husbands, Agwe (Loa of the Sea), so the undulation may be seen as ocean waves or the serpent. The movement should be fluid, and might appear in any body part. In this case, attention will be paid to the spine,] following the rest of the flow of this class experience.

Timing: The example here is in 3/4, but 6/8 is also appropriate. 3/4 metre, 95 bpm

Start: Dancers are in low plié with the torso bent forward at the waist. The head should follow the spine, and focus should be down in a frontward diagonal to start. Hands reset gently above the knee.

[ct. 1] Step forward with R foot, torso undulating.
[cts. 2–3] Torso undulates.
[ct. 1] L foot steps together with R, torso undulating.
[cts. 2–3] Torso undulates.
[ct. 1] Step forward with L foot, torso undulating.
[cts. 2–3] Torso undulates.
[ct. 1] R foot steps together with L, torso undulating.
[cts. 2–3] Torso undulates.

Repeat the pattern double-time for 4 sets. Repeat the foot pattern double-time again, adding an undulating sweep of the R arm toward the L, taking all 4 sets of 3 to completely cross the body with the arm. Repeat with the L arm moving R.

The focus should follow the hand as the arm sweeps in both directions.

Jumps

At this point, the instructor should give a series of jumping phrases, first to warm up the feet, then progressing to jumps in 2nd, and then jumps that send the dancers bounding into the air. Clear attention should be paid to alignment and the core should be active at all times without allowing the chest and shoulders to rise during the jumping (although shoulder isolations can be added). The Dunham Presentation of the Arms can inform how to use the arms. For example, for small, bright footwork such as jumps in 1st position parallel and turned out, the arms might cycle from Dunham Presentation Low to High. In bigger jumps in second, the arms might remain in Dunham Presentation in Second, which will enhance the student's attention to alignment. A variety of rhythms should be incorporated into this experience.

Final Combinations

A Dunham master teacher would likely end a class by teaching an excerpt from the Dunham repertory. For the purpose of this experience, the instructor should create a combination of movements from the class that most challenged the students. For example, diagonally from the corner, a sequence of Yanvalou R and L might be followed by an 8-count progression with isolations moving the dancers in a circle to the R then repeated L. This could bring them into a pattern of the Rocking Horse and then the Dunham Walk in a fast triplet exiting the space. In addition to a final focus on the unique movement qualities of the technique, this combination uses multiple rhythms and could even incorporate polyrhythm.

Lester Horton (1906–1953): Biographical Sketch

A fluke brought me to the Lester Horton school. A friend had shown me some Lester Horton movements and they seemed exciting and masculine. It was only after watching a number of classes that I finally got the courage to participate. Lester turned out to be the greatest influence on my career. . . . The technique I learned from Lester has continued to affect and influence me and my work . . . [it] continues to be an inspiration for my choreography.

—Alvin Ailey, *Revelations: The Autobiography of Alvin Ailey*

Much like Katherine Dunham, Lester Horton was one of the few pioneers of modern dance who made major sacrifices in order to bring black dancers to the concert dance stage. While he was not himself black, his work certainly has had significant influences on later artists of the African Diaspora. "He went inside the drum—all of those syncopated rhythms—Horton beat them out. [Horton wrote a number of percussion scores for his work.] So much of it is very African movement, but he made it a technique by breaking it down into dance information that can be imparted and trained in the studio. It was as if he had been to the jungle himself and witnessed those things."[46] Horton hadn't been to the jungle, though, or to the Caribbean as Dunham had. Instead, his major cultural influences were indigenous to the United States.

Growing up in Indianapolis, Horton developed a deep interest in history at an early age—regional Civil War stories were the first historical concerns to capture his attention. Later, as part of the Nature Study Group at the local library, Horton found his true ethnocultural passion in the study of the area's indigenous peoples:

> One of his first excursions was to the mysterious Indian mounds near Anderson, built by the first known inhabitants of the area, a vanished people who were referred to only as the Mound Builders. There was some speculation at the time as to whether the mounds had served as a setting for some forgotten ceremonial rite or as a place of burial. The youngster was fascinated by these unanswered questions and began to haunt the Children's Museum . . . [with its] splendid displays of American Indian arts and artifacts.[47]

His interest in indigenous peoples was as much about familial heritage as historical fascination, as one of his great-grandmothers had been full-blooded Algonquin and other native heritage was also present.[48] While there would be divergences along the way to founding a dance company

Judith Anderson, Carmen de Lavallade and Lester Horton, ca. 1953.

and establishing a dance technique with its own historical merit, nearly everything Horton pursued in his life was sourced in his early inquisitive examination of native ideas.

Studying native culture led him to develop an interest in a branch of zoology involving the study of snakes—an area of interest that for a time he intended to pursue as a vocation. In fact, after high school, he even began studying design and drawing to help in his classification work with the snakes.

During his lifetime, Horton would tell a variety of stories about what led him to dance—a 1922 Denishawn performance, a Wild West show, and a performance by Anna Pavlova.[49] Likely though, the snake designs he was working on led him to his first examination of tribal dances, which in turn led him to study concert dance[50] and ballet with Madame Theo Hawes (Italian) and later with Adolph Bolm (Russian). In 1925, Horton was cast in a local production choreographed by a Denishawn teacher, Forrest Thornburg, who liked Horton so well that, "[b]etween rehearsals Thornburg taught Lester some Denishawn dances and Lester, in turn, aided the choreographer in rehearsals, proving to be an adept assistant."[51] The experiences he had with ballet left Horton dissatisfied, and while he went on to briefly attend the Pavley-Oukrainsky School in Chicago, the technique was not for him.

His love of dance and native history finally merged when Horton met William and Clara Bates, the couple responsible for establishing the Indianapolis Theater Guild. The Bates' ideas for the Guild stemmed from the work in the Little Theater movement that swept the nation in the early part of the last century—a movement that believed in creating rich communal cultural experiences. As part of the Guild's early work, Clara Bates produced a performance of Longfellow's poem *The Song of Hiawatha*, and remembering having seen Horton perform with Hawes, invited him to participate in the project. This led to Horton's first fieldwork, learning and recording traditional native dances:

> Arrangements were made for several trips to Indiana reservations so that Lester could study at first hand the dances he would be performing and teaching for *Hiawatha*. The following spring he spent several weeks in Santa Fe where, through some of William Bates' business and professional connections, Lester was given the opportunity to learn from excellent Indian performers who taught him dances as well as complex chants. . . . The costumes and accessories he sketched while in Santa Fe were later reproduced in large quantities for the pageant.[52]

Despite his young age, Horton was named art director and dance master for the Guild. (The experience was his first opportunity to experiment with creating costume pieces and props, which would later be a signature of his approach to total theater.) Clara Bates was so impressed with Horton that she paid his tuition at the John Herron Art Institute, and insisted he live in the family's carriage house. After the successful *Hiawatha* production, Horton eventually moved to Chicago and later to Los Angeles, which served as a home base for his continued study of indigenous dance forms that clearly became the foundation of his modern dance. This is where similarities between Horton and Dunham begin:

> Among the tribesmen of the Western plains can be found rhythms not un-like those of the Dalcroze system, an approach to the canon form in music, and social dancing, apart from the religious ceremonials. . . . The religious symbol of the Hopi snake dance has a counterpart in the Damballa of

Haitian Voodoo. . . . The basic steps among all primitives have a recognizable affinity, the variations being mainly in the body movements.[53]

Horton's early works were often solos, and as he grew in choreographic skill, he honed his work by employing an economy of movement, but not of scale. Much native dance is based on group form, and he took every opportunity to work with larger groups of dancers. His roots in the pageantry of *Hiawatha* and proximity to Hollywood fueled his tendency toward spectacle. Despite the Great Depression, 1934's *The Painted Desert*, for example, used a cast of one hundred dancers. His vision was changing at this point and the content of his work began to shift that year as he officially formed Lester Horton Dance Group.

Like their New York counterparts in the 1930s, Los Angeles modern dancers felt the weight of their sociopolitical times. Antifascism was a major theme in the works being made, and the leftist concern for workers' rights led West Coast dancers to organize around similar themes as dancers on the East Coast were doing. Horton began to embrace the "vital experience" as a basis for choreography as he turned to the social and political in his work.

> The intense commitment of [Communist] Party workers in his group and the strength of his belief that the central humanistic ideas were morally correct led to a radical change in his work over a period of just a few months. He gave up on his beloved pageant-like compositions and ethnically based dances to concentrate more intently on developing a style based on a new purpose: to make dances which would influence and, perhaps, instruct. . . . By 1936, Horton had emerged as a choreographer intensely involved in the problems of his time. "The dances are propaganda," wrote the *American Dancer* critic, "but they are good dances in themselves." *Dictator* was the quintessential agitprop piece in the repertory during this era . . . a powerful direct piece with little left to the imagination.[54]

At the same time, however, Horton himself never joined the Party, although he and his dancers were often the target of far right (and frequently pro-Nazi) press attacks in Los Angeles. Legendary dancer Bella Lewitzky, an original member of Horton's Group, was herself questioned in the 1950s by the House Un-American Activities Committee. Alvin Ailey recalled that at the time of the McCarthy hearings, "the rumor was that Bella wanted Lester to publicly denounce them. Lester didn't do so, and that, it is said, led to more conflict between them."[55] In fact, Lewitzky left the company not long after that. The press at the time frequently referred to the Horton Group as a "cooperative," a denigration, implying that there was something sinister about the company's democratic mode of operation. They, however, viewed themselves as a family and,

Lester Horton.

Esther Brown, Alvin Ailey, and Joyce Trisler in Lester Horton's Combata de Amor, *ca. 1953.*

while Horton was clearly in charge of the choreography, everyone shared responsibilities when it came to doing the research on the subject matter for new dance ideas he generated:

> When a dance about a particular culture was projected, the art, music, history, and movement patterns of the people were studied. It was understood that company members would do research assignments and share their findings at the next meeting. This work was not intended to affect Horton's choreography directly, but rather to give the dancers a frame of reference upon which to build characterizations.[56]

Company members also shared responsibilities for helping Horton create the costumes, props, and stage decor. Those responsibilities later extended to keeping the theater clean, once Horton established the Lester Horton Dance Theater in 1946 (following the return of some of the company's male dancers at the end of World War II), one of the first American theaters permanently dedicated to modern dance.

Horton's company is also "believed to have been the first modern dance troupe in America to be racially integrated."[57] If that isn't entirely accurate, it is clear the company was definitely among the first. Horton's biographer, Larry Warren, noted, "Horton's easy rapport with members of minority ethnic groups living in the Los Angeles area was a revelation to the members of the company. Integration, for him, had never been something to work toward; it simply was a fact of life."[58] Lewitzky recalled that early on in the company's development, one of the first nonwhite members was Renaldo Alarcon, a Mexican-American, who helped to expand the group's cultural understandings.[59] Lewitzky also remembered Horton's sensitive treatment of racial terrorism in his dance *Chronicle,* which in 1937 was the company's largest success to date. In the work, Horton turned a critical, though tactful, eye on America's development as a nation. The final section, originally called "Incitation" was reworked (and renamed "Terror, Ku Klux Klan"), and the piece ended with what reads like an abstracted lynching. Lewitzky said, "The curtain went down and then went up again, and there was silence. We thought, "Oh, you know, it was a turkey. Then came a deafening roar as the whole house stood up."[60] Ailey, the most wildly successful of a number of successful alumni from the company, recalled in his autobiography that in the later 1940s and early 1950s:

> It was quite revolutionary . . . to have a mixed company with two black people as lead dancers. But being on the West Coast helped. There are a lot of black people, Asians, and Mexicans in Los Angeles, so the idea of fusion was strong. Martha Graham managed a mixed company on the East Coast (in the late fifties she had Mary Hinkson and Clive Thompson),

though not to the extent that Lester did. Lester was in the vanguard, and what he did was inevitable. He realized that you have to use the best dancers regardless of color.[61]

Lester Horton is largely better remembered for his technique than for his choreography. Because there was so much less modern dance on the West Coast—although there was certainly a modern dance community there—dance critics were not particularly well versed on the subject matter. For Horton, his dances would frequently be found confusing by one critic, and at the same time clear by another. So, there was often disagreement over the quality of his work—although not necessarily the caliber of his talents (recall here the Clive Barnes quote at the beginning of this chapter).

In addition to the works mentioned thus far, Horton made dances for several Hollywood films, including *Phantom of the Opera* (1943). His notable stage repertory included *The Beloved* (1948, a violent duet set to text from *The Song of Solomon*), *Voodoo Ceremonial* (1932, a spectacle piece based on W. B. Seabrook's *Magic Island*, costumed in black shrouds and green masks), and *Departure from the Land* (1939). During this time, the Group's prestige was growing, and "its concerts became big events in the [Los Angeles] community."[62] This paved the way for an invitation to stage Stravinsky's *Le Sacre du Printemps* at the Hollywood Bowl in 1937. Warren noted of *Sacre*:

> This was the first time the work would be staged on the West Coast, and the first anywhere by an American choreographer. . . . Like the Diaghilev Ballets Russes production in 1913, *Sacre* raised a storm of protest. . . . There was shouting and cat-calling and people headed for the box office . . . [be- cause audience members found] movements were unfamiliar, disturbing, and, to some, obscene. Some critics, however, felt otherwise. . . . The modern realism, forthrightness and stark ugliness incorporated by the Horton Group suited the music.[63]

Horton's most famous work is likely *Salome* (1934), a choreodrama examining the pathology of decadence. After the piece first premiered, Horton made numerous changes to it on a seemingly regular basis until his death in 1953. In his historical review of the work, Richard Bizot observed, "Tracing the succession of Horton *Salomes* will reveal an intensifying of his [Horton's] effort to coordinate all elements of theater, including dance, into a unity."[64] Of the Horton works that survived past his death, *Salome* has likely been staged most often. By the time the Dance Theater closed in 1960, some of America's most famous dancers had worked there, including Alvin Ailey, Janet Collins, Carmen de Lavallade, Bella Lewitzky, James Mitchell, Carl Ratcliff, Joyce Trisler, and James Truitte.

Lester Horton: In the Studio

In the summer of 2009, I was talking with friends following Ruth Andrien's Taylor class at the American Dance Festival, when I noticed two young women across the gymnasium with a video camera. One was filming the other as she executed a series of the Fortifications and other work from the Horton technique. At one point, she made a descent into a Side Lunge Sit and then labored as she made her ascent. I watched her go through the movement phrases several times before I approached her and asked her to repeat the Lunge sequence again. As she returned to standing, the work—the effort—required from her working thigh (in this case, the right) was clear on her face. Nothing about her movement was efficient. There was no economy of movement because her body was not working as an integrated whole, and she was relying almost entirely on the right thigh to hoist herself back up. Instead of trying to explain the kinesiology and biomechanics behind a clear execution of the descent/ascent, I slapped my own lower abdomen (over the pyramidalis) and drew my hand upward in a slow spiral toward my sternum. The dancer's eyes grew larger, and after she went through the movement again, there was a big smile on her face because this time there was much more fluidity in the movement since it had required much less effort.

Now, certainly there were several other things that should have been adjusted in how this young woman was working, but I use the example to illustrate several important points about Horton technique: Horton was interested in developing a corrective method of dance training, and one way that played out is in the elimination of arbitrary movements. *The technique is streamlined*, so that each body part is structurally integrated into the larger whole. While limbs may certainly move on their own, they always have a relationship with the other parts. It is also impossible to properly (and safely) execute Horton movement without working from an engaged core. The core strength developed in this technique helps to protect the lower spine—and the knees. Horton paid great attention to the human body's structure, stating:

> I am sincerely trying now to create a dance technique based entirely on corrective exercises, created with a knowledge of human anatomy . . . a technique having all the basic movements which govern the actions of the body; combined with a knowledge of the origin of movement and a sense of artistic design.[65]

"Horton makes you strong. It makes you powerful, but it's hard work. I remember in high school when I first started taking Thelma Hill's class, I could hardly walk for a week," recalled Keith Lee, former principal dancer for American Ballet Theatre.[66] "I was so glad I'd had that training, because when Alvin [Ailey] came to choreograph *The River* on ABT, he really used a great deal of Horton technique in the movement, the women were even doing laterals en pointe."

After leaving ABT, Lee spent several years as Ailey's ballet master, but even after moving on to make his own work, he continued to teach Horton technique. *In fact, I studied with Lee while he was teaching at Shenandoah University, and it was in his studio that I first began to understand the fluid power of the technique.* That is one of the important things to keep in mind about the training system: *while the work is powerful, it must remain fluid so that it never becomes brittle in the body.* As Ana Marie Forsythe, chair of The Ailey School's Horton Department, noted in an interview in 2007:

> Horton's technique isn't limited to a concept of one or two movements and their contrasts. The technique is dynamic and dramatic, develops both strength and flexibility, and works with an energy that is constantly in motion. The primary focus of many beginner-level Horton studies is creating length in the spine and hamstrings. There is also an emphasis throughout all levels on developing musicality and performance qualities.[67]

When my colleague Elijah Gibson was performing with Giordano Jazz Dance Chicago, he began studying Horton. Since becoming an assistant professor at Shenandoah University, he has taught the technique both in modern dance class and as a regular component of his jazz class. As we discussed the strengthening and lengthening elements of the technique, Gibson observed that "every single muscle in the body is active all the time. Everything has to be engaged. You are always reaching and pulling at the same time with the arms, legs—even the hips—and simultaneously, the core is supporting the lower back."[68] This kind of oppositional energy is often referred to as *dynamic tension,* but I prefer the idea of fluid tension with Horton, as it is both supple and explosive. As Horton began developing his training system, he was not particularly interested in creating dancers who looked like him. He wanted to foster the uniqueness of the individual in his dancers, to train them quickly and make them strong, versatile performers.

"Horton believed in getting the body warmed up and blood flowing quickly," Forsythe said, "so class begins standing, rather than sitting, like some other modern techniques." Codified Horton technique incorporates seventeen "fortification studies" (among other elements), each focusing on a different idea, such as descent/ascent and laterals, or body parts such as the Achilles tendons or abdominals. Class then progresses across the floor, with movement phrases, turns, and single-foot arch springs, which is a jump from one foot. In the video series that she made with fellow Horton technique master teacher Marjorie Perces, Forsythe also said because the lines are so clean and clear, "this makes [the technique] very accessible to even beginning dancers or nondancers."[69] Likewise, Lewitzky said, "[Lester] built his technique on my body, so his technique felt to me like the only way anyone should move . . . and it should feel like it's from your body too, not laid on your body."[70]

Keith Lee and Sally Wilson in Alvin Ailey's The River *(which fused ballet and Horton technique) for American Ballet Theatre.*

One hallmark of a Horton class is that once students have learned the basic material, most of the class flows with few interruptions. This gives students the chance to really focus on the body-mind connection and to explore the performance opportunity in the studio. Horton clearly believed that performance began in the technique class, not on stage, and that is evidenced in his training methodologies.

Lee said students should note that "because so much of the technique requires you to balance off-center, in order to be confident in all those places you have to attend to your posture—your placement. The Horton experience encompasses every part of dance. Students need to use everything they've got, and really hang on the teacher's words. Give the teacher anything they ask for and this work can help transform you."[71]

Vocabulary: Before getting started, here are a few descriptions for the basic positions of the arms and feet you will encounter in this training series.

The Feet: Periodically in Horton technique, you will be working with one leg parallel against one turned out. Generally though, here are the positions of the feet you will encounter in the series that follows. Parallel 1st, 2nd, and 4th—the feet are in parallel, two inches apart in 1st and about hip/pelvis apart in 2nd. Natural 1st, 2nd, and 4th—the placement is the same as above, but the hips are turned out with the feet at roughly 45 degrees. Wide Natural 2nd—the feet are at 45 degrees but are now wider apart than the shoulders.

The Arms: *Natural Low*—arms are at your sides, palms inward, about an inch or a little more from the body. *Middle Parallel*—palms face inward as the arms extend horizontally forward to shoulder height. *High Parallel*—palms face inward as the arms reach overhead in line with the shoulders. *2nd*—palms face the ground while the arms reach to the sides in line with the shoulders. *Closed Egyptian*—the elbows are bent at 90 degrees as the arms extend forward from the shoulders, the palms are turned toward your face. [Note: there are additional arm positions, but you will not need to know them for the following experience.]

In the Center

Preparation—Relevé/Plié: Engage the core.

Timing: 6/8 metre, 70 bpm

Start: Stand in Parallel 1st, arms in Natural Low. On the preparation, arms open through 2nd and rise to High Parallel Energy should be flowing through the spine upward through the fingertips and downward through the heels. The breath flow should be relaxed and consistent, flowing in a smooth circular pattern without ever being held. The head floats on top of the neck, chest is down, and ribs are drawn together, but not locked so that breathing is hindered. The pelvis is neutral. Allow the energy to be fluid throughout the body to the point that you must lengthen even more to contain the energy, and this leads you into relevé.

[cts. 1–6] Relevé by lengthening upward until your heels rise off the floor, taking all 6 cts.

[cts. 1–6] Slowly lower by lengthening the legs downward, reaching the heels toward the floor while energy continues upward in opposition.

[cts. 1–12] Repeat.

[cts. 1–3] Demi-plié.

[cts. 4–6] Straighten.

[cts. 1–6] Repeat.

[cts. 1–6] Grand plié, arms move to Middle Parallel on descent.

[cts. 1–6] Straighten, arms return to High Parallel.

[cts. 1–12] Repeat.

[cts. 1–3] Relevé.

[cts. 4–6] Lower R heel (lengthening the Achilles) to the ground with a straight leg, L leg remains bent and the L foot is in forced arch.

[cts. 1–6] Repeat on the L.

[cts. 1–2] Relevé.

[ct. 3] Lower.

[ct. 4] Turn out to Natural 1st.

[cts. 5–6] Tendu R foot to natural 2nd, arms in 2nd.

Repeat the entire sequence in Natural 2nd. Repeat it in Natural 4th with R foot front and then again L. Return to Parallel 1st, arms in Natural Low. Relevé, balance, and close your eyes. Lower with the eyes closed, still working for length in both directions. Check your alignment with your eyes still closed. Check again after opening the eyes.

[cts. 1–6] Roll down through plié until the hands touch the floor, head forward along the spine.

[cts. 1–6] Roll up, straightening the legs.

[cts. 1–3] Repeat roll down in plié.

[cts. 4–6] Roll up.

[cts. 1–3] Repeat roll down in plié.

Elijah Gibson demonstrates the Horton Flat Back.

[cts. 4–6] Roll up.

[cts. 1–6] Roll down, straight legs.

[cts. 1–6] Roll up.

[cts. 1–3] Roll down, straight legs.

[cts. 4–6] Roll up.

[cts. 1–3] Roll down, straight legs.

[cts. 4–6] Roll up.

Flat Back Series

[Note to teachers: Help students to care for their lower back. Correct issues like swayback. It is important that they use their core strength during the entire movement.] In the Flat Back Front, the core is always engaged. From Parallel 2nd with arms in Natural Low, reach the top of the head up and out until the spine is long and moves the torso forward into a "table top" position where the torso and legs form a 90-degree angle at the hips.

Basic Flat Back

Timing: 6/8 metre, 70 bpm

[cts. 1–3] Move torso forward to Flat Back.

[cts. 4–6] Return to standing, being sure to use abdominal activation to support the spine.

Repeat this 4–6 times.

Flat Back with Arm Reach

Timing: Same

[cts. 1–3] Move torso forward to Flat Back.

[cts. 4–6] Remain in Flat Back, and as the arms reach sideways and move into High Parallel, rotate the palms to face each other.

[cts. 1–3] Return to standing.

[cts. 4–6] Rotate the palms outward and press arms into Natural Low.

Repeat 4–6 times.

Flat Back with Arms in High Parallel

Timing: Same.

Start: Raise arms to High Parallel

[cts. 1–3] Move torso forward to Flat Back.

[cts. 4–6] Return to standing, arms remain in High Parallel

Repeat 4–6 times.

Flat Back with Demi-plié

Timing: Same.

Start: Arms in High Parallel.

[cts. 1–3] Move torso forward to Flat Back.

[cts. 4–6] Demi-plié.

[cts. 1–3] Straighten legs.

[cts. 4–6] Return to standing.

Repeat 4–6 times.

Flat Back Back Bend

Timing: Same.

Start: Arms in High Parallel. Engage the core.

[cts. 1–3] Move pelvis diagonally forward, fingertips reach upstage.

[cts. 4–6] Return to standing.

Repeat 4–6 times.

Primitive Squat

Always keep the core engaged in this series. This supports the spine and helps you to return to standing. The movement lengthens the gastrocnemius and the Achilles, and strengthens the supporting muscles around the knee.

Timing: 4/4 metre, 80 bpm

Start: Parallel 2nd with arms in Middle Parallel.

[cts. 1–4] Lengthen in the spine in both directions, engage the core, and descend into the Primitive Squat position (see the illustration).

The author in the Primitive Squat. Always be sure to track knees over toes, and don't allow them to roll in or open out—stay in true parallel.

[cts. 1–4]   Deepen the core engagement as you ascend to standing.

Repeat at least 4 times. Relevé, arms to High Parallel Balance and lower.

Lateral Series

"The abdominal muscles must be activated to support the back each time the body is in any lateral position to prevent strain and injury to the body. In laterals the stretch of the torso and the arms to the side results in a shift of weight and a pull of the hip to the opposite side. This muscular compensation enhances maximum sideward flexibility."[72] Also, keep in mind Gibson's comment about everything constantly reaching in all directions at once—even the hips here must reach away from the arms.

Timing: 6/8 metre, 75 bpm
Start: Wide Natural 2nd, arms in High Parallel.

[cts. 1–3]   Lift the L side as you reach the fingertips to the R and the hips L. Hips must remain facing front at all times, even as they shift to the L.
[cts. 4–6]   Engage the core even more, especially the L oblique, and return to standing.

Repeat R and L at least 4 times, then on 2 cts. and 1 ct.

Lateral with Flat Back

Notice the movements are progressively getting a little faster as we go.

Timing: 6/8 metre, 85 bpm

[cts. 1–3]   Lateral R.
[cts. 4–6]   Rotate to Flat Back toward stage R.
[cts. 1–3]   Rotate back to Lateral.
[cts. 4–6]   Return to standing.

Repeat 4 times, then on 2 cts. and 1 ct.

Lateral with Horizontal Swing

Timing: 6/8 metre, 90 bpm

[cts. 1–3]   Lateral R.
[cts. 4–6]   Flat Back R side.
[cts. 1–3]   Torso flows horizontally to the L.
[cts. 4–6]   Lateral L.
[cts. 1–3]   Return to standing.
[cts. 4–6]   Relevé and lower.

Repeat 4 times, then on 2 cts. and 1 ct.

Fortification No. 1 (Achilles Tendon Stretch)

Only the first half of this study is used for this experience.

Timing: 4/4 metre, 70 bpm
Start: Parallel 1st, arms Natural Low.

[cts. 1–2]   Relevé.
[cts. 3–4]   While still in relevé, slide R foot forward and rotate into Natural 4th (L foot remains in Parallel), lower the heel while the arms move into an L-shape (L forward, R in 2nd).
[cts. 1–4]   Flat Back over and the arms change to reverse the L-shape.
[cts. 1–4]   Return to standing as the arms change sides again.
[cts. 1–8]   Repeat Flat Back and return to standing, making the same arm changes as before.
[cts. 1–4]   Point the R foot, close Parallel 1st.

Repeat on the L, then on 2 cts.

Foot Work and Brushes

This is a sequence I sometimes use in place of Fortification No. 2 (The Plié Study), which is designed to strengthen and warm up the feet.

Timing: 3/4 metre, 95 bpm
Start: Parallel 1st, arms in Natural Low.

[cts. 1–3] Peel the toes off the floor so they fan open and you feel a slight stretch in the metatarsal arch.

[cts. 1–3] Contract the metatarsal arch, drawing the pads of all your toes down to the floor—the arch should lift off the floor and you'll be balanced on your heels and pads of your toes.

[cts. 1–3] Release the foot to neutral, pouring it back onto the floor naturally.

[cts. 1–9] Repeat.

[cts. 1–3] Relevé.

[cts. 1–3] Lower straight leg.

[cts. 1–6] Repeat.

[cts. 1–3] Peel R foot off the floor, starting with the heel, until the big toe comes off the floor.

[cts. 1–3] Replace the foot.

[cts. 1–6] Repeat L.

[cts. 1–3] Relevé.

[cts. 1–3] Lower straight leg.

[cts. 1&] Brush R tendu, close.

[cts. 2&] Brush R tendu, close.

[cts. 3&] Brush R tendu, close.

Repeat L, then again with leg raising to 45 degrees R and L. Repeat with leg to 90 degrees R and L.

[cts. 1–3] Relevé and rotate to Natural 1st to lower. Repeat the entire sequence in Natural 1st with arms in 2nd. After the final relevé in Natural 1st, tendu the R foot into Wide 2nd. To complete the sequence

[cts. 1–3] Peel the toes off the floor so they fan open and you feel a slight stretch in the metatarsal arch.

[cts. 1–3] Contract the metatarsal arch, drawing the pads of all your toes down to the floor—the arch should lift off the floor and you'll be balanced on your heels and pads of your toes.

[cts. 1–3] Release the foot to neutral, pouring it back onto the floor naturally.

[cts. 1–9] Repeat.

[cts. 1–3] Grand plié and straighten.

[cts. 1–3] Relevé.

[cts. 1–3] Lower.

[cts. 1–3] Grand plié.

[cts. 1–3] While in grand plié, roll the heels up into relevé.

[cts. 1–3] Straighten the legs while in relevé.

[cts. 1–3] Balance.

[cts. 1–3] Roll down and close Natural 1st, arms to Natural Low.

Deep Forward Lunge Series

The entire body is active here. This is not a passive stretch, so energy flows in all directions, and each muscle should be alert (which is not the same as tense!).

Timing: 4/4 metre, 50 bpm

Start: In the center, feet Parallel 1st, arms in Natural Low. Step into a deep lunge on the R foot, hands on the floor on either side of the foot. Track the knee in line with the second toe, but avoid having the knee pass the toes.

[cts. 1–16] Accent the pelvis toward the right heel, pulse the hips forward. This is not a bouncing action, just a slight accented pulse.

[cts. 1–4] Transfer the weight onto the L foot and the hands, step R foot back to the L, then move the L foot between the hands.

Repeat 4 times, deepening the stretch a little more each time. After the final repetition, step both feet forward between the hands in Parellel 2nd, engage the core, and return to standing by coming through a Flat Back. Step the feet into Parallel 1st as the arms come to Natural Low.

PROGRESSIONS ACROSS THE FLOOR

Leg Swings

Really be certain that you are working with a swing action in the hip. You don't want to kick at this point. This series travels stage L to stage R.

Timing: 3/4 metre, 70 bpm
Start: L leg in Natural 1st, arms in 2nd.

[cts. 1–3] Brush the R foot forward so the shin becomes parallel with the ceiling.

[cts. 1–3] Brush the R foot back so the thigh is parallel to the floor.

[cts. 1–3] Brush the R foot front again.

[cts. 1–3] Step outward in a smooth gliding step on the R foot.

Repeat across the floor. Repeat, adding the spine in an overcurve toward the leg as it swings front and an arch back as it swings back. Core is always engaged and the hips are front.

Elementary Balance

From stage L to stage R, you'll be working your standing leg in Natural 1st against the leg in motion in Parallel for part of this sequence.

A variation of the Deep Forward Lunge by students in the author's Beginning Horton class at Northwestern State University of Louisiana.

Timing: 6/4 metre, 65 bpm
  Start: In Natural 1st, arms in Natural Low.

[cts. 1–3] Lift the R knee forward through parallel (knee is bent and lower leg is at a 90-degree angle with the thigh) as the arms come to Middle Parallel.

[cts. 4–6] R leg opens to 2nd, palms rotate inward and arms open to 2nd.

[cts. 1–3] Together, the torso moves into Flat Back Back Bend and the pelvis moves forward.

[ct. 4] Rotate palms toward ceiling on the downbeat.

[cts. 5–6] Contract the core upward, bringing the pelvis to neutral and the torso upright, arms to High Parallel.

[cts. 1–3] Rotate R thigh to Table.

[cts. 4–6] Stretch into Flat Back as R leg extends into high arabesque.

[ct. 1] Turn R hip under to parallel on accented 1, but don't drop the level of R leg. [ct. 2] Bend the knees as the arms fold into Closed Egyptian, torso rounds over.

[ct. 3] Bring R knee forward as in the beginning, L knee straightens and arms return to Natural Low.

[cts. 4–6] Walk forward three cts.

Repeat on the L, continuing to travel across the floor.

Elementary Front T Balance Study

This is a basic introduction to the Front T and it emerges from the study above, so you'll start out the same way and move from stage L to stage R. This time, though, there is no backbend or pelvic press.

Timing: 6/4 metre, 55 bpm
  Start: In Natural 1st, arms in Natural Low.

[cts. 1–3] Lift the R knee forward through parallel (knee is bent and lower leg is at a 90 degree angle with the thigh), arms come to Middle Parallel.

[cts. 4–6] R leg opens to 2nd, palms rotate inward and arms open to 2nd.

[cts. 1–3] R thigh rotates to Table, arms to High Parallel.

[cts. 4–6] Stretch into Flat Back, R leg extends into a straight line with the spine (instead of the high arabesque you just did) so that arms, head, torso, and legs are all in one level line.

[ct. 1] R hip turns under to parallel on the accented 1.

[ct. 2] Bend the knees, arms fold into Closed Egyptian, torso rounds over.

[ct. 3] R knee comes forward as it did in the beginning, L knee straightens, arms return to Natural Low.

[cts. 4–6] Walk forward three cts.

Repeat on the L, continuing to travel across the floor.

IMPROVISATION

"Lester Horton used improvisation spontaneously in class as the students were moving across the floor. He would call out various parts of the body for the students to add to the basic phrases he had established."[73] This is a good place to include a traveling improvisation of some sort at the teacher's discretion. Ideally, the assignment will add humor, which is also a part of the Horton tradition. Working with level changes, staccato movement, and big locomotor turns that eat up lots of space are good at this point as a contrast to the detailed, concentrated work the class has experienced so far.

Side Hip Push, Figure 4, and Lateral T Balance

Keep the rib cage together throughout this sequence.

Timing: 3/4 metre, 75 bpm
Start: Face downstage in Natural 1st, arms Natural Low, move stage L to stage R.

[cts. 1–2] Step R, pushing the right hip out to the R so the weight shifts over the R foot. Simultaneously, raise the arms through 2nd, move the R arm to a high diagonal as the R hip continues to push R, L arm moves parallel to the L leg which is now lengthened diagonally, foot pointed. Legs, arms, head, and hips are all reaching outward.

[ct. 3] R hip pushes so far out the L foot has to step across the R to catch the weight, circle R arm over the head, arms finish Natural Low.

[ct. 1] Step R into Side Hip Push as above.

[ct. 2] Plié, folding into the Figure 4 Squat accenting the flexed L foot as you place it just above the R knee, turning this Figure to the L for one full turn.

[ct. 3] Step the L foot across the R.

[ct. 1] Step out to the R, arms come to High Parallel.

[ct. 2–3] Moving through High Lateral, fulfill the Lateral T position.

[cts. 1–2] Hold it.

[ct. 3] Return to standing, L foot crossing over R, arms in High Parallel.

Step R to repeat the entire phrase across the floor. Repeat toward stage L. Additional variations include completing the Lateral T in 1 ct., or the T can be a jump where the T is fulfilled at the height of the jump (not in the landing). You can also promenade the T toward the direction of the hands.

Jumping Study

This study is a combination of jumps from the Horton system. It incorporates the Double-Foot Arch Springs, Unaccented Runs, and the Stag Jump.

Timing: 4/4 metre, 110 bpm
Start: Stage L in Natural 1st, arms in Natural Low. Move R.

[ct. 1] Double-Foot Arch Spring by jumping from two feet and landing on both feet in plié.

[ct. 2] Repeat.

[cts. 3–5] Run in plié on balls of the feet 3 steps starting on L foot, arms in 2nd.

[ct. 6] Spring into Stag Jump: R leg comes forward until the thigh is parallel to the ceiling, knee bent to 90 degrees; L leg moves backward into the Stag, R arm is in 2nd, L arm is straight out in front of the L shoulder.

[ct. 7] Land on both feet in plié, arms to Natural Low.

[ct. 8] Stag Jump L leg leading, reverse the arms.

[ct. 1] Double-Foot Arch Spring turning half turn to the R.

[ct. 2] Jump half-turn R again.

Repeat the sequence.

Final Questions

1. How did your in-studio experiments compare with or inform your experience once you explored the class materials? How did the material feel in your body? What differences did you find in your body-mind as you participated in these in-studio experiences?

2. What did you learn about music?

3. How might you use the philosophical ideas in Dunham's work to inform your dancing or your teaching?

4. What ideas did the flow of the Horton materials give you about the structure of a technique class?

5. How do sociocultural realities like race, gender, sexual identity, and economic status affect technique and how do you (or your students) experience class? How do those factors influence the genesis of training methodologies?

Works Cited

Ailey, A. & Bailey, P. (1995). *Revelations: The autobiography of Alvin Ailey*. New York: Birch Lane Press/Carol Publishing Company.

Anderson, J. (1992). *Ballet and Modern Dance: A concise history*. Princeton, NJ: Princeton Book Company.

Aschenbrenner, J. (2002). *Katherine Dunham: Dancing a life*. Urbana and Chicago: University of Illinois Press.

Barnes, C. (1967, December 3). Genius on the Wrong Coast. *Los Angeles Herald Examiner*.

Barzel, A., Turbyfill, M., & Page, R. (1983). The Lost Ten Years: The untold story of the Dunham-Turbyfill alliance. In V. A. Clark & S. E. Johnson (Eds.), *Kaiso! Writings by and about Katherine Dunham* (pp. 177-188). Madison: University of Wisconsin Press.

Bizot, R. (1984, Spring). Lester Horton's *Salome*, 1934-1953 and after. *Dance Research Journal*, 16(1), 35-40.

Clark, V. A. (1994). Performing the Memory of Difference in Afro-Caribbean Dance: Katherine Dunham's choreography, 1938-1987. In V. A. Clark & S. E. Johnson (Eds.), *Kaiso! Writings by and about Katherine Dunham* (pp. 320-340). Madison: University of Wisconsin Press.

Dunham, K. (2005). Dunham Performing Arts Training Center as a Focal Point for a New and

Unique College or School. In V. A. Clark & S. E. Johnson (Eds.), *Kaiso! Writings by and about Katherine Dunham* (pp. 551-556). Madison: University of Wisconsin Press.

_____. (2005). Early New York Collaborations. In V. Clark & S. E. Johnson (Eds.), *Kaiso! Writings by and about Katherine Dunham* (pp. 125-149). Madison: University of Wisconsin Press.

_____. (n.d.). (Library of Congress Staff, Interviewer). Katherine Dunham on the Need for Dunham Technique, Video #38. [Video interview]. Washington, DC: Library of Congress.

_____. (2005). Performing Arts Training Center as a Focal Point for a New and Unique College or School. In V. A. Clark & S. E. Johnson (Eds.), *Kaiso! Writings by and about Katherine Dunham* (pp. 551-556). Madison: University of Wisconsin Press.

_____. (1951). Southland Program: A dramatic ballet in two scenes. In V. A. Clark & S. E. Johnson (Eds.), *Kaiso! Wiritings by and about Katherine Dunham* (pp. 341-344). Madison: University of Wisconsin Press.

_____. (1964). The Dunham Schools. In V. A. Clark & S. E. Johnson (Eds.), *Kaiso! Writings by and about Katherine Dunham* (pp. 479-480). Madison: University of Wisconsin Press.

Dunham Pratt, M. C. (2009, July 7). Katherine Dunham. Interview by J. Legg.

Forsythe, A. M. & Perces, M. B. (Directors). (2002). *Lester Horton Technique: Intermediate Level* [Motion Picture]. United States: Kultur International Films.

_____. (1990). *Lester Horton Technique: The Warm-up* [Motion Picture]. United States: Kultur International Films.

Franko, M. (2002). *The Work of Dance: Labor, movement and identity in the 1930s.* Middletown, CT: Wesleyan University Press.

Gibson, E. (2009, April 25). Lester Horton Technique. Interview by J. Legg.

Graff, E. (1997). *Stepping Left: Dance and politics in New York City, 1928–1941.* Durham, NC: Duke University Press.

Gottschild, B. D. (1996). Digging the Africanist Presence in American Performance: Dance and other contexts. Westport, CT: Greenwood Press.

_____. (2001). Stripping the Emporer: The Africanist presence in American concert dance. In A. Dils and A. Cooper Albright (Eds.), *Moving History / Dancing Cultures: A dance history reader* (pp. 332–341). Madison: University of Wisconsin Press.

Hill, C.V. (1994, Fall). Katherine Dunham's *Southland*: Protest in the face of repression. *Dance Research Journal*, 26 (2), 1–10.

Holmes, J. (2009, November 5). 'Postracial America' One Year Later. *The Huffington Post*. http://www.huffingtonpost.com/jamie-holmes/postracial-america-one-ye_b_346967.html.

Lee, K. (2009, June 3). Lester Horton Technique, part 1. Interview by J. Legg.

_____. (2009, June 5). Lester Horton Technique, part 2. Interview by J. Legg.

Legg, J. (2008, November 7). *Dancing Blackness*. [Lecture]. Winchester, VA: Shenandoah University.

_____. (2008, May/June). Katherine Dunham Technique: Why you should investigate this modern master's work—plus what to expect in class. *Dance Spirit*, pp. 74–77.

_____. (2007, January). Modern Focus: Horton Technique. *Dance Spirit*, pp. 94–95.

Lloyd, M. (1949). *The Borzoi Book of Modern Dance*. New York: Dance Horizons.

Manning, S. (2001). Watching Dunham's Dances, 1937–1945. In V. A. Clark & S. E. Johnson (Eds.), *Kaiso! Writings by and about Katherine Dunham* (pp. 256–266). Madison: University of Wisconsin Press.

Martin, J. (1931, August 30). "The Dance: A repertory movement; Stravinsky's *Petrouchka* opens the Dance Center's season of Experiment—a novel theater and production," *The New York Times*.

_____. (1940, February 25). The Dance—A negro art: Katherine Dunham's Notable Contribution, *The New York Times*.

_____. (1946, November 17). The Dance: Dunham, Schoolmarm Turned Siren or Vice Versa; In *Bal Negre* at the Belasco, *The New York Times*.

Osumare, H. (2007). *The Africanist Aesthetic in Global Hip-Hop: Power moves*. New York: Palgrave.

Perces, M. B., Forsythe, A. M., & Bell, C. (1992). *The Dance Technique of Lester Horton*. Princeton, NJ: Princeton Book Company.

Perpener, J. O., III. (2005). *African-American Concert Dance: The Harlem renaissance and beyond*. Chicago: University of Illinois Press.

Pierre, D. B. (2005). A Talk with Katherine Dunham. In V. A. Clark & S. E. Johnson (Eds.), *Kaiso! Writings by and about Katherine Dunham* (pp. 248–250). Madison: University of Wisconsin Press.

Rose, A. (1990). *Dunham Technique: "A Way of Life."* Dubuque: Kendall/Hunt Publishing Company.

_____. (2008, February 19). Katherine Dunham. Telephone interview by J. Legg.

_____. (2007, May 27). Katherine Dunham. Telephone interview by J. Legg.

Warren, L. (1977). *Lester Horton: Modern dance pioneer.* New York: Marcel Dekker.

CHAPTER 4

The Next Generation

José Limón

Erick Hawkins

[M]ost nations in the world have a ministry of culture in some form, whereas the United States does not. Indeed, the very notion seems politically inconceivable in this country. . . . Comparative investigation of State[i] support for cultural projects, examined in historical perspective, provides grist for the mill of anyone inclined toward a belief in American exceptionalism, by which I mean difference, not superiority.

—Michael Kammen, Culture and the State in America, in *The Politics of Culture*

As with any history, certain historical demarcations used in this book may seem arbitrary or artificial. They are designed, however, to help us see dance events not as singular, novel occurrences in a dance vacuum, but rather as intertwined with broader societal developments. Nowhere is that likely more evident than when considering 1946 as the start of the late period in modern dance. The emergence of modern's next generation of leaders coincides with an era of tremendous social, economic, and political change in the nation. By 1946, male dancers like José Limón, Alwin Nikolais, and Murray Louis who had placed dance careers on hold while serving in World War II returned home eager to pursue careers in the artform again. At the same time, Doris Humphrey's health concerns forced her to stop performing, and Limón, her protégé, created his own company with Humphrey as its first

---

[i]Following the practice in political science, State is capitalized in Kammen's remark as it refers to general activity across governments. Where it is in lowercase, state refers to a specific government, in this instance, the United States.

Kristina Berger in Erick Hawkins' Cantilever.

artistic director, thus marking a pivotal transition between first and second generation modern dance leaders. Finally, 1946 was also a critical year in the establishment of America's Cold War policies—policies that clearly initiated a cultural war with the Soviets as much as they had the political war, greatly affecting the financial stability of several prominent modern dance companies in the latter part of the era.

Kammen is correct in stating that America has never engaged a cultural czar (although a Bureau of Fine Arts and a Cabinet-level Secretary of Art were proposed as long ago as the late 1930s).[1] Justin Lewis, Professor of Communication and Head of the Cardiff School of Journalism, Media and Cultural Studies at Cardiff University, goes a step further to say that American political parties actually have no real cultural policy at all.[2] Lewis, however, points out that a lack of coherent policy does not always keep the state from tinkering with an "array of cultural industries and activities" through planning, regulation, and subsidy.[3] He goes on to identify two basics ways that Western nations often approach culture:

> The first is for government to abstain from cultural policy altogether, leaving a society's cultural life in the hands of free market forces. . . . The second is for the government to base a cultural policy on fairly traditional, narrow notions of arts and artistic value, thus limiting the state's role to the protection of a limited selection of cultural activities, such as drama or classical music.[4]

American policy certainly oscillated between these two ideas, often with great volatility, in the last century. Political support for or opposition against arts and cultural funding, however, has not always fallen neatly along party lines and members of both dominant parties have been as likely to embrace state involvement in cultural production as they have been to reject it. We will see that the state has, nevertheless, frequently turned to the arts either to address domestic economic concerns or to further its political agenda—particularly in countering fascism and in containing Communism in the last century. We will, therefore, consider the late modern period against a backdrop of World War II's conclusion and the rise of the Cold War. The impact of the ideological body politic on the dancing body of the era cannot be overestimated, especially given Western efforts toward global democratization.

To understand the era's cultural climate and the influence this had on dance far into the second generation of the artform, we need to take a step back to the Great Depression, and the state's first major engagements of the arts. As historian Julia Foulkes, Associate Professor of History at The New School (whose work centers on art and urbanization) noted of the era, "Poised at the perilous moment after the stock market crash of October 1929 and the start of a new decade, modern dancers steeped themselves in the social, political, and aesthetic issues of the day."[5] She also observed that, "Modern dancers explored theories of government, the relationship between workers and artists, and the political meanings of different kinds of dance."[6]

The Confluence of American Art and Politics

We saw in Chapters 2 and 3 that the 1930s was a crucial decade for the development of American concert dance. While we are looking primarily at modern dance in this book, it should be pointed out that as the originators and mavericks in the preceding chapters were establishing their bodies of choreography and training systems, Ruth Page had a successful ballet school and company in Chicago, George Balanchine and Lincoln Kirstein established the School of American Ballet (1934), and their companies (American Ballet and Ballet Caravan), along with Ballet Theatre, were all improving training opportunities for ballet dancers as well. What has not been discussed thus far is the fact that all of this work was being done during the Great Depression (roughly 1929–1939)—the period of deepest global financial catastrophe in the last century. We also need to consider more closely that concurrent to the work of the modernists and ballet artists was the work of leftist dancemakers and labor unions in New York City. Since the late 1980s, scholars including Stacey Prickett, Elizabeth Cooper, Julia Foulkes, Lynn Garafola, Ellen Graff, and Mark Franko (see Chapter 3 for more on the work of Graff and Franko) have provided extensive insight into the work of dance as a mechanism for political action in the decade, and the extent to which concert dance was radicalized for both community and professional stage by dance artists who may or may not also have been Communists.

Graff points out that, "The Communist Party, USA (CP), enjoyed its most influential decade during the 1930s."[7] Franko noted, "Whether aimed at revolution, management, or entertainment, mass action in the thirties depended on the social organization of cooperative movement on a mass scale."[8] Graff also illustrated that in 1931,

> a Workers Cultural Federation was formed after a delegation of American artists returned from the Soviet Union with directives for attracting proletarians, intellectuals and blacks into their ranks, as well as for organizing agitprop [agitation and propaganda in the form of leaflets, plays, dance presentations, etc.] theatrical troupes. In New York City 265 delegates, claiming to represent some 20,000 members from 130 different groups, met to endorse the proposition that "culture is a weapon."[9]

Although sympathetic professional artists from nearly every artistic genre produced radical art, innumerable amateurs also participated in classes or performances citywide through labor unions or community houses. The Needle Trades Workers Industrial Union and many others fostered workers' dance groups, and the Workers' Dance League (which became New Dance League in 1935) organized cooperative group action based on the idea that "Dance Is a Weapon in the

Revolutionary Class Struggle." A distillation of the goals of this work—by Communists and non-Communists alike—was a struggle for an egalitarian society through a level playing field of labor. It was the workers' wage, in this view, that would demonstrate civil equality regardless of race, gender, or other social identifier. An affiliated group, the New Dance Group, also arose at this time (1932) and established itself outside of the unionist structure as an academy dedicated to training working-class dancers (as separate from "elitist" dancers at modern dance schools such as Graham's), offering training for ten cents per three-hour class.[10]

Unemployment was a major point of focus for participating artists and labor groups engaged in this dance-related activity. As early as March 6, 1930, the CP organized a demonstration for "International Unemployment Day" and may have had as many as 100,000 participants.[11] Note that it would be nearly three more years before the United States unemployment rate reached its height in the Great Depression, topping out at 25 percent or 10,000,000 unemployed Americans.[12] Then, in December 1933, the Roosevelt Administration created the "skeleton organization of the first [federal] art program, the Public Works of Art Project (PWAP)" within the Treasury Department,[13] which was funded via the Federal Emergency Relief Administration. While PWAP ended in 1934, three subsequent programs emerged during the 1930s: The Section of Painting and Sculpture, the Federal Art Project of the Works Progress Administration (WPA), and the Treasury Art Relief Project (TARP). Note that only the Section of Painting and Sculpture was not related to economic relief for the artists. Of the four projects, it was the WPA programming that marked the first budgetary allocation for culture in America—an allocation that was ultimately eliminated owing to Congressional opposition to Communism. It was here, albeit briefly, that the state first supported dancers—modern dancers in particular—and fostered the creation of their art.

WPA and the Federal Dance Project (FDP):

Established in 1935, the WPA sought to provide government employment to the masses of Americans without jobs. Initially, four of the WPA's projects focused on work in the arts: the Federal Arts Project, the Federal Theatre Project, the Federal Music Project, and the Federal Writers Project. (A variety of other projects addressed general cultural preservation, such as the Historical Records Survey and the Survey of Federal Archives.)[14] The Purpose Statement in the *Manual for Federal Theatre Projects of the Works Progress Administration* is a perfect illustration of the goals of these projects:

> The primary aim of the Federal Theatre Project is the re-employment of theatre workers now on the relief roll: actors, directors, playwrights, designers, vaudeville artists, stage technicians, and other workers in the theatre field. The far-reaching purpose is the establishment of theatres so vital to community life that they will continue to function after the program of the Federal Project is completed.[15]

Originally employed via the Theatre Project's New York regional subdivision, dance artists soon called for their own discipline-specific unit, "shaped by the sense of mission characteristic of the federal projects in the arts and by the special commitment to left-wing politics that governed the New York theatre project."[16]

Helen Tamiris is widely credited as the driving force behind the Federal Dance Project's creation—she had developed extensive management, organizational, and fundraising experience through her own company as well as leading projects such as Dance Repertory Theatre and serving on the board of the Concert Dancers' League (see Chapter 2 for more on Dance Repertory Theatre). In an effort to secure funding for the dance project, a committee of fifteen dancers (including Doris Humphrey, Charles Weidman, and Don Oscar Becque) formed the Dance Association with Tamiris as its chair. In that capacity, Tamiris lobbied WPA Director Harry Hopkins and Federal Theatre Project Director Hallie Flanagan for the establishment of a dance-specific WPA program, with Flanagan in turn lobbying Congress for project funding. The Federal Dance Theatre emerged in 1936 with Becque as its director, and an executive committee of Tamiris, Humphrey, Weidman, Felicia Sorel, and Senia Gluck-Sandor. The initial budget allocation was $155,000 with which the committee was to hire 185 dancers and create eight productions in its first eight months.[17]

From its inception and throughout its short existence, the Project was fraught with difficulties and controversies. As early as March 1936, the WPA halted the hiring process for all the arts projects despite the fact FDT had taken on only eighty-five of the 185 dancers it was originally allotted. Periodic protests by groups of dancers began as early as April 1936—in this case, in reaction to the continued hiring moratorium—resulting in the arrest of the participants. By that fall, furor erupted over Becque's leadership style and a variety of his decisions, which ended with his dismissal in December. (In its first eight months, FDT had created just three productions—only one of these was a new work, the other two were stagings of preexisting works.)[18] Lincoln Kirstein then joined as director, only to leave three weeks later—the internal politics and temperaments of the FDP proving unnavigable. As it turned out, FDT was constantly strife-ridden, and choreographers contended with numerous delays and budget cuts. By 1937, FDT was rolled back into the Federal Theatre Project. In 1939, a month after the final work Tamiris made for the Project, The Federal Arts Project was shut down by an act of Congress. Republican Congressmen Martin Dies and J. Parnell Thomas of the House Un-American Activities Committee (HUAC) sought to eliminate Communists and their supporters from all government agencies, and the Federal Arts Project was a clear target because many in its ranks had joined or associated with the CP. (One estimate indicates that the CP grew from 12,000 members in 1929 to 100,000 in 1939.)[19]

One place where Congress and American artists found common ground was over mounting concerns about fascism and the threat of a new war in Europe. As early as 1936 and the first meeting of the Dance Congress, American dancers joined in a stand against fascism, its stagnating impact on creative endeavors, and its wars of aggression.[20] Numerous dance leaders boycotted the 1936 Olympic Games in Germany, including Graham, Humphrey, Weidman, Kirstein, and Tamiris. Later that fall, the name of the Wigman school in New York was changed to the Hanya Holm School (see Chapter 5 for more on this). By 1937, artists were making profound works supporting the Loyalists in the Spanish Civil War in their battle against fascism. Even Graham, who had previously not engaged in political dance, made *Chronicle, Immediate Tragedy*, and *Deep Song* as part of the antifascist effort. Three years later, the Germans invaded Paris on June 14, 1940, and as Serge Guilbaut, Professor of Art History at the University of British Columbia, put it:

> Americans saw in the fall of Paris the death of a certain idea of democracy. For them Paris stood for the triumph of individualism. . . . For Paris to fall without a shot being fired was more serious still, because it represented the symbolic destruction of Western culture. . . . Fascism was said to be a reversion to the Dark Ages, when men, unaccustomed to the civilizing benefits of Christianity, behaved like beasts.[21]

The propaganda of the Nazi Party embraced art, film, and literature but rejected modernism —the Nazis destroyed modernist art across Europe. In its efforts to take on some of Europe's traditional roles, the United States became the defenders of Western culture prior to entering the War, and embraced the modernist, avant-garde aesthetic. In 1940 and 1941, the government's most public demonstration supporting modernism was "Buy American Art Week," which demonstrated an investment in democratic art. (In fact, the simple act of modernist painting was eventually read as political action against Hitler.)[22] In 1941, Lincoln Kirstein's American Ballet Caravan received $140,000 from the U.S. State Department for a semiofficial Good Neighbor tour of Latin America, marking the first government-sponsored international dance tour. The company visited all but two South American nations during the six-month tour in the hope of averting Nazi cultural infiltration of the region by offering a demonstration that democratic culture was alive and well.[23]

The defeat of fascist regimes in Germany and Italy at the end of World War II paved the way for a renewal of anti-Communist efforts in the U.S. Congress. In 1945, HUAC was elevated from a special investigative committee to a standing committee—this distinction was solidified in the Legislative Reorganization Act of 1946 (paving the way for McCarthyism later). HUAC was invested with broad authority to investigate subversive and un-American propaganda and activity, and charged with making recommendations to Congress for necessary remedial legislation.[24] Also in 1946, George F. Kennan (U.S. attaché in Moscow) wrote "The Long Telegram," identifying key conceptual/ideological differences in U.S.-Soviet relations (February), British Prime Minister

Winston Churchill first referred to Soviet-block countries as the Iron Curtain (March), and Chief White House Counsel Clark Clifford synthesized the concerns of numerous federal officials regarding U.S.-Soviet relations for President Truman in the Clifford-Elsey Report (September). In effect, 1946 set the stage for Cold War policy, and in March of the following year, the Truman Doctrine was announced—the U.S. doctrine of containment regarding global Communism. A push began in the early 1950s to increase the international visibility of U.S. cultural production as we confronted Communist expansion. Because the Soviets preferred realism and rejected modernism, avant-garde modernist art became a vital cultural asset in the atomic age,[25] as it had in the West's antifascist front. Modernist dance was central to that effort.

President Eisenhower solicited Congress in 1954 for emergency funding to support the export of American culture abroad. In a letter dated July 27, he wrote, "I consider it essential that we take immediate and vigorous action to demonstrate the superiority of the products and cultural values of our system of free enterprise."[26] The President's Emergency Fund for International Affairs was passed in August. The provisions for the $5,000,000 Fund included (among other items) $2,592,000 to establish the State Department's global export of American culture. The Kirstein/American Ballet Caravan Latin American Tour in 1941 and New York City Ballet's reception at the 1952 Berlin Cultural Festival had already proven that American dance companies were more than capable of representing the nation at the highest levels. When the touring program was instituted, the American National Theatre and Academy (ANTA) assisted the State Department in arranging tour details. ANTA also organized a panel of eminent national dance leaders (choreographers, directors, and critics) to evaluate potential companies for participation in the program. In the fall of 1954, the State Department launched its first tour, sending the José Limón Company to the Inter-American Economic and Social Council in Rio de Janeiro, and the UNESCO conference following it in Montevideo. In addition to the high caliber of Limón's work, his "fluency in Spanish helped the audience achieve greater understanding of the originality and value of American modern dance."[27] When attention was turned to the Eisenhower Administration's international region of greatest concern, Asia, Martha Graham's company was chosen for that tour. From October 1955 to February 1956, Graham toured nine Asian countries where the group "conquered; her company was seen by cheering thousands . . . the foreign press and heads of state applauded."[28] Over the next few years, the Dance Panel struggled with considerations of "high art" over entertainment in choosing companies—avant-garde work was also a particular challenge to the Panel. In time, however, Merce Cunningham, Erick Hawkins, and Paul Taylor were approved for tours. Alvin Ailey's company became the first African American company enlisted for the tours in 1962—the company was chosen to offset images of America as a racist nation in the midst of the civil rights movement.

At the same time the State Department tours were exporting art, consideration was being given to the future of culture at home. By 1958, groundwork was laid for a national center for culture—a vision fulfilled when the Kennedy Center for the Performing Arts opened. Then, in 1965, the National Endowment for the Arts was established to provide direct support in the development and implementation of American creative activity. The path of Congressional support for public arts funding has been a tumultuous one—with opposition reaching back into the 1930s (see Chapter 7 for more on the National Endowment for the Arts). Choreographers and dance companies have long had to rely on grants and fellowships from private charitable trusts in order to stay afloat, particularly given the unpredictable funding practices of the U.S. Congress over the years. It is thanks to nonprofit organizations like the Andrew W. Mellon Foundation, the John D. & Catherine T. MacArthur Foundation, the Ford Foundation, and the John Simon Guggenheim Memorial Foundation that companies, choreographers, scholars/critics, and students are often able to continue participating in the artform that is our life's work.

Core Ideas

....

Observations and Experiments

Journal I: Nature—the elements, animals, plants, even smoke—are all instructive objects of study in preparing for this chapter's experiences. Notice how gentle rain falls, unrestricted from the sky, and how it rolls down the window. Watch water flow unencumbered in a gutter, down a drain, or along a quiet creek. Notice how there is no effort, only motion. Observe a waft of smoke moving upward without resistance. Spy on a cat to see how noiselessly it moves, and how it moves efficiently from its center regardless of whether it's moving quickly or lazily. Note that when a cat swats a fly, it uses effortless contraction and decontraction—it's not that the cat doesn't use its muscles, it just knows when and how much effort to put behind the action. Watch a tree blowing in the breeze. Observe the overcurve energy—it isn't limited to the uppermost limbs, but resonates without hesitation from the roots upward. Pay attention to the recovery from the overcurve, and how the path of motion is simply redrawn

backward along the initial course of motion. Take notes on these observations.

Journal II: Visit a playground with a swing set and a basketball court. Go for a swing and let yourself experience the momentum. Notice the sensation of that motion in your body and the energy sequence in the action. Trace the impetus, release, and recovery. Track the speed of the motion from the height, moving in a downward arc through the depth of the undercurve, and upward again on the other side. Bounce a basketball and notice the effects of gravity and rebound. Pay attention to your own breath and how it influences your movement.

Experiment I: While notably different, there are several similarities in the Limón and Hawkins training methodologies. First, there is their use of rhythm, and second is the way dancers use kinetic energy to help produce efficient movement—in fact they have even been referred to as the first release techniques, although that perception isn't exactly accurate because they both employ a broader effort spectrum than that idea implies. It is on the latter concept that these studio experiments will focus.

Timing: 8 cts.

Start: Stand in parallel, feet slightly apart, core activated, and each part of the body dynamically aligned knees over ankles, hips over knees, rib cage over hips, shoulders over rib cage, and head on top of shoulders.

Preparation: Close your eyes and check the main weight centers in the body: the pelvis, rib cage, and head. Sense what it is for each center to be aligned without relying on the mirror, then open your eyes and check visually. How did what you felt match up with the alignment you saw in the mirror?

From that neatly organized place—standing as tall as possible, and fully focused in the present—begin a roll-down series. Each movement takes 8 counts (music isn't needed, the instructor can count the class through this). Be sure to keep the shoulders and chest open throughout, and place the hands lightly on the sides of the thighs and allow them to slide as needed. Be sure to think about each movement before you execute it, then feel the movement happen.

[cts. 1–8] Send energy through the top of the head, lengthening the body even more, and create a slight overcurve as you roll the head forward (incorporating only the head and neck).

[cts. 1–8] Restack the head on top of the shoulders.

[cts. 1–8] Overcurve, roll the head forward until the shoulders join the roll about halfway down to the waist, allowing the weight of the head and shoulders to pull you forward.

[cts. 1–8] Roll back up.

[cts. 1–8] Roll forward, bend at the waist.

[cts. 1–8] Roll back up.

[cts. 1–8] Roll forward (making sure the weight of the head, shoulders, and chest carry you forward), bend the knees until fingertips touch the floor (if possible).

[cts. 1–8] Roll back up.

[cts. 1–8] Roll all the way down until the palms touch the floor (if possible).

[cts. 1–] Roll back up. Reconnect with your starting alignment.

Restack your alignment, repeat to the side L and R, going only as far as the knee bends.

Experiment II: Without counts this time, play with how subtle changes in the weight centers can initiate and influence movement.

Start: In parallel, check alignment and maintain full body alignment throughout this exploration.

Initiate a shift in the pelvis to the R and see how the rib cage and head respond, what happens in the spine, and how far to the R you can take your pelvis before you actually have to step to the R. Notice what happens in the rest of the body as you take that step. Try the same thing leading with the rib cage and then the head.

Stand in 1st position. Initiate a sideward weight shift R by lifting your pelvis up to establish an overcurve that causes the R foot to slide to the side into a plié. Try to reverse the overcurve, shifting the weight back to 1st.

Repeat the idea using an undercurve, then reverse to close. Notice the sensations you experienced in the two ideas. Try both with the rib cage and head leading. You can also play allowing the weight centers to initiate a lean that takes you into a wider stance, front, side, and back—possibly taking you into such a weight shift that you fall into a lunge. Try the leans again, and see if you can use the kinetic energy to motivate locomotion. Notice what happens if you walk with the weight of your head forward or run with the weight of the pelvis shifted to one side. Explore other kinds of movement you can create using these weight centers and the idea of weight shift. Be sure to take some notes on your findings.

Technical Genesis

José Limón (1908–1972): Biographical Sketch

Children do not walk to school. They run, skip, hop, leap: they dance to school, or into the dining room, or up the stairs to bed. The adolescent is notorious for his nervous, jittery dances. And love's young dream: imagine our early romances without a waltz by moonlight! We discover the rapture and intoxication of love during the dance. And even maturity finds a new dimension to the weary business of existence during the sedate ritual of the ballroom: a suspension, a surcease, an inexplicable lifting of the spirit.

—José Limón, *On Dance,* in *The Vision of Modern Dance*

There is a humanness in José Limón's work and in how he related dance to everyday life. His dances are dramatic, and many are content-driven, peopled with iconic characterizations. Dance critic Walter Sorell once said, "Limón has a very personal way of communicating the inner drama of his characters. There is a certain grandeur . . . in his gestures; there is an intensity in the rapport between the dancers on an emotional and intellectual level."[29] The duende, the soul and passion, of his work is also the foundation of his technique. Ann Vachon, director of the José Limón Institute and former member of his company, said his technique was founded on humanism, "and what humanism means applied to movement and to training. There is an acceptance of nature's effect on the body—weight, breath, and effort are important aspects of the technique."[30] Carla Maxwell, artistic director the José Limón Dance Company, said, "José's work has always been lifegiving because it is so full of hope and harmony, even in his most extreme tragedies."[31] Limón himself stated, "I deplore the artist who makes of his art a withdrawal from the travail of his time; who sterilizes and dehumanizes it into empty formalism; who renounces the vision of man as perfectable . . . who forgets that the artist's function is perpetually to be the voice and conscience of his time."[32]

José Limón demonstrating in the studio at Jacob's Pillow, 1946.

Born in Culiacán, Sinaloa, Mexico on January 12, 1908, Limón was the oldest of eleven children who grew up in a cultural environment—his father was a musician/composer who served as director of the State Academy of Music. Even as a youngster, Limón demonstrated artistic talent himself: "It was taken for granted by everyone, including myself, that I was destined for a painter's career."[33] The part of his childhood spent in Mexico was shrouded by death and the Mexican revolution. He watched as two of his siblings died of untreatable maladies, and saw his uncle shot through a window in their home as the war raged. He also witnessed the execution of a stranger by a firing squad, recalling later "the sound of the volley and the violent desolation of a woman weeping."[34] By the time he was seven and his family had immigrated to the United States, Limón said

> I had seen and felt many things that seven-year-olds should be spared. . . .
> I had learned that living was a precious and unpredictable business and that
> to cope with living one had to have *valor*—courage. And I was soon to
> learn that for the rest of my life I was to be a translator and conciliator. It
> would be my task to translate . . . to reconcile many disparate and contra-

dictory cultural habits and ways of living, and to resolve hostilities within and around me.[35]

In high school, Limón studied music (voice and piano) and art—both of which certainly informed his career as a choreographer. He also majored in art briefly at UCLA before hitchhiking to New York in 1928, where he planned to join the art scene. "The rapture," he said, "the sense of liberation at having found, at last, the *magnum desideratum*, was almost more than I could bear. I walked on clouds. Life was a radiant, golden dream come true."[36] The art world in New York though seemed bent on imitation of masters like Manet, Renoir, and Picasso. Searching for a different set of artistic ideas, Limón turned to El Greco (Doménikos Theotokópoulos), the Greek Spanish Renaissance painter and sculptor whose work merged Byzantine ideas with Western traditions. Unfortunately, Limón noted, "The more I studied his work . . . the more I came to the fatal recognition—fatal, that is, to my life's ambition—that he had done all I hoped to do and done it supremely well. New York now became a cemetery, and I a lost soul in torment."[37] It was during these days of lost ambition, that Limón's dream changed quickly, however, leading him on an unexpected path. A friend, Charlotte Vaughn, took him to see his first dance concert, a performance by Harald Kreutzberg. Limón later recalled:

> Suddenly, onto the stage, borne on the impetus of the heroic rhapsody, bounded an ineffable creature and his partner. Instantly and irrevocably, I was transformed. I knew with shocking suddenness that until then I had not been alive or, rather, that I had yet to be born. There was joy, terror, and panic in the discovery . . . and now I did not want to remain on this earth unless I learned to do what this man—Harald Kreutzberg—was doing.[38]

His search for answers about "what this man was doing" led him first to Isadora Duncan's recently released (posthumously) book *My Life*. Then, two of Limón's friends, who had gone to school with Charles Weidman in Lincoln, Nebraska, sent him to the Humphrey-Weidman studio, where he began his dance training and met his future wife, Pauline Lawrence. Of the birth of a dancer, Limón said:

> You pant, sweat, and hurt. You learn that you are. You learn that the past— the *jarabes*[ii], the bullfights, the painting, the Mexican in you, the fearful passage to the land of the *gringos*, the wounds, the deaths—have been only a preparation for this new life.[39]

[ii] A *jarabe* is a traditional mariachi song noted for its mixed metre.

At twenty-two, just two years after his New York arrival, Limón found himself on stage in Doris Humphrey's *Lysistrata*, where he had "been judiciously placed in the back line of the chorus . . . [and] where he abandoned himself nightly in the bacchanal."[40] There had been an earlier stage appearance in a smaller piece by Charles Weidman, *Rhythmic Patterns of Java* (1928), but it had been cast with students in technique class. *Lysistrata* marked Limón's first audition, which came after numerous hours "at the studio, early, very early, working on the stubborn body. Power of muscle I had in abundance. It was suppleness that I lacked,"[41] he said. It was on one such morning that Humphrey looked into the studio and said:

> I'm glad to see you working so hard. For a while I had my doubts about you, and was thinking of telling you not to waste your time but to go back to your painting; you'd never make a dancer. Now I think you're going to be one of the world's extraordinary people.[42]

Limón was moved along quickly in the developing technique at the Humphrey-Weidman studio, and in their growing repertory. When men were added to Humphrey's 1931 masterpiece, *The Shakers*, Limón was among them:

> I found performing *The Shakers* a deeply moving experience. It was a tough, demanding assignment. It has influenced me in an infinite number of ways, both as a performer and as a choreographer. It helped to mold me and led me always to seek an impassioned formalism. I have repeatedly, over the decades, tried to achieve the compelling dramatic power of Doris' abstractions and failed. I have found myself imitating or plagiarizing her.[43]

His own choreographic explorations began in the days following the close of *Lysistrata*, investigating movement in the basement of a building where he served as the maintenance person. He remarked of that work, "The attempt to fill the vast, eternal emptiness of space and time is indeed an act of arrogance and presumption. I didn't know this, and being young I didn't know I didn't know it. All I knew was that I wanted to put movements together, to make a dance."[44] There are two versions of the story regarding the vehicle through which Limón made his first compositions, Limón's version and Eleanor King's. I present both here in brief for historical consideration. *According to Limón:* Working with three of Doris's women—Letitia Ide, Eleanor King, and Ernestine Henoch (Stodelle)—he formed his first company, The Little Group, premiering at the Humphrey-Weidman Studio. The concert of seven works, created in a few short months, was possible, he said, only because I drove the girls and myself with merciless determination. We rehearsed night and day."[45] *According to King:* It was Charles Laskey who initiated the Little

Group's organization. Laskey was a new dancer in Weidman's group of men who seemed to have numerous ideas about thematic materials for new compositions. Early meetings consisted of Laskey, King, Limón, Ernestine Henoch (Stodelle), and Cleo Atheneos. By the time the Group was ready to get off the ground, however, Laskey was finding greater success dancing for Balanchine. Atheneos did not remain long either due to her increasing involvement with teaching. It was then that Letitia Ide joined the Group, completing the final quartet.[46] While Laskey may have been the group's original organizer, it is likely that Limón did become the driving force as he suggested upon Laskey's departure. What is clear despite other discrepancies, though, is that Limón's early works "primarily dealt with pure movement . . . experimenting with what his body was beginning to accomplish as a dancer. His painter's eye composed the groupings of dancers; the musical structures came easily from his early training and lifelong love of music."[47]

As he delved more deeply into dancemaking, he also continued growing in the repertory at Humphrey-Weidman, becoming Humphrey's most important protégé, originating roles in *New Dance*, *Theatre Piece*, *With My Red Fires*, and *Passacaglia*. Limón began to develop a commanding stage presence, marked both by dignity and an animal quality in his movement range. He was guided by what Humphrey had mentioned during a discussion in one of her classes, as Limón put it, "that a dancer's movement was revelatory of the inner man, his nature and his spirit. . . . This admonition made a tremendous impression on me. It has followed me as a sort of artistic conscience throughout my long career."[48] On his own, he later raised such questions as, "What disciplines, what exercises were there to make the inner man a worthy source of that gesture you owed to yourself and to your fellow man? What rigors, what self-denials, what immolations?"[49] By 1937, he received one of the first choreographic fellowships from Bennington School of the Dance. The work he created, *Danza de la Muerte*, was his response to the Spanish Civil War. In his memoir, Limón said the style of the movement

> was of a rugged sculptural formality. The opening was a solemn commemoration of brave men fallen in battle, an elegiac tribute by comrades who would follow in their footsteps and by women bearing a double burden of mourning, both for the dead and for those about to die. . . . I remember this as a good, strong, young piece. It was full of my immaturities but also of my virtues. It was a stepping-stone . . . the decades would give me surer footing, better balance, more wariness.[50]

The next summer at Bennington (1938), Martha Graham created *American Document* and invited Limón be the leading man in the piece—her first work for a man. He went to "Doris and Charles for advice and guidance. They were both quite dispassionate. They said the choice was entirely up to me . . . they reminded me that she was a formidable and all-consuming personality.

I would run the risk of being swallowed up artistically."[51] While he was not concerned about the possibility of being swallowed, he was loyal to his mentors, and turned down Graham's offer. Erick Hawkins instead took the role, and became both Graham's first male soloist as well as her husband. Limón's sense of loyalty was not enough, however, to overcome a rift that developed between him and Weidman in 1940. Taking his leave from Humphrey-Weidman, he returned to California where he briefly worked with former Graham dancer May O'Donnell.

Not long after the move, Limón began an intense correspondence with Pauline Lawrence—who in turn left New York to marry Limón. Lawrence, who herself had long been a major force in the Humphrey-Weidman Company, was not content to allow Limón to linger long away from the thriving New York dance scene and soon convinced him to return. In 1942, Humphrey welcomed Limón back into the company. Humphrey and Weidman had begun to drift apart by that point as well, and Limón took Weidman's place as the male lead in Doris' works. Limón also created his

José Limón in Chaconne.

solo *Chaconne* in 1942, the first work where he "found a way to set his inventive movements in a strong emotional and thematic context . . . [which] marked his maturing as a choreographer."[52] That same year, with America's increased participation in World War II, Limón was drafted and stationed at Fort Lee in Virginia. He was able, however, to choreograph shows there at the camp, and returned to New York when on leave for more serious choreographic work.

In 1946, with the war over, Limón returned to New York where, by this time, Humphrey's arthritis had forced her retirement from the stage. Her relationship with Weidman had also grown so distant that she turned their studio over to him. With Lawrence's support and prodding, Limón founded his own company that year and he asked Humphrey to serve as his artistic director. The first work the company premiered was Humphrey's *Lament for Ignacio Sanchez Mejias*, the dramatic story of a bullfighter's death based on the eponymous Federico García Lorca poem, which served as an excellent transition piece for the new collaboration. *The Story of Mankind* followed in that year, and *Day on Earth* came next (1947). With *Day*, it became clear that the relationship was working well for both Limón and Humphrey. Limón looked to her not only for the dances she made for his developing company, but also continued to rely on her guidance of his own choreography. For Humphrey, the fact that she could not demonstrate the movements she desired forced her to find new ways to choreograph, and pushed her continued growth. These new dances she was making were not reductive of her former ideas, but rather "ranged further in theme and characterization, often cued stylistically to Limón's personality or to those of other dancers rather than her own."[53] Dance critic Marcia Siegel said, "*Day on Earth* is for me just about the best surviving example of the combined humanistic and kinesthetic possibilities of modern dance."[54] Humphrey continued to make some of her greatest works for the new company, including *Night Spell* (1951) and *Ritmo Jondo* (1953), guiding her protégé until her death in 1958.

Limón once said of his own creative process, "My first requisite is an idea. I cannot function with abstractions, or with what is called absolute dance. I work out of the emotions, out of human experience, mine or those about which I have read or heard. Certainly there has to be a deeply felt motive or subject."[55] This is clear from the first dance he made for his new company, and in much of the repertory that followed. *La Malinche* (1947)—based on tales of the conquest of Mexico[56]—is driven less by p   in the essence of each character, and th   motivation and interplay among the ch   s seminal work, *The Moor's Pavane* (1949),   original cast after they had been perform   miere, "I was more than usually shaken   e public, to be an impertinence, an almos   d not to make a 'dance version' of Shakes   ce to find a form which might prove valid   nge or paraphrase."[58] To that end, Limó   s rather than . . . trying to duplicate its a   naracters, each doomed by his or her flaw   rocess of deterioration, perhaps several in

The Limón Company in The Traitor.

> Limón has a very personal way of communicating the inner drama of his
> characters. There is a certain grandeur, with a touch of the archaic, in his
> gestures; there is an intensity in the rapport between the dancers on an
> emotional and intellectual level, and there is a specific ambience created
> through emotional communication of the dramatic intent through facial
> expression as much as body movement.[60]

In *The Traitor* (1954), the choreographer used Judas' betrayal of Christ as a means of exploring his concerns about the McCarthy Hearings and the trial of Ethel and Julius Rosenberg. Watching fellow choreographer Jerome Robbins' HUAC testimony—May 5, 1953, where he admitted membership in the Communist Party's Theatrical Transient Group and named eight other members—probably seemed a contemptuous act to a man like Limón, for whom loyalty meant so much. It is also not inconceivable to think that the professional breaks between Weidman and

Humphrey, and Weidman and Limón, may have informed *The Traitor's* heightened emotional state as well.

Works like *The Emperor Jones* (1956) continued Limón's iconic characterizations. *There Is a Time* (1957) is indicative of biblical themes in the repertory, while *Missa Brevis* (1958) can be read as an act of faith. *Missa Brevis* served as the choreographer's response to man's inhumanity during World War II, particularly it's devastation in Poland. In the work, we ultimately see the coming together of community and the triumph of the human spirit over war's ravages.

Thematic ideas drawn from his Mexican heritage continued to inform his works like *The Unsung* (1970) and his final dance, *Carlota* (1972). Other works were brighter in theme: while *The Winged* (1966) was inspired by mythological beings, it was largely about flight. *Dances for Isadora* (1971) was a tribute to Isadora Duncan. *A Choreographic Offering* (1964) was an homage to his mentor, Humphrey, and used motifs from some of her greatest works. "*Choreo*," as the work is often called, is one of the few truly abstract works in the Limón repertory, yet Limón's humanism comes through with great clarity.

Decades after his death in 1972, Limón works are frequently included in the repertories of dance companies and university programs, and the company he founded continues to present his works around the world. In addition to the Limón-Humphrey repertory, the company performs works by Anna Sokolow, Donald McKayle, current artistic director Carla Maxwell, and former company members like Clay Taliaferro.

José Limón: In the Studio

"José liked to see risk," according to Vachon, who had studied with Limón at The Juilliard School and Dance Player's Studio before joining the company. "For José, modern dance was about the spaciousness of America. You would earn a compliment if you ate up a lot of space in class. Using the weight, and allowing the pelvis to propel you forward let's you take huge risks in any direction."[61] As a result, the technique is dramatic, not precious. It is human and accessible. "The technique tends to make generous teachers," Vachon said. "It precludes putting people down or shaming students."[62]

In a general examination of Limón's training methodology, we see three basic influences: the work of his mentors Humphrey and Weidman, his own teaching experience, and the ideas of the dancers he worked with early in the company's development.

Humphrey-Weidman

A review of the vocabulary list later in this section will show the interconnectedness of Limón's technique and Humphrey's discussed in Chapter 2. What has not been discussed in this book, however, is the influence of Charles Weidman on the training conducted at the Humphrey-Weidman Studio—which, in turn, had an obvious impact on Limón. Weidman shared the lyricism of

Humphrey's dance style, and incorporated "his own powerfully vigorous approach to jumps, turns, and floor-work."[63] In her book on Weidman, Jonette Lancos, professor of dance at State University of New York at Geneseo, noted that he was dedicated to developing male dancers and "began offering free lessons to men, with the stipulation that once they enrolled they would pay $2.00 for missed lessons."[64] He also frequently made dances for all-male casts, such as *Steel and Stone* (1931) and *Traditions* (1935). "[Weidman] not only influenced the next generation of men dancers with his choreography but through teaching his technique, special men's workshops, and his repertory at the Bennington College Summer Dance School from 1934–1941."[65] Limón recalled that Weidman

> was always interested in the intrinsic abilities of the male dancer, and devoted much thought and time to devising a syllabus of technical studies quite distinct from that of women. He taught classes composed entirely of men where the emphasis was distinctively masculine. The entire vocabulary of the dance came under a close scrutiny in terms of what men could or could not do.[66]

(There is also speculation among some of Limón's former dancers that Limón actually influenced Weidman's method of training—in that he may have been the one who encouraged Weidman to solidify his ideas.)[67]

The use of gravity and emphasis on articulating musicality are both central in the Humphrey/Weidman/Limón lineage. While still members of Denishawn, Humphrey and Weidman had seen a performance by the Swedish dancer Ronny Johansson, who used weight to explore gravity rather than to attempt defying it. According to Lancos, "Johansson's new use of gravity sparked an idea for both Humphrey and Weidman in their new technique and movement style. For Humphrey, it was the fall and recovery principle and for Weidman, it was rebound theory."[68] Limón remembered that at the Humphrey-Weidman Studio

> there was much concern about weight and substance of the body. Both our teachers abandoned the traditional concept that the body had to appear free of all gravitational pull and movement devoid of all effort. The weight of the body should be recognized and exploited. . . . Elevation, soaring into the air, would in consequence have more drama, more meaning. It would become a triumph, a conquest.[69]

The application of weight—of gravity—coupled with effort are critical elements of Limón's dances. In the repertory, dancers are challenged to "move through space with varied effort," said former Limón principal dancer Clay Taliaferro. "It's like playing on an effort scale. The use of weight and effort in *Emperor Jones* is different than in *A Choreographic Offering*. Then you have *Pavane* which is also different from *Jones* in the use of the pelvis, which helps you to drive through space."[70] Limón's former assistant and company member, Daniel Lewis, noted:

> The Limón dancer continually confronts gravity, exploring the full spectrum of movement that exists between freedom from gravity and complete subservience to its power, between the moment of suspension just as the body is airborne and the moment the body falls or sinks to the earth—the range of movement Doris Humphrey called the "arc between two deaths."[71]

Taliaferro also noted that it was the powerful, masculine way of dancing in Limón's work that attracted him to dance in the first place. "I was the last dancer invited into the company before José's death, which was incredible to me. José was the reason I started dancing. I saw him on television as a teenager and knew that this was what I wanted to do"[72]—which calls to mind the inspiration Limón found in Kreutzberg's performance decades earlier.

With regard to musicality and rhythm, Humphrey and Limón had both had musical training in their youth, and rhythm was central to Weidman's work: "rhythmic variety made Weidman's technical series and choreography difficult to perform, exciting to watch, and essential in mastering his movement style."[73] There is also often an emphasis on compositional elements in the technique classes of this lineage focusing on rhythm, dynamics, motivation, and design as presented in Humphrey's *The Art of Making Dances*.[74] (That is certainly true in Humphrey and Weidman classes, and it may be true in a Limón-based class as well, depending on the teacher.)

Limón As Teacher

Much of Limón's training system evolved when he joined the faculty at The Juilliard School, and although he was not interested in creating a codified technique, the year-end exams at Juilliard required that he prepare materials in that direction. Vachon recalled, too, that as his Juilliard teaching continued, "movement materials from class became choreographic material later. Teaching then had an impact on Limón's choreography: He hadn't trained his original dancers—everyone was a soloist in those earlier works, and they had been trained elsewhere. At Juilliard, he had a chance to watch larger groups dancing, and that influenced some of his later dances,"[75] such as *A Choreographic Offering*.

Dancers Informed Technical Development

As Limón continued his work at Juilliard, company members who were also teaching, like Betty Jones, Ruth Currier, and Lucy Venable, contributed their own ideas to the evolving training philosophy. Lewis noted that Jones taught "the principles of alignment and breathing as developed by [Lulu] Sweigard."[76] Sweigard was one of the founders of ideokinesis, a somatic body-mind practice designed to develop sound alignment through imagery. It is interesting to note that because Limón's technique is not codified, there is still room for Limón-based teachers to bring other ideas into the training. "We want dancers to be safe," Vachon noted. "We want risks to be taken in the space, but not with the dancer's health. As a result, there is a good deal of consideration for developing healthy bodies. Many Limón teachers have a strong interest in somatics."[77] In addition to continued interest in Sweigard's ideas, other teachers incorporate material from the Bartenieff Fundamentals, and Jennifer Scanlon, former associate artistic director and principal dancer with the Limón Company, noted the importance of Alexander technique in her class.[78]

Limón and Ballet

Students with ballet training who come to a Limón class may find some similarities. "Because ballet was so important at Juilliard," Vachon observed, "it did have a little influence on his work at the time. In fact, as José's student, I was taking his class both at Juilliard and at Dance Player's. At Juilliard, we had part of our class at the barre, but everything was done in the center at Dance Player's. Pina Bausch was studying at Juilliard then and performed in Humphrey's *Passacaglia* and José loved the height of her leg [from her ballet training]. *A Choreographic Offering* is a hybrid in the way he used the legs."[79] Taliaferro also noted, "José turned to ballet to help him get back in shape when he returned from the army. Even by the time I joined the company, he was still doing a lengthy series of tendus at the barre in his own warmup."[80] The length of leg line, the way the foot works with the floor and the sense of dynamic alignment are all places where we can see similarities between Limón training and ballet training. Of course, his classical relationship to music is likely the most evident correlation of all—particularly when looking at the fluidity in a work like *A Choreographic Offering*. Taliaferro also pointed out, however, that the use of breath is extremely different between ballet and Limón. In Limón, "the breath grounds the body, and produces volume in the torso."[81] So, while influences of ballet may exist, students should approach Limón ready to experiment and to explore movement from the inside out, avoiding the simple recreation of someone else's shape.

Limón Class Structure and Concepts

In an interview I conducted with Jennifer Scanlon in 2006, she noted:

> Each teacher will likely have a different approach to conveying Limón class material. Some may start with running, walking, or body, leg, and arm swings to explore certain concepts, then build exercises from there. Others may adhere more closely to a set series of exercises that moves from seated

floor movements through center work and progresses with jumps and across-the-floor phrases.[82]

The influence of the breath on movement, and the impact of the weight of each body part are central to Limón technique. Developing a sense of how the two can work together helps a dancer to gain an understanding of gravity. Isolations are also an important component of the technique. In fact, Taliaferro observed that "José's use of isolation is one of the most obvious differences between his technique and Doris'."[83] This includes isolations of smaller body parts like the hands, but also of the big joints as well. "I didn't have technique with José," Taliaferro said. "I hadn't had lots of fall and rebound. Much of my training had been with Graham people, and he recognized that. He said I'd learn by dancing his repertory. I learned from him by rehearsing the dances over and over to the point of exhaustion, developing a full-bodied awareness. When I got to company class, though, the joint work helped me understand things like fall and rebound, how to use the breath and the exhale."[84]

Vachon stated, "Rhythm is also a major focus in classes. Most teachers employ an assortment of rhythm, often complex rhythms. Subdivision of the beat is very important. A 6/8 is comfortable for Limón movement, but teachers try to mix up metres in class. It's also important to focus on the overall musical phrasing. Most of us prefer live accompaniment to recordings,"[85] and both piano and percussion can be used effectively.

Being completely present and aware of your body is critical in the technique. Scanlon said, "José was interested in human wholeness, and it is key in his work that the whole person participates—mind, body, and spirit."[86] Taliaferro recalled, "José talked about the 'orchestrated body.' He saw an entire alphabet in the body—in the breakdown of the body and the major joints. It was helpful to me to see it as a grammar of the body, complete with punctuation. I loved that whole-bodiedness of the technique—the use of the back even in a gesture. The specificity is what creates the drama. For example, there is a moment in *Pavane* where Emilia uses the leg like an accusatory finger, and it becomes an oppositional duet with space."[87] A more general example of that specificity is that when doing a swing, a sense of drop is important—the dancer has to release the joint in order to allow suspension to occur. Limón also used imagery to help dancers in his work. "José was a musician and a painter," Taliaferro said, "and those things traveled with him. Some of his movement was like drawing [in space]. He would give you images sometimes like, 'Here you are circling the sky or cutting space' to help you understand what he was seeing in the movement."[88]

Limón Technique Today

"Limón is a creative technique," Taliaferro observed, "and it will continue to grow. Its principles are organic."[89] Nearly four decades after Limón's death, modern and ballet companies worldwide continue to perform his repertory, and choreographers like Taliaferro continue to use the technique in making their own dances. Teachers also continue to turn to Limón in the classroom, which has led Vachon and her colleagues at the Limón Institute to begin a series of teacher workshops. "We're not teaching vocabulary in these workshops. These workshops are for those who have a Limón background. We are devoting time to each principle—for example, breath and its effect on movement." The workshops operate based on the philosophy of keeping the technique accessible. "The technique will never be codified, and we have no intention of creating a teaching certification."[90] Teachers are welcome to offer Limón-based classes, and these workshops help them delve more deeply into the principles that are foundational to the technique. "So many people say that Limón is like coming home. Ruth Currier said that back in the 1940s, and people are still reaffirming that today. It is a celebration and acceptance of our humanity. It is not an envelope. It continues to expand as needed."[91]

PRACTICAL LESSON PLAN

Experiencing Limón Principles Through the Swing

Contributed by Ann Vachon, Director of the José Limón Institute

Ask everyone to reach for their dance bag or a backpack, preferably something weighted down with notebooks and shoes. First swing it in a low arc back and forth, experiencing the weight and the rhythm of the swing. Allow the arc of the swing to become wider, and notice how the bag feels lighter as it reaches a higher point—how your body feels freer, released, buoyant, as the bag swings higher.

Pay attention to the changes in speed, how the "falling" is faster than the upswing, which slows until it almost stops (suspends . . .) Pay attention to your stance—how have your legs and abdominal muscles engaged to support this activity?

Put the bag down and try this same sequence with a swinging leg, starting with the low arc and

the strong experience of gravity and then proceeding to a larger, higher arc, with a greater sense of freedom. Now try to experience the actual weight of your arm (we are so used to gesturing freely with our arms that it's hard to remember that they also have mass and weight, and that it takes effort to lift an arm). Experience this by lifting and dropping an arm. Now try swinging an arm, first in a low arc and then allowing greater freedom. How might you breathe with this? Experiment with finding a way to coordinate your breath with the drop/release and the upswing/suspension of the arm swing. Add a drop of the pelvis (a plié) with the drop of the arm and an out-breath. Add a rise to half-toe with the suspension at the end of the swing, on the in-breath.

Finally, pick up your prop again and imagine that it is a pail full of water. Begin to swing it, timed to the rhythm of your breath. Allow the arc of the swing to increase only as much as your breathing allows—but finally let it swing overhead. Isn't this ecstasy? Not a drop of water fell on you, and you were utterly daring and free at that moment!

Riding the Wave—A Look at Succession

Created by the author

In order to quickly understand succession, let's jump to another dance genre: break dancing. The most basic b-boy movement, the wave, is a successional movement. Hold both your arms out to the sides parallel to the floor. Lift your L fingertips up slightly; as you dip them back down, raise the middle knuckles, and as you let the motion continue up your arm, each joint in natural sequence raises and lowers in response until the movement rides through the body, across the shoulder, and out the R fingertips. Send the wave back through and out the L again. That's all successional movement is—just a sequential path that movement flows along through individual body parts, or the entire body. The old-school "dolphin" and torso "ripples" are other examples of successional movement in hip-hop/b-boy.

Stand in parallel, let your head roll forward so its weight draws the body forward toward the ground. The weight of your head will carry the shoulders forward, adding the chest and continuing forward. When you reach the point that you are bending at the hips, add a little bend in the knees until your fingertips brush the floor. Inhale, and let the breath initiate movement at the base of the spine, which sequentially unfurls the back until you are upright, on straight legs, with your alignment returned to neutral. You can also try this to the side (R and L), stopping at the waist, bending the knees, while keeping the chest open (don't let the top shoulder roll forward). Try it again to each side, drawing the

opposite arm across the body in an arc, so that the hand is over the top of the head when the torso is at its full range of motion to the side and you are in the depth of the knee bend. As the spine returns to upright and the knees straighten, let the arm rise with the torso, then let the weight of the hand lead the arm back to the side and down, so that the arm has now made a full circle.

You start to get an idea about the orchestra of the body as you pair the succession of the spine, the circle of the arm, and the bend/straighten of the knees. You can play with this same combination walking across the floor—try it taking a full 8 cts. (8 steps) to complete one side, then the other side. Try it in 4 cts. and then in 2 cts. Try this on top of a triplet (you may need to reduce your range of motion in the spine/torso). Think of other ways to move successionally and how those movements can move across the floor.

Make sure that you are thinking about the inhale and exhale of the breath. As you experiment with succession, notice what happens in the core, what you need to do to stabilize while standing still, and what adjustments you have to make while in motion.

Momentum, Rhythm, Time, Space

Based on a movement pattern created by Clay Taliaferro

Below is a series of movement experiences that introduce momentum, rhythm, time, and space as they might be encountered in a Limón class. It begins with a basic 16-ct. phrase that is then altered to experiment with some of the Limón principles like suspension and swing. After a dancer tries the basic phrase, there isn't a particular order that has to be adhered to in going through these ideas. Feel free to pick and choose—but start with the rather didactic basic phrase that includes the path pattern of forward, back, and curve. At the end of the series, there is a choreographic assignment to help the dancer further explore one of the ideas below.

Always connect to your breath in this encounter. Exhale as you run forward, inhale as you run backward. What breathing best assists your movement? You want to "stop on the spot," which means being precise, ensuring clean, clear transfers of weight/changes of direction. Also, remember always to be completely present. Be as mindful of stillness as you are of movement. *It is important that the runs stay metric: stepping on each beat in order to experience the struggle (inherent kinetic drama) involved in the change of direction.*

Basic Sequence

Start: Start: On R foot.

[6 cts.] Run forward, slap outside of thighs on cts. 1, 3, 5.

[4 cts.] Run backward, slap on cts. 2, 4.

[6 cts.] Run a circle to the R with a slight lean into circle, slap on cts. 1, 3, 5.

Repeat starting on L.

Suspension Sequence I

Start: On R foot.

[6 cts.] Run forward, slap outside of thighs on cts. 1, 3, 5.

[4 cts.] Step into relevé on 1, suspend on 2, 3, 4, arms at side, look directly ahead, or circle arms overhead and lift the gaze skyward.

[6 cts.] Fall forward into circular run 1, slap outside of thighs on cts. 1, 3, 5.

Repeat on L foot.

Suspension Sequence II

Start: On R foot.

[6 cts.] Run forward, slap outside of thighs on cts. 1, 3, 5.

[4 cts.] Step into relevé in 2nd position forming an X: step right on 1, raising the R arm, step L on 2, raising the L arm, flexing both wrists, suspend on 3, 4.

[6 cts.] Run in circular path, slap outside of thighs on cts. 1, 3, 5.

Repeat across the floor, starting R for each 16-ct. phrase.

Repeat full sequence coming back on the L.

Small Jump Sequence

Start: On R foot.

[6 cts.] Run forward, slap thighs on 1, 3, 5.

[4 cts.] 2 small jumps in parallel or 1st position, landing either on 1&3 or 2&4.

[6 cts.] Run in circular path, slap outside of thighs on cts. 1, 3, 5.

Repeat on L foot.

Choreographic Exploration

Taking the idea of the basic 16-ct. phrase and the exploration of momentum, design your own short study. You may add any locomotor movements you wish. Just be sure to continue working with direction or weight changes. You might also vary your counts and tempi. For example, the 6s might be fast while the 4s are two times slower. Or if like you could break down the 16-ct. phrase differently, perhaps using a 3 and a 2. However you vary the counts or tempi, though, be clear and stay true to the rhythms. You might also play with syncopation.

Erick Hawkins (1909–1994): Biographical Sketch

Isadora Duncan was the first major dancer in the West to intuit a kinesiological truth: that human movement starts in the spine and pelvis, not in
the extremities—the legs and arms. That is: human movement, when it
obeys the nature of its functioning, when it is not distorted by erroneous
concepts of the mind, starts in the body's center of gravity and then—in
correct sequence—flows into the extremities . . . she conceived the essence
of movement to lie in transition, not in position. When she says, "Study
Nature," she means "flow organically," in arcs, like . . . the gallop of a horse,
the wave on the beach . . . not like a man's mind-contrived, inorganic machine, which essentially cannot move but only take positions.

—Erick Hawkins, *Pure Poetry*, in *The Modern Dance*

Erick Hawkins saw clearly the interrelatedness of the world around him, "how we dance
stems from our total philosophical view," and that "[t]he body is not divided from the mind, the
soul."[92] The convergence of metaphysical and aesthetic ideas from Eastern thought and the
emerging Western movement sciences (kinesiology, ideokinesis) of the mid-twentieth century
were foundational to the training practices he established, and to his body of choreography. Born
in Trinidad, Colorado, in 1909, "Hawkins' lifelong pursuit of literary and philosophical ideas can
be traced to his early interest in classical studies, consolidated by a major in Greek civilization at
Harvard."[93]

He recognized the ancient Greeks as the originators of Western art, appreciated their admiration of the human body, and valued their strong aesthetic sensibilitites. It was also during his days
at Harvard that Hawkins was first introduced to Eastern philosophy in general, and Zen specifically. A classmate had given him a copy of Okakura's *Book of Tea*, which introduced Hawkins to
Eastern culture, and not long after Suzuki's *Essays in Zen Buddhism* fostered his awarenesses of
Eastern thought.[94] Years later, works like F. S. C. Northrop's *The Meeting of East and West* and
Eugen Herrigel's *Zen in the Art of Archery* led him to realize that "the quality of the dance must
be effortless, achieving a oneness of body and soul."[95] Hawkins himself became such a prolific
dance- philosopher that dance critic Walter Sorell said, "If Erick Hawkins had not become a dancer,
I could envision him as an American revivalist teaching the scriptures of Buddhism, Taoism, or
the philosophy of Confucius to the Indians in the Dakotas, in the mountains of Colorado, or in
the Mesas in New Mexico."[96] In fact, the concept of "dancer as priest" was one that Hawkins
himself espoused.[97] Hawkins' second wife (he was married to Martha Graham during his time in
her company) and long-time musical collaborator, Lucia Dlugoszewski, observed:

Erick Hawkins in Early Floating, *1961.*

Like Dante, Erick was not afraid to embrace elegance and beauty or the mythic grandeur of the human condition. Whether he approached technique or choreography, whether his originality veered into the philosophic, the aesthetic or the poetic or just the sheer fun of being alive, he was always on an adventure.[98]

Because of the marriage of philosophy and movement sciences inherent in his work, his ideas about dance preparation are perhaps better described not as a technique, but as a philosophy or theory of training. "As far as Hawkins is concerned, there is no 'Erick Hawkins dance technique.' His goal has been to understand the true nature of the human body and of human movement in order to find beautiful dance art. The sciences of anatomy and physiology have made it possible for dancers to comprehend exactly the structure and function of the human form."[99] The clarity and sensuality of the human body in its most natural manner of movement sounds like liberation when read against Atomic Age, Cold War politics. The philosophies and poetics of "beautiful dance art" today can certainly be read as diametrically opposed to the oppressive tension of McCarthyism. In his homage to Hawkins after the artist's death, dance critic Alan Kriegsman observed that Hawkins "cared little for material reward or superficial popularity,"[100] which in the postwar years of material excess was itself a social commentary. None of that is to superimpose poltical statement on Hawkins' work, but it does contrast his dance art with that of many of his contemporaries.

Discovering Dance

Like Limón before him, Hawkins was first inspired to dance following a performance by Harald Kreutzberg (in concert with Yvonne Georgi) in 1930, and later began his dance training with Kreutzberg. In 1934, he enrolled at the School of American Ballet (eventually becoming the first student to teach for Balanchine), and began performing and choreographing for Lincoln Kirstein's Ballet Caravan from 1936 to 1938. According to Renata Celichowska, former Hawkins dancer and current director of the 92nd Street Y Harkness Dance Center, "Throughout his career, Hawkins frequently mentioned his admiration for Balanchine's creative genius in weaving dance and music together and for his unquestionable commitment to his artistic vision."[101] Hawkins said of his decision to leave ballet, "Ballet did not satisfy me because it was too much like a diagram and, for me, too much of the indescribable pure poetry of movement had to be left out," and that ballet had developed out of "extremely unsensuous attitudes toward the body."[102] With regard to ballet training, he noted, "The underlying feeling of balletic technique is in an opposite direction to sensing the beauty of cooperation with nature—with the nature in us, the nature we are, and are a part of, rather than trying to dominate nature."[103] He went on:

It is significant that the official symbol of the School of American Ballet is Leonardo da Vinci's drawing of a man's body . . . ready for scientific measurement and ready for scientific (rather than felt) relationships. The change to a fresher and more comprehensive principle is what makes modern dance.[104]

The perception of the male dancer as "supernumerary" in ballet was also a concern to Hawkins.[105] One of the elements in Kreutzberg's work that had originally caught Hawkin's attention was the masculine energy of Kreutzberg's dancing.

While Chapter 5 includes a broader discussion on gender in modern dance, it is important to note here Hawkins' early concerns about being a male dancer:

> After I had started my first dance training, for two years I did not write my family to tell them what I was doing. When a young man has arrived at his vocation and is put in the terrible position that his vocation in the world's eyes is a questionable one for a man, you can see what trouble he is in.[106]

Dance critic Marcia Siegel's observastions about the male in dance, especially ballet, in this era support the nature of Hawkins' concerns: "If gender in dance defines itself in terms of sexuality, as it so frequently seems to, some men have chosen the role of androgyne . . . the male adopts a nonaggressive sex role in order to push dancing beyond the limits set by conventional masculinity."[107] Hawkins eventually spent a summer observing indigenous ceremonial dance traditions of the American Southwest, discovering the importance of men in traditional dance forms. In speaking of concert dance years after this experience, he noted:

> It is the specialization in our dance in which it is not demanded of men dancers that they be complete men and complete artists, carrying on their art in relation to everything else in the world, that has given dancing for men its bad name and its insignificance. Dance for men in America has no prototypic underlying ritual and myth such as the matador in the Spanish bullfight has to give him his challenge, his commitment, his worth and his honor. But unless something equivalent to this is finally created in the soul of the American people, a man's dancing will always be inconsequential. A man dancing will have to go far beyond entertainment. A man dancing will have to stand for what a man can become. He will really have to be a hero, in his body, his mind, his spirit.[108]

His sense of the masculine, however, was not based on preconceived ideas and his training did not convey a sense of machismo. Dlugoszewski recalled her first meeting with the man who later became her husband: "When I first met Erick Hawkins I had never been up close to a dancer, especially a male dancer," she said. "I came to my first rehearsal with him and he met me bare-chested. . . . Every male bare torso that I had ever known had a kind of armored hardness of muscles across the chest." She found, though, that his chest had a "delicate sensibility" developed through his approach to dance training. There was a "vulnerability, an expressive physicality of tenderness that I never expected a man to possess."[109]

Hawkins joined Martha Graham's company in 1938 after leaving Ballet Caravan, becoming the first man to dance for her. In time, he helped her to build the managerial components of the company, became her lover, and eventually her husband. Siegel asserted that in terms of Graham's choreography,

> Hawkins literally embodied the sexual side of her life and her dance. He made it possible for her to push through the themes she'd dwelt on for the first decade. Not only sex but theatre itself opened up. She began to make dances that were a little less abstract, a little more dramatic, dances with stories an audience could relate to. The neophyte Hawkins walked in on *American Document* during the creative process and immediately influenced the way it turned out.[110]

Dance historian Maureen Needham Costonis agreed that "The whole tenor of Graham's creativity changed with this introduction of the kinds of dramatic tension inherent in male/female interaction. Critics could no longer jibe at Miss Graham's 'grim' and 'sexless' dances, but instead commented on her innovative use of a 'positive male presence' in the person of Erick Hawkins."[111] Celichowska indicated that when Hawkins first saw Graham's work, it "immediately spoke to a kindred 'American' spirit in Hawkins and he quickly became interested in developing his dancing in this direction."[112] Celichowska further observed:

> The complete commitment to their art form was a prevalent characteristic of both Graham and Hawkins as artists. Hawkins often related an observa-tion he made while performing with Graham in *Appalachian Spring*. It struck Hawkins how intently Graham experienced each moment of the piece, whether she was moving or standing still. This total involvement with the performing moment became a lasting influence for Hawkins.[113]

The two artists were deeply interested in an American art, in a theater that encompassed the sum total of theatrical production elements, and some of Graham's most potent work from the era reflected Hawkins' own interests in Greek civilization. On this ideal of an American art, Hawkins said:

The idea that American dance could use the European technique and psychology as a basic stock appears false to me. There comes a time in a nation's culture, as in an individual's life, that he must do his own work and speak out of his own core. No matter how humble the modern American dance may be, it knows where it is going. At this moment, I would say the direction, not speed, counts.[114]

Hawkins recalled that Graham's *Letter to the World* (1940) "was a more mature statement in dance than had ever been done in the West up to that point."[115] Celichowska recounted that Hawkins had said that among other reasons for his break with Graham, "was that Graham's artistic approach and technical theories stressed an obvious 'willfullness' of the body, which became increasingly fraught with tension."[116] Hawkins said:

> The acceptance of effort as a norm of movement has permitted all kinds of aberrations in Western dance art: tight corsets for men and women, an aggressive or militant athleticism [that] is opposed to poetic sensibility, and a sad and perverse lack of true animal grace. The notion that the body is trained to move well through effort, through work, through domination, through "making the movement happen," through the tightening of muscles in order to do the movement, is common to theorists in academic ballet and to practitioners in modern dance, since there are no longer any vestiges of a theory in modern dance.[117]

In Hawkins' work, there is a sense of a democratic body, and an egalitarian relation between woman and man. He said in a lecture at the Smithsonian Institution in 1978:

> Now there is one aspect in human relations which has seldom in the world's history been squarely faced by all parties: the relations between men and women. Right in the lifetime of everyone listening to me, there has been an enormous change in consciousness about men and women and their relationship. What disagreement still! Women opposing the Equal Rights Amendment even lack a common point of view themselves! I have, in my lifetime watched the forging of a "normative ideal" of how the male and female components of human life are to be looked at with justice and happiness.[118]

Graham was the dominant presence in her own life, and in her own art. While Hawkins influenced her exploration of myth in the beginning, the characterizations were her own. The goddess in her dances held dominion of the stage. Siegel compared Hawkins to Ted Shawn, noting the similarities between them after the dissolution of their marriages to Ruth St. Denis and Martha Graham, respectively: "[Hawkins'] career seems uncannily similar to Ted Shawn's— the effort to find validity as a dancing male, the frustration of trying to work with a dominant woman. But where Shawn's subsequent style stressed the heavy, masterful qualities, Hawkins decided to avoid all agressiveness and conflict."[119] Hawkins said:

> Throughout the dance, for me, the delight would be to show the identity of man and woman, not their struggle for domination, not their aggressiveness toward each other. . . . The Western world is waiting for a new statement of the beautiful relationship between man and woman. Neither Christian nor Greek tradition gave many patterns of it. . . . Only a few poets today speak to me of this: e.e. cummings who can say "one's not a half two. It's two are halves of one." . . . In Western art, movement has *never* achieved this.[120]

These issues of the masculine in dance, and the relation of the genders are indicative of the choreographer's far-ranging philosophy. In a statement he wrote in 1959, he spoke more broadly about what he was working toward in his art, the direction he wanted American dance to take:

· ·

Statement of Erick Hawkins[iii]

I would like to see pure fact occur in the art of dance and pure fact is the rebellious rediscovery of the innocence of the materials. Only when one has the innocence of the materials can there possibly be created the tender gesture which is the only real relationship of people to one another on stage.

I would like to see choreography of such immediacy that the dancer could momentarily resolve that baffling paradox of thought and action, and the naked beauty of real motionlessness would happen on stage.

I believe in the possibility of choreography of such immediacy that time could be sensed in its most difficult and yet most haunting dimension, time sensed instant-by-instant, a kind of time freed from space.

Thus, dance in America today would be an art worthy of being experienced, watched, understood, appreciated, discussed, and criticized, on the level of the other mature arts—poetry, painting, sculpture, architecture, and music.

And it would be not only a mature art, but a really modern art! Thus, American dance would contribute its own unique insights to the new, exciting aesthetic principles of the other arts of today.

I would like to see dance as a modern art in America today, to realize that it is possible to explore movement in and for itself, to delight directly in the innocence of its own materials and its own being—more like the work of a Calder, a Miró, a Brancusi, a Tobey, a Varèse, an e.e. cummings, a

Morris Graves—and realize it doesn't always have to revel in *Sturm und Drang* but rather in the pure fact of movement, which is our poetic experience of "now."

I would like today's dance to stop "interpreting" music, to stop its slavish dependence on music, whether "good" music or "bad," such as jazz. I would like to see dance challenge composers to write a live new music, written now for dance itself.

I would like to see our dance, as a modern art, throw away all its crutches, all its eclectic borrowings, and find its own deep physicality, its own sensuousness, its own passionate intensity. I would like dance to create its own theatre of pure fact, which is immediacy. I would like to see audiences know how to look not just with their eyes, but with their whole body, and look in time, instant-by-instant, and perhaps sense that ultimate innocence of pure movement or, even more astonishingly, pure motionlessness.

[iii] Statement of Erick Hawkins appeared in his book *The Body is a Clear Place and Other Statements on Dance.* Reprinted by permission of the publisher, Dance Horizons.

This philosophy affected every aspect of Hawkins' work, and is indicative of his approach to total theatre. Celichowska observed, "From the cut of the costume on the dancer's body to the quality of craftsmanship in the set, to the clear tones created by a violin or piccolo, to the sensitively designed light on the dancers, Hawkins believed that all aspects of a dance work were equally important."[121] About music, Hawkin's said, "I am one of the very few choreographers and dancers who will never use records or tapes for a live dance performance."[122] Of records, he said, "Records make us deaf. . . . We are practically completely deaf from "Muzak" and we need even louder and stranger sounds to break through our callousness and indifference. . . . The living musician reinforces the living dancer to make the audience come alive."[123] If he was to be engaged in new dance, Hawkins believed new music neccesary, particularly since, to him, new dance must be rhythmic in order to attain beauty—a new body discipline and new movement vocabulary demanded this new music. To this end, commissioned musical compositions were critical, and he would allocate the bulk of a new work's budget for the creation of the music.

From the first work he made after leaving Graham's company—*openings of the (eye)* (1952)—through the end of his life, Dlugoszewski was Hawkins' most important collaborator, creating numerous musical instruments needed to execute the complex scores she wrote for him. Dlugoszewski, who composed her first chamber music as a teenager, studied piano at the Detroit Conservatory of Music before studying physics and mathematics at Wayne State University. In 1952, she moved to New York, where she trained in music analysis with Felix Salzer, piano with Crete Sultan, and composition with Edgard Varèse. In the 1950s, Dlugoszewski began designing her instruments, including the timbre piano, "a conventional piano whose strings are struck with beaters and played with a variety of bows and plectra, or pieces of wood, metal, and ivory. She later created percussion and friction instruments, constructed by the sculptor Ralph Dorazio, for musicians performing for Hawkins."[124] In many of their collaborations, according to Celichowska, "Hawkins first created the dance and then Dlugoszewski composed music as an independently coexisiting theatre of sound that could relate to the movement either by evoking it or momentarily demolishing it. The unique approach to their collaboration created theater in which the movement and music are seemlessly interwoven."[125] Highlights from their collaborations include the seventy-five-minute-long *Here and Now, With Watchers* (1957) for one female and one male dancer with a pianist on the timbre piano; the fifty-minute *8 Clear Places* (1960) and *Geography of Noon* (1964) both included a percussionist performing onstage with the dancers, and *Sudden Snake-Bird* (1960) with a musical score using only bell sounds.[126] Examples of Hawkins' dances where his philosophies are easily recognizable on stage include *Early Floating* (1961), *Angels of the Inmost Heaven* (1971), *Classic Kite Tails* (1972), *Greek Dreams, with Flute* (1973), *Death is the Hunter* (1975), *Plains Daybreak* (1979), *Summer Clouds People* (1983), *Killer of Enemies: The Divine Hero*, and *Intensitites of Wind & Space* (1991).

Hawkins also collaborated with sculptor/designer Ralph Dorazio, visual artist Ralph Lee, and lighting designer Robert Engstrom. Additionally, Hawkins served as the costumer designer for his dances under the pseudonym Tad Taggart. Celichowksa noted that "[b]ecause he felt them to be such an integral part of the dance, Hawkins would always have a rehearsal version of the costume made before choreography began."[127] After Hawkins' death in 1994, Dlugoszewski served as artistic director of the Erick Hawkins Dance Company from 1996 until her own death in 2000, and during that time, she choreographed four works for the company.

In the following section, we will see how Hawkins' concerns and ideals merged in his training philosophy and the development of his choreography. Unlike many of the other generators of training methodologies in this book, Hawkins began developing his process before he started making dances for his new company. Where Graham, for example, had retrogenerated her technique through ideas extracted from her choreography, Hawkins wanted to establish a way of dancing that was more natural in its origination in the body than what he had encountered up to then in his dance experience. In essence, Hawkins picked up where he thought Duncan had left off decades earlier.

Erick Hawkins: In the Studio

The same principles of good body movement that apply to a dancer walking across a stage apply to that dancer walking from home to the theatre. Hawkins is deeply concerned with the interconnectedness of all human experience and the way that we can enrich our understanding of our lives through studying dance. By the same token, anything we observe in our

Kristina Berger in Hawkins' Greek Dreams, with Flute.

daily lives or anything we read or any work of art we experience may illuminate our dance training.

—Beverly Brown, Training to Dance with Erick Hawkins,
in *Erick Hawkins: Theory and Training*

In her essay Brown noted, "Two serious injuries, first one of his knee and then of his lower back, caused him to question the dance training he received. . . . Hawkins felt that since so much could be known through science about the human body, there surely must be a way for a dancer to train" that would prevent career-threatening major injuries and reduce minor, frustrating ones as well. "By studying anatomy and physiology, a dancer can learn not to violate the nature of his body and therefore, to do 'natural dancing.'"[128] Hawkins himself explained, "It turned out that my instruction as a beginning dance student and later as an apprentice/artist was inadequate. Injuring myself through ignorance, a quite common occurrence in athletics, dancing, and daily life,"[129] inspired Hawkins' quest for a normative ideal for preparing the dancing body. He said that "[t]he concept of a 'normative ideal' asks a person to quietly look at something in human culture and fathom possibilities that are dormant. . . . The word 'normative' means a general standard, a norm, and hence, is positive in feeling. An 'ideal' means having the imagination to conceive of a way to arrive at unexplored but sensed, larger possibilities. . . . One aspect of the abundant life is a healthy body and for that, we need a normative ideal."[130] Nada Diachenko, a professor of dance at the University of Colorado at Boulder and former soloist with Hawkins' company, observed that Hawkins "wanted to make dance based on the way the body is put together. The 'normative' is about our natural organization at birth, the body's basic organization. This allows you to strip away that which interferes. From this perspective, distortion in choreography is okay, but we don't want to train that [into the body]. It is a balanced way of training that helps the dancer make conscious choices," and working from that deep body-knowledge and understanding helps the human spirit to be more present in the dance.[131]

Think-Feel

Hawkins training encourages a modulation of effort as a key to efficient movement. "Erick believed that good dance doesn't have to be effortful," recalled Katherine Duke, artistic director of the Erick Hawkins Dance Company. The body is "made a certain way," she said, "and allowing the body to work naturally is more effective than trying to make the body do something else."[132] Working in that manner then allows the dancer to move more efficiently, which reserves additional energy that can be put toward performance. (See Appendix A for more on efficient movement.) That movement effeciency stems from Hawkins' normative philosophy, and itself is a stark contradiction to the social circumstances of the late modern era, correlating directly to the contemporary reading of Hawkins' training and artistic philosophies I discussed earlier. In fact, Celichowska recalled, "When I first saw the company, I was preoccupied with trying to find traditional ballistic relationships in the movement. Erick's performance attitude was so different from what I was used to seeing. In Western culture, with the consumer idea that bigger is better, movement tends to be tension-filled. The difference was unsettling when I started with Hawkins. I felt like I couldn't dance at first."[133] In order to confront ballistic, tension-filled movement and dance in a more normative manner, the dancer must recognize that, as Hawkins said, "tight muslces can't feel," and he developed the idea of "think-feel" to encourage that new way of moving.[134] Brown pointed out:

> If we hold our muscles inappropriately tight for a long time we will not feel movement happening in our body. We will feel tightness. When our muscles are too tight, we try to relax them, but relaxation often becomes confused with passivity, and passivity is hardly appropriate for someone desiring to dance.[135]

Diachenko also said that while we tend to think in terms of contraction and release, "Erick used 'decontraction' to juxtapose contraction."[136] (This juxtaposition forms the training's key element, and makes an interesting comparison with Graham's contraction and release.) Hawkins placed contraction and decontraction on a continuum where, at each end, the body is in a state of non-movement. Most movement occurs at the midpoint of that scale, both in terms of dance and pedestrian motion. Brown noted that when students first approach Hawkins-based training, they are

> very tight and unable to decontract when asked to do so. Thus, in the beginning classes a great deal of time is spent learning to decontract and to identify how much decontraction is appropriate in different movement situations. Movements practicing decontractions are given priority until students have sufficiently awakened their kinesthetic awareness and are properly prepared to execute strong or vigorous movements with appropriate economy of energy.[137]

All of this helped to create a free-flow quality in Hawkins' work. "He was really one of the first dancers to approach body-mind work," Diachenko noted. "He incorporated ideokinesis and imagery into his training"[138] and his work is sometimes referred to as one of the first release techniques in dance. (*Kinesis* is motion; *ideo* is the idea, the sole stimulation in the process.) Hawkins combined "the metaphysical and aesthetic ideas from the Orient with our Western kinesiological science" which created a balance of opposites akin to yin and yang, the balance of doing and not doing[139]—bringing the focus to a sense of lightness, varied dynamics, and clarity in the dancing.

Ideokinesis is based on the work of Mabel Elsworth Todd and her students Barbara Clark and Dr. Lulu Sweigard. Clark's work with dancers led to a practice she called "mind-body" work. Sweigard's work demonstrated that Todd's teaching method of thinking rather than doing produced measurable changes in the relative position of skeletal parts and that the changes were quite consistent, and she developed an approach to teaching called "neuromuscular reeducation." Numerous dancers looked to Sweigard for reeducation, and as preparation for this work, she frequently required that they study anatomy and physiology. "Dancers who persisted in their studies with Sweigard gradually realized her work was clearly not an alternative to medical treatment but a means of optimizing the coordination of the healthy body, thus distinctly advantageous to any one seriously pursuing the art of dance."[140]

Celichowska observed that imagery can be used during both moments of stillness or of motion in order to influence both involuntary (e.g., cardio-respiratory activity) and voluntary movements (dancing and pedestrian activities). She noted:

> The goal of using imagery in involuntary movement is to increase one's sensitivity to optimal muscular coordination. Although muscles do not activate without nervous excitation, the central nervous system can fall into a pattern of engaging certain muscles during habitual movement patterns, whether or not these muscles are truly needed. It is as if to lift a leg the message from the brain is translated from "lift leg" to "engage all leg muscles." As a result, the muscles of the leg get into the habit of prematurely tensing and overworking. The primary movement goal becomes secondary to the activity of muscular contraction. By using movement imagery in moments of stillness, the dancer can correct these overworked neuromuscular patterns. Thinking a movement or imagining change within the body, gives the body the opportunity to return to innate, more efficient movement patterns.[141]

This relational dialogue between body and mind is critical in Hawkins' training, and leads to the "think-feel" process. This dialogue creates a body-mind unity that allows the body to simply do the movement, rather than requiring a situation of "forced" and inefficient movement. Hawkins regularly used these basic images (in addition to a variety of others): the "teeterbabe" (a baby bouncer) support of the pelvis, the "boomerang" swing of the legs, the "tasseling" flow of the arms and legs, and the ascending and descending curve of a "spiral staircase" through the axis of

Katherine Duke in Hawkins' Heyoka.

the leg.[142] (See Hawkins Principles below for more on imagery.) Celichowska also pointed out that Hawkins placed great importance on a teacher's continued development and renewal of their favorite images, staying fresh in order to remain effective.[143]

Hawkins' Principles[144]—A Brief Overview[iv]

Celichowska stated, "Basic dance training on the physical capabilities and laws governing the human body offers endless possibilities. Each investigation of a different joint, muscle, neuromuscular pattern, or physical principle can lead to further movement refinement and countless movement combinations." Here are just a few considerations from Hawkins.

The Body's Center of Gravity: The Pelvis—In Hawkins' movement imagery, movement is initiated from the pelvis, the body's gravitational center. Gravity, Weight, Balance, and Alignment—Gravity and its impact on ideal anatomical alignment affects all human movement, whether standing or sitting. This informs our sense of weight, and the practicalities of how we balance that weight.

Contraction and Decontraction—These principles influence the experience of doing and not doing. As Brown stated, "When a dancer alerts himself to efficient use of muscle energy by trying always to place his body weight where he will be able to maintain balance most easily, when he moves with full awareness of the amount of contraction and decontraction in his muslces, he is sensitizing himself to the pull of gravity."[145]

Arcs, Curves, and Momentum—The relevence of physics to dance can't be overstated. Within these principles, for example, Hawkins examined "the force of motion acquired by a moving body as a result of the continuance of its motion." There is a relation here between Hawkins' ideas and the Humphrey-Limón tradition if we consider the "Arc Between Two Deaths" and "Fall and Recovery."

Flow and Transitions—Here, Hawkins was connecting with Isadora Duncan's belief that movement lies in transitions rather than positions. Clarity of shape and line are certainly important, but the emphasis is on an organic evolution from position to position, and through sequential motion. Motion may be expressed in qualitative terms or as existing on a Bartenieff Effort Continuum between bound and free flow. The flow of Hawkins' movement is often described as being free rather than bound. The movement is fluid. Hawkins noted that, "Correct human movement is correct by virtue of one quite simply stated kinesiologically observed, and tested

---

[iv] This is just a rudimentary list of Hawkins' principles. For more detail, see Celichowska's *The Erick Hawkins Modern Dance Technique*, Princeton Book Company, 2000.

principle: Just do the movement. . . . The end of the journey in the study of *Zen in the Art of Archery* is to learn to permit the arrow to shoot itself."[146]

Form—Hawkins said that "there is a 'classicism' in the world of nature and of art where form takes on a 'violent clarity' . . . that is utterly simple, utterly without anything extra.[147] As Celichowska remarked, for Hawkins, "the dancer is forever striving to make the body 'a clear place.'"[148]

What is Rhythm? Is Music Sound?—Because Hawkins wanted the dancer to "listen to and experience their own inner song and rhythm," music was not used in class. This placed an importance on "being on the pulse of the movement, of obeying the rhythm of the body and of knowing the rhythmic structure of a movement."[149]

Dynamics—The relationship between "flow and the forming of things is one of the most exciting relationships in dance and is one that encompasses the idea of energy levels or dynamics. The use of dynamics in dancing predicates the aesthetic power of choice. A strong shape or angular form need not always be executed with bound flow, nor does free flow exculsively suggest subdued movement or shapelessness."[150]

Imagery and the Principles

Now that we have a cursory idea of some of the core principles, let's consider the application of two of the images mentioned above.

1. *Principle:* The Body's Center of Gravity: The Pelvis
    Image: Teeterbabe

    The center of gravity in an object is the point around which the mass of that object rotates. In a standing human, this is generally in front of the second sacral vertebra, so it is seated in the pelvic girdle. Celichowska noted that this center may shift: lifting the arms overhead raises the center; in a flatback the center actually shifts outside of the body.[151] Hawkins based the teeterbabe image on a child's teeterbabe device. The child is lowered into the teeterbabe, which supports its weight in the pelvic region like a swing seat. Unlike a swing, though, the teeterbabe allows the legs to hang with complete freedom without flexion in the thigh socket. For the dancer, this image helps to create a sensation of lifting and resting the pelvis and spine on top of the legs, which encourages a buoyant lift in the pelvis and eliminates a sense of "sitting into the legs."

2. *Principle(s):* The Body's Center of Gravity: The Pelvis Arcs, Curves, and Momentum
    Image: Undercurve and Overcurve

Diachenko asked, "How do you get a ball through space? You throw it underhand [undercurve] or overhand [overcurve]."[152] Just as you make these arcs in space as you throw a ball, you can also make them as you shift the weight of your pelvis in stationary movements or in movements that travel through space. Think of these curves or arcs as a U that may be rightside up or inverted. Quick shifts of weight on the top of the leg are the focus of a number of sequences during the center floorwork of the Hawkins class, but they may be found in traveling patterns as well. A simple movement such as a walk that begins on straight legs, moves through steps in plié, and returns to straight legs uses an undercurve. Likewise, a walk using relevé uses an overcurve. A chassé uses both. These curves or arcs can create loops and figure 8s (more imagery) and can help the dancer to follow through with the momentum generated by the initial force that created the movement. The dancer, in effect, takes advantage of the continued energy by allowing "movements their most efficient and organic execution." Celichowska noted, "Just as there are no straight lines in the body, there are no straight lines in human movement. All human movement describes arcs and curves."[153]

3. *Principle:* Contraction and Decontraction
    Image: Tassels

In active decontraction, the limbs will "respond organically to movement initiated from the torso. The movement pathways these loose limbs follow are similar to the natural momentum paths of the loose end of a rope, or a tassel on the end of a hat or curtain."[154] To understand how this image is applied to movement, consider a Hawkins "tassel-leg turn": This begins with the pelvis "spiraling toward or away from a weight-bearing leg. As the pelvis continues to spiral over the ball of the standing foot, the non-weight-bearing leg unleashes in response to the impetus of the pelvis. If properly decontracted and integrated with the pelvis, the weight of this trailing leg will acquire enough momentum to continue 'tasseling' around the pelvis and spine beyond the initial pelvic impetus."[155] If you have ever played a game of tether ball, you have seen this wrapping and unwrapping concept in action.

This is at best a surface look at only three of the many images frequently used in Hawkins training. Each of these images, however, is derived from everyday items, and their relationship to dance movement is easily recognizable. They create a recognizable sensation in the body from their first introduction, and when allowed to spend time in a think-feel dialogue, the body-mind responds well to the images while in stillness as well as when in motion.

A traditional ninety-minute Hawkins class includes floor, center standing, and traveling sequences, all of which continually focus attention on the power of your center of gravity. "We begin seated on the floor," Duke noted, "because that takes the weight off of the legs, which makes it easier to let go of tension."

EXPLORING IDEAS ORGANIZED AROUND THE THIGH SOCKET

For this experience, we move through the traditional floor-standing center-traveling progression, but rather than approach a number of different exercises, this material is an exploration of the thigh socket. In separate interviews, Katherine Duke, Diachenko, and Celichowska all suggested that *the most important element of the training students should experience in a first Hawkins encounter is the use of the thigh socket* (hip joint). Duke pointed out that, "This is the largest joint in the body," where the head of the femur meets the pelvis (at the acetabulum on the ilium). She said, "It's important to get students to think about where the leg begins. It doesn't simply

Kristina Berger, Jeff Lyon, and Katherine Duke in Erick Hawkins' Cantilever. *This image provides three different perspectives of the thigh socket.*

start there where the thigh creases."[156] For example, the psoas actually attach all the way up at the twelfth thoracic vertebra and are part of the complex pelvic muscular system that aides in the initiation and control of movement from the body's gravity center. So, you really are working from that high attachment down through the thigh socket and into the leg.

This series of experiments is just that: experimentation. For a variety of reasons, Hawkins did not present his theories and practical ideas as a codified technique. In part, he recognized that some elements of his approach were informed by other movement specialists. At the same time, he also believed that one cannot actually teach someone to dance, but that what a teacher does is to help students find their own entry into natural (normative), organic, true principles of human movement. The sequence you are about to experience is a synthesis of ideas from Hawkins' own classes and the artist-teachers I interviewed for this section (Celichowska, Diachenko, and Duke), informed by my own experience in trying to develop an embodied understanding of Hawkins' use of the thigh socket. Focusing movement initiation in the front of the body is sometimes a new concept for trained dancers. Hawkins' wife Dlugoszewski stated, "Erick's breakthrough vision of singling out and putting a laserlike focus on the front muscles of the legs and torso, making them the sole source of control in initiating movement in all the other muscles of the body, was a great intuitive insight into technique. . . . It generated an animal essence of extraordinary sensuousness in the performances of his dancers."[157] On the surface, this sequence will look easy. It is deceptive. It takes time to achieve.

Before you begin, take a minute *to find your center of gravity* (COG). Place your hand on your lower ab-domen so that your index finger is below your naval. The bottom of your pinky finger will fall roughly at your COG. Rather than sitting on the surface of your abdomen, think of the COG as moving from the surface deep into your torso, as though it were connected to the 3rd or 4th lumbar vertebra. Also, keep in mind the importance of imagery. Think-feel as you move through this sequence.

DISCOVERING THE THIGH SOCKET CREASE

A Hawkins class is typically done without music, and teachers usually count students through movement sequences. This helps the dancer to understand rhythm as it applies to movement, rather than as rhythm applies to music.

FLOOR WORK

Lengthening the body

Timing: No cts.

Start: Lying on the back, legs extended "beneath" you, feet a little wider than hip distance apart (even wider if that helps to let go of tension in the pelvic region). Arms may extend down along the torso or out to the sides. A helpful image for this entire experience is lying in warm sand, which supports the body and eliminates muscular tension. Allow the weight to drop into the floor (sand) by dropping the breath into the floor. Feel the back surface of the body touching the floor, and lengthen the muscles out along the floor. Gently jiggle the legs as though they are hanging down so that their weight encourages the thighs to decontract. Now simply let the legs go so that they fall into their natural alignment. Do they rotate open at that thigh socket or do they rotate inward? Take time to "sense gravity resting back into the body while the pelvis, thigh sockets, and legs are free of their weight-bearing function."[158] Stay "alive" in this moment as you experience the weight sinking into the floor. "Moments of stillness allow time during which images of safety and yielding into gravity can be incorporated into the dancer's coenesthetic sense."[159]

Simple thigh socket flexion

Timing: No cts.

Start: Extended on the floor, bring your attention to the front of the thigh socket, to the psoas. Try to initiate movement with a gentle flexion of the psoas, allowing the muscles in the abdomen to respond naturally. Additional muscles/ligaments—the lower back and hamstrings—are not needed in this activity, so allow them to remain decontracted. Think-feel this experience. Think about only creasing the thigh socket. As you crease in the thigh socket, you may feel the thigh lift slightly off the ground, the knee may bend a few degrees, and the ankle may flex, all in organic response. That is natural. Do not try to "manufacture" the response. The amount of movement in knee and ankle will depend on how your body is put together.

Repeat at least 4 times without counts.

Repeat at least 4 times on a moderate 4-ct.

[cts. 1–4] Crease.

[cts. 1–4] Decontract.

Constructive Rest

Initiated by Mabel Todd and developed by Lulu Sweigard, the Constructive Rest position is a good place to decontract the back muscles, particularly in the lower back. Keep in mind, that decontraction is not a passive release, but rather a yielding sensation. Stay with the image of warm sand and the sensation of gravity taking you into the sand.

Timing: No cts.

Start: Extended on the floor, flex the thigh sockets, draw the heels in toward the sitz bones, and organize the legs/feet so they are parallel. Wrap the arms over the torso and allow the weight to sink deeper into the sand. Continue to widen and lengthen the lower back, taking pressure out of the lumbar region.

In this position, you may also work with a partner. Another dancer should straddle your legs, lift one leg at a time, and manipulate the leg in the thigh socket. Your partner will simply reach under your leg so the "crook" of your knee is in the "crook" of their elbows (both arms together), and gently lift upward. Just let the leg hang momentarily, encouraging all of the muscles and ligaments to decontract as the weight of the pelvis sinks toward the floor. Think-feel a decontraction of the small ligaments that attach the head of the femur to the pelvis. This is a gentle process! A yielding, but again, avoiding passivity. Your partner may also gently move your leg in small circular or figure-8 patterns if you are having difficulty decontracting in the stillness of the "hanging" leg. Your partner then releases your leg (foot back to the floor) and then repeats on the other leg. Once complete, assist you partner through the same experience. Both of you should take care not to strain your back when lifting your partner's legs.

Note: While you are the partner on the floor, you may leave your arms across the torso as in Constructive Rest, or extend them out to the sides as needed for comfort.

After both partners have been assisted, return to the Constructive Rest position and extend arms out to the sides.

Thigh crease/gentle lift

Timing: Moderate 2 cts.

Start: Constructive Rest, arms out to sides, take a moment to focus, to think-feel the psoas as you did in the simple thigh crease experience. With the fingers, trace a line from the center of the thigh socket upward to the center of the knee and back down again. Use just enough of a "massaging" energy so that you still have a sense of the line traced line once you remove the fingertips from the leg. Try to focus your initiation to the front of the leg where you've just traced that line. Allow the thigh socket crease to deepen, the head of the femur drops into the pelvis, and the thigh moves backward toward the torso until the foot peels away from the floor. Disengage the psoas, and pour the foot back into the floor.

Repeat R and L at least 4 times on your own time.

Repeat at least 4 times on a moderate 2 cts.

[cts. 1–2] Crease/lift.

[cts. 1–2] Open the joint/pour foot into the floor.

This doesn't require a large range of motion. The whole idea is to focus on not just flexing/creasing in the joint, but on the contraction of muscle.

Leg circle or loop

Timing: Lilting 8 cts.

Start: As above. With a buoyant, circular quality initiate flexion in the psoas, let the femur drop into the pelvis and the thigh drop toward the torso. Allow the joint to open into rotation as the momentum takes the knee through a looping pathway to the side, and the foot in motion arcs around the stable foot. Let momentum carry the leg (let it "boomerang") back along the same pathway into parallel, pour the foot back onto the floor.

Repeat on your own several times, and remember to think-feel. Continue to spread the back out in all directions on the floor as well as the arms. Try not to let the pelvis "fly" off the floor—use the weight of the pelvis to continue yielding into the sand, which will help to keep you connected to the floor.

Repeat on 8 cts. with a great circular quality to the pulse.

Before coming to sitting for the next sequence, drop both thighs into the pelvis, increasing the crease, and gently swivel the pelvis in a small figure-8, just to encourage decontraction in the lower back. Replace the feet on the floor, pour body over to one side, allowing the weight of the head to circle you around as you fold into a seated position. Let the torso roll up, bring the weight onto the sitz bones, and extend the legs into 2nd position. Keep the torso in a nicely organized alignment, in a plumb line.

The image of the plumb line comes to us through the building trade, where a weight is tied to a cord (it looks like a clock pendulum, only with a point at the bottom of the weight) and this is suspended from the top of a door or window to ensure that both sides of the frame are symetrical and that the top (and bottom if it's a window) is level and well balanced before components are nailed into place. Imagine if the frame was "out of plumb" or unlevel. The door or window would not fit, or at the very least would not close as it should. In dance, the image of a line down the center of our body helps us to ensure that both sides are symetrical, and that the shoulders and hips are level.

Seated thigh crease

Timing: Moderate 2 cts.

Start: Come to sitting, legs extended in front of you. As you did while lying on the ground, jiggle your legs around, and when you let go, observe how they are naturally organized, rotated inward or outward. Consciously organize your legs so that they are linearly aligned, knees and toes facing skyward. Keep the thigh sockets, knees, and ankles soft. As before, intiate by flexing/contracting in the front of the thigh socket. Allow the head of the femur to fall backward into the pelvis, which will encourage a slight bend in the knee and a flexing of the ankle. Just as before, don't manufacture that response. Let it be a natural, organic response. As you uncrease, think of "opening" the joint, make sure the torso stays on its axis.

[cts. 1–2] Crease.

[cts. 1–2] Open.

Repeat 8 times on both sides.

Repeat 8 times with both legs in unison.

Before coming to standing, take a few moments to gently stretch the front of the thigh socket (the psoas). You might use a back bridge or gentle lunges to offset the work you've been doing in the psoas.

CENTER WORK

Knee bends (pliés) and relevés

The sequencing of these knee bends will be simple and direct. The focus is on using the weight of the pelvis and that big joint we've been working on to initiate this movement, rather than only considering the knees and ankles in the process. Think about the image of the teeterbabe, and think about the organization of your legs as you did on the floor. Lift the pelvis up and place it on top of the legs, so that the legs "dangle" beneath the pelvis—don't "sit" into the legs. Allow the weight of the pelvis to carry you downward so that the knees and ankles respond. For this sequence, just focus on demi-pliés parallel, 1st and 2nd positions. Think-feel a nice, circular, buoyant energy. Just allow the arms to be by the sides. Really put your attention on the pelvis and thigh sockets.

Timing: Bright but sustained 8, 4, and 2 cts. Tendu between positions on 4 or 2 cts.

1. Place the pelvis on top of the legs, plié on 4 cts., rise on 4 cts. Repeat 4 times on 8 cts. in parallel 1st and 2nd.

2. Repeat four times on 4 cts. in parallel 1st and 2nd.

3. Repeat 8 times on 2 cts. in parallel 1st and 2nd.

4. Plié on 2 cts., relevé on 2 cts., 4 times in parallel 1st and 2nd.

Sensous feet/thigh crease

This sequence is a quick foot warmup in parallel, with a quick thigh-socket crease. The 3-3, 2-2 rhythm pattern is a standard in Hawkins training and with it, a number of possibilities exist for sensous footwork.

Timing: 3 cts./2 cts.

1. Peel R foot on 1, toes come off the ground on 2, pour foot back onto floor on 3. Peel the foot on 1, toes come off the ground on 2, pour foot back onto floor on 3. Demi-plié 1, 2. Straighten 1, 2.

2. Repeat entire sequence on L foot.

3. Peel R foot on 1, replace on &, peel foot on 2, replace on &, peel foot on 3, replace on &. Peel L foot on 1, replace on &, peel foot on 2, replace on &, peel footon 3, replace on &.

4. Demi-plié on 1, straighten on 2. Demi-plié on 1, straighten on 2. Repeast on L foot.

Initiate a crease in the front of the thigh socket by drawing the foot up off the floor until the toes meet the standing ankle. Pour the foot back onto the floor as the psoas decontracts.

[ct. 1] Crease the thigh socket to draw foot up.

[ct. 2] Toe of working foot touches standing leg ankle.

[ct. 3] Decontract and pour foot onto floor 3.

[ct. 1] Relevé, lower.

[ct. 2] Repeat relevé, lower.

Repeat sequence on L foot.

Small jumps

Maintain the buoyant energy you have been working on. Keep the image of the teeterbabe and use the idea of allowing the pelvis to initiate the movement. Notice how the legs are organized in the air and in the landing. Play with metre and rhythm to see how different counts or syncopation affects the buoyancy of the jumps.

Timing: Bright 8 cts.
Start: In parallel 1st and 2nd.

Take a series of 8 small, bright jumps in each position.

TRAVELING

Walking and momentum

Because we have only made a slight weight shift at this point during the foot sequence, take a moment and think about how the weight of the pelvis moves your body through space. Take a walk across the studio. Think about the torso's plumb line, and keep it on that upright axis as you move forward without letting it shift forward or fall backward in the walk. Lift the pelvis up and place it on top of the legs as you did in the knee-bend work. Walking in parallel, allow the weight of the pelvis to carry you forward as it shifts from one thigh socket to the other. Try to avoid additional contractions in the body that aren't required in the act of walking.

Undercurve and overcurve

Throughout, focus on the momentum of the pelvis. Let that do as much of the work for you as possible.

Explore chassés and full-out runs as well. Notice where the natural undercurves and overcurves are, and what happens if you add a little verticality into the the traveling movement—perhaps a bright light elevation (not quite a full-out "jump," but a slight spring or bounce).

Timing: Brisk 4 cts.

[ct. 1] As you continue walking, take a regular step.

[cts. 2–3] Pass through demi-plié as you step.

[ct. 4] Return to straight legs as you step.

[ct. 1] Regular step.

[cts. 2–3] Pass through half-toe.

[ct. 4] Regular full foot.

Repeat both plié and half-toe sequences.

Runs with thigh crease

Run across the floor, stopping on one leg—try three runs, stopping on the fourth. Allow the weight of the pelvis to shift forward over the top of the femur, increasing the crease in the thigh socket. Notice how far forward you can allow the pelvis to shift until its weight pulls you off balance and you fall forward into the next run. Try the run on half-toe and examine the same idea. Notice how your sense of balance changes as you move. Don't forget your upper body through these processes. Remember the plumb line—encourage the three main weight centers—the pelvis, rib cage, and head—to work together. Remember to think-feel. Avoid unnecessary contraction in the body. After the experience, be sure to include another psoas stetch as part of the cooldown process.

Final Class Discussion Questions

1. As you have moved through the experiences in this chapter, what have you learned about your relationship with gravity?

2. How aware were you of momentum while going through the movement experiments in this chapter? What did you learn about your own body's response to momentum?

3. In the introduction to this chapter, we looked at the impact of politics and funding on modern dance training during the central and late modern periods. What do you think is the current "State of the Union" in terms of the relationship between dance (or arts in general) and American politics? How does that relationship affect dance funding? Dance training?

Works Cited

Beckh, E. (1960). Government Art in the Roosevelt Era: An appraisal of federal art patronage in light of present needs. *Art Journal*, 20 (1), 2–8.

Bird, D. & Greenberg, J. (1997). *Bird's Eye View: Dancing with Martha Graham and on Broadway*. Pittsburgh: University of Pittsburgh Press.

Brown, B. (1979). Training to Dance with Erick Hawkins. In R. Lorber (ed.), *Erick Hawkins: Theory and Training* (pp. 8–27). New York: The American Dance Guild.

Celichowska, R. (Writer and Director) (2000). *The Erick Hawkins Modern Dance Technique* [Book and DVD]. Highstown, NJ: Princeton Book Company.

_____. (2009, May 31). Renata Celichowska on Erick Hawkins. Interview by J. Legg.

Cooper, E. (1997, Autumn). Tamiris and the Federal Theatre 1936–1939: Socially relevant dance amidst the policies and politics of the New Deal era. *Dance Research Journal*, 29 (2), 23–48.

Dalzell, J. (2010, June). *Teacher's Wisdom: Jennifer Scanlon. Accessed October 10, 2010, from Dance Magazine*: http://dancemagazine.com/issues/June-2010/Teachers-Wisdom-Jennifer-Scanlon

Diachenko, N. (2009, June 23). Nada Diachenko on Erick Hawkins. Interview by J. Legg.

Duke, K. (2009, May 31). Katherine Duke on Erick Hawkins. Interview by J. Legg.

Federal Theatre Project. (1935). *Manual for Federal Theatre Project of the Works Progress Administration*. U.S. Works Progress Administation.

Foulkes, J. L. (2002). *Modern Bodies: Dance and American moderism from Martha Graham to Alvin Ailey*. Chapel Hill: The University of North Carolina Press.

Franko, M. (2002). *The Work of Dance: Labor, movement and identity in the 1930s*. Middletown, CT: Wesleyan University Press.

Garafola, L. (2005). Lincoln Kirstein, Modern Dance, and the Left: The genesis of an American ballet. *Dance Research: The Journal of the Society for Dance Research*, 23 (1), 18–35.

Guilbaut, S. (1983). *How New York Stole the Idea of Modern Art: Abstract Expressionism, Freedom, and the Cold War*. Chicago: The University of Chicago Press.

Graff, E. (1997). *Stepping Left: Dance and politics in New York City, 1928–1942*. Durham, NC: Duke University Press.

Hamm, C. (1980). John Cage. In *The New Grove Dictionary of Music and Musicians* (pp. 597–603). Washington: Grove's Dictionaries of Music, Inc.

Hawkins, E. (1966). Pure Poetry. In S. J. Cohen (Ed.), *The Modern Dance: Seven statements of belief* (pp. 39–51). Middletown, CT: Wesleyan University Press.

_____. (1992). *The Body Is A Clear Place and Other Statements on Dance*. Pennington, NJ: Princeton Book Company.

Humphrey, D. (1995). *Doris Humphrey: An artist first*. (S. J. Cohen, Ed.) Pennington, NJ: Princeton Book Company.

Kaiser, M. M. *The Art of the Turnaround: Creating and maintaining healthy arts organizations*. Hanover, NH: University Press of New England.

Kammen, M. (2000). Culture and the State in America. In G. Bradford, M. Gary, & G. Wallach (Eds.), *The Politics of Culture: Policy perspectives for individuals, institutions, and communities* (pp. 114–140). New York: The New Press.

King, E. (1978). *Transformations: A memoir by Eleanor King / The Humphrey-Weidman era*. New York: Dance Horizons.

Kriegsman, A. (1972, August 2). Erick Hawkins: The dance as priest. *The Washington Post*, p. B6.

_____. (1994, November 25). Erick Hawkins, The Modern Man. *The Washington Post*, p. B1.

Lancos, J. (2007). *Reclaiming Charles Weidman* (1901–1975). Lewiston, NY: The Edwin Mellen Press.

Larson, C. (1939). The Cultural Projects of the WPA. *The Public Opinion Quarterly*, 3 (3), 491–496.

Legg, J. (2006, October). Focus Modern: Limón technique. *Dance Spirit*, pp. 123–125.

Lewis, D. (1984). *The Illustrated Dance Technique of José Limón*. Hightstown, NJ: Princeton Book Company.

Lewis, J. (2000). Designing a Cultural Policy. In G. Bradford, M. Gary, & G. Wallach (Eds.), *The Politics of Culture: Policy perspectives for individuals, institutions, and communities* (pp. 79–93). New York: The New Press.

Limón, J. (1966). An American Accent. In S. J. Cohen (Ed.), *The Modern Dance: Seven statements of belief* (pp. 17–27). Middletown, CT: Wesleyan University Press.

_____. (1979). On Dance. In J. M. Brown (ed.), *The Vision of Modern Dance* (pp. 97–104). Princeton, NJ: Princeton Book Company.

_____. (2001). *José Limón: An unfinished memoir*. Middletown, CT: Wesleyan University Press.

_____. (2001, Spring). Letter to Pauline, Betty and Lucas on the occasion of the 10th Anniversary of *The Moor's Pavane*. (N. Owen, Ed.) *Limón Journal: A publication from the Limón Institute*, pp. 2–3.

Louis, M. (Writer). (1973). *Dance As An Art Form* [DVD].

Lubow, A. (2009, November 8). Can Modern Dance Be Preserved? *The New York Times Magazine*, pp. 38–43.

Macaulay, A. (2007, November 25). 50 Years Ago, Modernism Was Given a Name: *Agon*. Accessed 5 November 2008, from *The New York Times*: http://nytimes.com/2007/11/25/arts/dance/25maca.html?_r=1&pagewanted=print

Matt, P. (n.d.). Welcome to Ideokinesis. Accessed 16 February 2011, from http://ideokinesis.com.

Mazo, J. (1977). *Prime Movers: The makers of modern dance in America*. New York: William Morrow & Company.

Morris, G. (2006). *A Game for Dancers: Performing modernism in the postward years, 1945–1960*. Middletown, CT: Wesleyan University Press.

Needham Costonis, M. (1991, Fall). Martha Graham's American Document: A minstrel show in modern dance dress. *American Music*, 9 (3), pp. 297–310.

New Music Box (2000, May). Lucia Dlugoszewski, Composer and Choreographer, Dies at 68. Accessed 24 January 2010. http://newmusicbox.org/news/may00/obit_ldlugoszewski.html.

Owen, N. (Ed.) (1997, Spring). The Dance Heroes of José Limón. *Limón Journal: A publication of the Limón Institute*. New York: José Limón Institute.

Popkin, S. (1979). Introduction. In R. Lorber (ed.), *Erick Hawkins: Theory and training* (pp. 4–7). New York: The American Dance Guild, Inc.

Prevots, N. (1998). *Dance for Export: Cultural diplomacy and the Cold War*. Middeltown, CT: Wesleyan University Press.

Siegel, M. (1985). *The Shape of Change: Images of American dance*. Berkeley: University of California Press.

_____. (1993). *Days on Earth: The dance of Doris Humphrey*. Durham, NC: Duke University Press.

_____. (1993, Spring). Marthology. *The Hudson Review*, 46 (1), pp. 183–188.

Sorell, W. (1986). *Looking Back in Wonder: Diary of a dance critic*. New York: Columbia University Press.

Taliaferro, C. (2010, September 27). Clay Taliaferro on José Limón Technique. Interview by J. Legg.

Terry, W. (1957, October 27). Experiment? Joke? Or War of Nerves? *New York Herald Tribune*.

The National Archives. (1995). *Records of the Work Projects Administration*. Accessed August 26, 2010, from National Archives Guide to Federal Records: http://www.archives.gov/research/guide-fed-records/groups/069.html.

Vachon, A. (2010, September 29). Ann Vachon on José Limón Technique. Interview by J. Legg.

CHAPTER 5

The Avant-garde

Merce Cunningham
Alwin Nikolais and Murray Louis

"You know, [Cage] remarked, "I've never really liked dance." "What do you mean," I asked in utter bewilderment: "Why not?" Adopting an expression of mock disgust, he shook his head and said simply, "All those faces, all those (and he paused again for special emphasis)…bodies!" My motive for repeating this story is not to suggest that Cage's lifelong involvement with dance was fundamentally disingenuous. Quite the contrary. It's precisely this touch of puritanism in Cage that has lent a chastened rigor to the Cunningham/Cage aesthetic.

— Roger Copeland, *Merce Cunningham:*
The Modernizing of Modern Dance

Moving farther through the postwar years, we will see monumental shifts in the dancemaking process, the dance-music relationship, ideas about dance presentation, and the leadership of the artform. At the same time, critical shifts occurred in the perception and performance of gender and sexuality in American modern dance. This was particularly true across the decade of the 1950s as nonlinear narrative and abstraction became the cornerstones for much avant-garde work. In the brief discussion that follows, we will see that the

Merce Cuningham in his work Changeling, *1958.*

construction of gender and sexuality has been mutable, in flux in much the same way as every other aspect of modern dance. Historian Julia Foulkes (see Chapter 4), for example, observed that from the inception of modernism in the arts, painters and dancers presented the body—on canvas and stage—in new ways with "disjointed, angular compositions of body parts." She noted that what distinguished dance from other modernist art forms was composed of the individuals who participated in the work:

> [W]hite women . . . gay men, and some African American men and women. Women had leading roles on stage and off, replacing the common stage image of the sexual ingénue with that of the pioneering individual who moved her own body with disquieting, abrupt force. Gay men, too, recast the effeminate image of the sissy into a hardened, heroic, dancing American athlete.[1]

Anthropologist and dance scholar Judith Lynne Hanna points out that sexuality and dance are effectively conjoined as they "share the same instrument—the human body."[2] George Balanchine acknowledged that as well in discussing his abstract ballets when he said that simply by putting a woman and man on stage together, you create plot even if there is not a storyline, or inherent meaning in the movement. Hanna further pointed out:

> Dance is an eye-catching, riveting way for humans to identify themselves and maintain or erase their boundaries. Feelings and ideas about sexuality and sex roles (also referred to as gender) take shape in dance . . . [and] reflect and also challenge society's expectations for each sex's specific activities, whether dominance patterns or mating strategies.[3]

What we are talking about here is a national culture, and how identity (biological and psycho-emotional) relate to that culture.

Defining Culture

In 1871, British anthropologist Edward Taylor originally defined culture as "that complex whole which includes knowledge, belief, art, law, custom, and any other capabilities and habits acquired by man as a member of society." In contemporary cultural anthropology, culture is typically defined as "socially patterned human thought and behavior."[4]

We see these normative ideas mapped out in our culture. Forces of religiosity, economic and class structure, and political thought (among other factors) all predicate the normative expression of sexuality and the performance of gender across the societal spectrum, including the appearance of these identities on stage, in literature, television, sports, and even military service. The rise of modernism in the last century was concurrent with immense shifts in sociopolitical thought. For example, the struggle for women's suffrage presaged the work of Isadora Duncan and Ruth St. Denis by nearly five decades. When the 19th Amendment was at last ratified in 1920, Martha Graham and Doris Humphrey were dancing for Denishawn. All these women, major leaders in the New Dance, must have found inspiration in this social struggle—been buoyed and inspired to forge

An advertisement for the New York Denishawn School c. 1928. Note that "Mr. Shawn personally teaches a class for boys specializing in masculine technique and dances.

even more victories for women, and their art form. Women, in fact, dominated much of the modern dance field prior to World War II (save for Ted Shawn, Charles Weidman, and Lester Horton, and the handful of men who eventually danced for them). Helen Tamiris, in addition to being a leading choreographer, was also the powerhouse organizer and fundraiser of modern dance, unparalleled, really, by any similar work from male dancers.

Look, too, at the choreographies of any female dancers at the time. Foulkes's statement about the pioneering, disquieting, abrupt force of the new woman's dancing body is a far cry from the image of the sylph. She may have been referring to Graham's *Heretic* (1929), *Frontier* (1935), or *Chronicle* (1936), but the reference might easily be to any dance made by any number of women working in the era. The dancing female imagery of Pearl Primus, Jane Dudley, Sophie Maslow, Hanya Holm, and any number of other dancemakers was the visage of woman as strong, potent, and in control of the space around her. On the whole, this was different from the appearance of woman in the works of Duncan and St. Denis, where the female was still soft, pliable—and, well, feminine—in a premodernist context. That image was all but gone though by the end of the 1920s.

Concurrently, men were addressing head-on what dance critic Marcia Siegel referred to as "the specter of homosexuality."[5] American mythos has long presented the founding, protection, and proliferation of our national identity as a victory solely at the hands of white, heterosexual, Christian men. In this mythos, the Holy Trinity of Machismo is the most prominent of our public images: the cowboy, the soldier, the football star.

Where any gay man participated in those categories of heroism, he was expected to serve in silence. In public presentation, the American male dancer almost always felt the same need to present a non-gay, masculine front regardless of what his personal sexual identity might have been. (A notable exception to that might be certain male roles in Katherine Dunham's work.) According to Ramsay Burt, professor of Dance History at De Montfort University in Leicester, England, "There is a widespread reluctance to talk about dance and homosexuality."[6] After the breakup of Denishawn, Ted Shawn—who had a decades-long relationship with another man after leaving his marriage to St. Denis—founded what was likely the first all-male dance company in America. Shawn strove to break the stereotype of the male dancer as effeminate and foppish. In his dances, you saw "men being heroic—suffering, challenging, striking, striving . . . this preoccupation with the look of the body, the insistence that the body should look virile at all times, was Shawn's principal contribution to our choreographic development."[7] The physical aspect of Shawn's choreography presented a body prepared for work, for labor—in fact, many photographs of his Men Dancers show the company in industrial situations, in front of massive machinery engineered, built, and run by men. This epitomized the way in which both ballet and modern dance map cross-identity roles on the male dancing body, where gay men play straight roles. Dance critic Gay Morris also pointed out that "homophobia was tied to anticommunist rhetoric to an extraordinary degree in the postwar period. . . . Communists were routinely equated with effeminacy and homosexuality on a metaphoric level, while actual homosexuals were viewed as a threat to national security and the moral fiber of the country."[8]

The work of the avant-garde, on the other hand, might be referred to as genderless or asexual, but that is simplistic. As Roger Copeland indicates in the observation at the start of this chapter, the Cunningham/Cage aesthetic eschewed the use of gender as a choreographic device because they knew "how easily the body can seduce, how effortlessly it can push an audience's hot buttons; and [they were] eager to circumvent that sort of facile manipulation."[9] That is not to suggest that Cunningham's work cannot ever be said to have a sensuality—or even a spirituality. They are, after all, dances performed by human beings, and complex texts are inherent even where there is not narrative-driven meaning. In Nikolais, too, we see a clear rejection of using sex/gender roles in choreography. He gave us a macroview of motion where the human is seen as part of a larger whole.

While abstractionism and nonlinear narrative are paramount in Paul Taylor's repertory, so too are iconic characterizations of both man and woman. Suzanne Carbonneau, Professor of Performance at George Mason University, noted, "Taylor's men are men, and his women are women,"[10] as evidenced in works like *Arden Court* (1981) and *Sunset* (1983). Taylor constructs the power of both female and male characters through the virtuosic athleticism required of both sexes in works like *Esplanade* (1975). In fact, his most athletically demanding role, the lead in *Le Sacre du Printemps (The Rehearsal)* (1980), was made for Ruth Andrien, who pushed the limits of physical endurance perhaps more than any man had in Taylor's repertory. The sense of the athletic remained front and center when Taylor included same-sex relationships in *Piazzolla Caldera*

(1997)—gay could no longer be equated with effete in modern dance. Bill T. Jones and Arnie Zane had, of course, already blown the closet door off the dance stage nearly two decades earlier, and Matthew Bourne had re-envisioned *Swan Lake* two years prior with an all-male cast.

Iconic constructs of sexuality and gender were also vital to images of African American society as presented in modern dance. Dance historian Thomas DeFrantz, director of Women's and Gender Studies at MIT, noted that in the early days of Alvin Ailey's company, Ailey's stage persona was "built upon an impassioned flailing of his body through dance passages steeped in fiery cool. Ailey seemed to enjoy tempting his audiences with an exotic allure."[11] There was a hyper-masculinity in Ailey's movement—a machismo. DeFrantz noted that Ailey's mentor, Lester Horton, had "encouraged his company to see beyond common constructions of race and sexuality. Ailey gravitated to the vision of personal and sexual liberation, and poured himself into study to develop a weighty, smoldering performance style that suited his athletic body and his concern with the representation of masculinity."[12] In his quest to confront stereotypes of black dancers, Ailey pushed the envelop. His dances require men to demonstrate great technical mastery and animal power alongside rhythmic virtuosity. Like Taylor, Ailey also used iconic male-female roles. DeFrantz pointed out that in *Blues Suite* (1958), "Ailey used the dramatic narrative to essentialize black social dance as the site of sexual power negotiation." Blues dance then "is masculized to the degree it is construed to be (hetero)sexual."[13]

Core Ideas

. . . .

Observations and Experiments

Journal I: Observe yourself as you go through your day. Notice how your body feels as you move and how you perceive your own body in motion in daily life, outside the studio. Locate the impetus for movement in your physical self as you walk down the street: the weight of the pelvis, the chest, or the skull. Pay attention to your gait: long or short strides; quick and alert or calm or controlled pace. Really try to be aware of yourself in your body. See if you enjoy the feeling of motion in your body as you walk and if your walk tells you about how you perceive yourself. Consider what you radiate to others as you walk.

Journal II: Explore your internal sense of direction as you move through your day. Observe the sensations that occur in the body as you round corners and make sudden changes of direction. Take notes on how those changes affect your sense of self and your relationship to the space around you.

Experiment I: Make a short chance dance. Roll a die three times. The first number indicates the number of short phrases you will create for the dance; the second is the number of gestures you will need for each phrase, and the third is an approximate duration for each movement phrase. So, 6-2-5 indicates a dance with six short phrases, each with two gestures, and lasting roughly five seconds each. The entire dance then is only thirty seconds long. You can roll the die again to determine other elements like rhythm, level, and direction changes, or similar devices.

Experiment II: Stand outdoors and observe the space around you, noticing the terrain and the surrounding architectural elements. Observe how people make their way through the space, how their bodies interact with the space, and how their bodies relate to others passing through at the same time. Notice what happens to one body in the space when another changes direction and if there are places where people make noticeable rhythmic changes in their locomotion through that area. Draw an outline sketch of the space, and take it and your notes into the dance studio. Create a short phrase tracing the outline of your line drawing through the space. Incorporate some of the changes of direction you noted, the rhythms, and other purely physical/nonemotional reactions you saw. Determine what happens if a fellow dancer performs their dance phrase overlapping your own, in terms of reaction, changes in sense of rhythm and time, or a total change.

- -

Technical Genesis

Merce Cunningham (1919–2009) and John Cage (1912–1992): Biographical Sketches

> I used to be told that you see the center of the space as the most important: that was the center of interest. But in many modern paintings this was not the case and the sense of space was different. So I decided to open up the space to consider it equal, and any place, occupied or not, just as important as any other. In such a context you don't have to refer to a precise point in space. And when I read that sentence of Albert Einstein's: 'There are no fixed points in space,' I thought, indeed, if there are no fixed points, then every point is equally interesting and equally changing.
>
> — Merce Cunningham, *The Dancer and the Dance*

Merce Cunningham, leader of the vanguard movement in modern dance, died on July 26, 2009, just months after premiering his latest work, *Nearly Ninety*, in recognition of his own ninetieth birthday. In the course of a career that spanned seventy years and included nearly two hundred dances, Cunningham stirred controversy, inspired the search for new ways to create dance, and encouraged a progressive incorporation of technology into dance creation and performance/presentation.

He was famous for being a man of few words in the studio (both as teacher and choreographer) and also for allowing his pupils to find their own way, rather than showing them the way, all of which earned him comparison to a Zen master.[14] Cunningham was generous with college students—so much so that at one point his own dancers felt his communication with students was more direct than with them.[15] *During my years as an undergrad, and especially as a graduate student, I was fortunate to have periodic opportunities to speak briefly with Merce. The questions he posed in response to those I asked helped me to shape my own thoughts about dance, and how I found (and perceived) myself in the liquid architecture of dance.*

Dance critic Jack Anderson noted, "Three aspects of Cunningham's choreographic theories have been especially provocative: his use of chance and indeterminacy; his treatment of stage space as an open field; and his tendency to regard the components of a dance production as independent entities."[16] When Anderson wrote that in 1992, Cunningham was just beginning to use computer technology to craft his dances. So, in considering Anderson's statement, we should view technology as a fourth element. In the last fifteen years or so of his career, his repertory can be read not simply as modern art, but as a post-industrialist manifesto where the intersection of human thought and electronic information is literally mapped into the human body by way of computer-generated senses of shape, time, space, and rhythm.

In order to understand Cunningham, his choices, and his technique, it is also necessary to consider his creative and life partner, John Cage. Cage's artistic ideas complemented and fueled Cunningham's own in profound ways, and together they forged what is perhaps the most prolific collaboration in the American avant-garde.

Merce Cunningham

Cunningham was born on April 16, 1919, in Centralia, Washington, where his dance studies began when he was quite young. His parents were not particularly aware of the arts in general, but Cunningham noted:

> …they didn't stop me from tap-dancing when I was an adolescent. My father [a lawyer] said, "If you want to do it, fine. All you have to do is work at it." There was no special objection. It is curious perhaps, since my two brothers followed him, one being a lawyer, the other, a judge.[17]

Cunningham also said that as an eight-year-old, "More than dancing it was the idea of being on stage, in a theater that attracted me."[18] A few years later, his dance studies became more serious when he entered Maud Barrett's studio, where he pursued tap and ballroom, and began performing. Barrett had performed in the circus and in vaudeville, and her energy stunned

Cunningham.[19] His first touring experiences came with Barrett and her small company around Washington, and later on a month-long tour in California.

After high school, Cunningham spent a year at the University of Washington in Seattle, which he found unsatisfying. So the next year, he transferred to the Cornish School for Performing and Visual Arts, run by a family friend, Nellie Cornish, in Seattle. Cunningham attended the school with the intention of becoming an actor but continued his dance training as well. In addition to acting, diction, voice, and theater history, he studied eurythmics and dance composition. It was also there that former Graham dancer Bonnie Bird introduced him to Graham's technique. He later remarked, "I never had serious dance training before that. For months I could hardly crawl up the stairs, but I did it. . . . We had two technical classes a day, almost every day, plus all the rehearsals."[20] By his second year, composer John Cage had joined the staff at Cornish, playing for dance classes and directing the percussion orchestra, which he invited Cunningham to join. The two men began a relationship as life partners that lasted until Cage's death, and an artistic partnership that inspired the avant-garde art world for nearly fifty years.

During the summers following his two years at Cornish, Cunningham was able to attend the summer workshop at Mills College in Oakland, California. In 1938, the two workshop instructors were Bonnie Bird and Lester Horton. Cunningham served as Bird's assistant that summer, and Bella Lewitzky assisted Horton. In addition to teaching, Horton was also invited to stage a new work on the students; he cast Lewitzky and Cunningham in the principal roles. The work, *Conquest*, seems to have been the first in which Cunningham had the opportunity to work with a significant choreographer. Horton biographer Larry Warren noted that Cunningham later "recalled choreographic sessions in which Horton, seated in a chair and smoking a cigar, would somehow design ingenious lifts, and how Lewitzky bounded off into space at the slightest suggestion from the choreographer."[21] The choreography contained fast, complex rhythmical footwork, a trait Cunningham adopted. *Conquest* also contained several production elements that would become hallmarks of Cunningham's own work. Collaboration played a significant role in the production, as composer Lou Harrison also assisted with the decor design. Also, Horton had a tendency to make variations in the structure of his dances to the point that his dancers frequently did not know what would be performed until performance time.[22]

The regular faculty from Bennington School of the Dance was in residence teaching at Mills College in the following summer (1939), so Cunningham encountered Graham, Humphrey, Weidman, and Hanya Holm for the first time. While at Mills, Graham invited Cunningham to join her company, and even though he had never seen her dance, he made his way to New York and became her second male soloist.[23] He danced for the company from 1939 to 1945, creating roles in some of her most important works, including *Letter to the World* (1940), *Deaths and Entrances* (1943), and *Appalachian Spring* (1944). Not long after he began studying and performing in her company, Graham also suggested that he begin ballet training and made arrangements with

Lincoln Kirstein for him to study at the School of American Ballet. Cunningham later recalled Kirstein asking him why a modern dancer wanted to learn ballet, to which he responded that he really appreciated all forms of dance and did not have a particular predisposition to any specific form—[24] a fact that may have aided his vision when he began to develop his own technical ideas.

John Cage

John Cage was born in Los Angeles on September 5, 1912, to an inventor father and journalist mother. Although he was the valedictorian of his high school class, he was extremely displeased with his initial college experience and withdrew from school in favor of the education provided by nearly two years of exploring Europe, intending to be a writer. Upon returning stateside, his path led him back to music and periods of studying theory and composition with Adolph Weiss and Henry Cowell, and counterpoint and composition with Arnold Schoenberg.[25] In 1937 he moved to Seattle to become the composer-accompanist for Bonnie Bird's dance classes at the Cornish School.

As a composer, Cage was disinterested in the traditional preoccupation and reverence for harmony in musical composition, and he found as much value in silence as a component of composition as traditional sound elements. Time, for Cage, became a significant creative factor early in his career, as did nontraditional instrumentation. A prime example of his interest in both time and silence is his work *4'33"* (1959), a piece where he sat, in silence, for four minutes and thirty-three seconds—instantly becoming one of the world's most controversial composers.[26] Cage's reputation as an innovative composer was well established as early as the 1940s—in 1949 he received awards from the Guggenheim Foundation and the National Academy of Arts and Letters.

During this period, Cage began to explore Eastern philosophies including the *I Ching* (the Chinese *Book of Changes*). The *I Ching* is among the oldest known books in the world and is said to illustrate the universal Law of Changes that governs all action:

> Could we but analyze the pattern of Changes . . . and could we but relate
> our affairs to the proper point in the everlasting process of ebb and flow
> . . . we should be able to determine the best action to be taken.[27]

In its original use, information is accessed from the *I Ching* by tossing a set of coins or sticks and measuring the results against a set of sixty-four hexagrams. The pattern of the hexagrams determines the action suggested. For Cage and other musicians interested in aleatory (chance) music, the chance operation (flipping the coins or a similar procedure) helped to determine the order of musical material in creating and/or performing a score. The toss of the *I Ching* coins, for instance, determined the outcome of *Music of Changes*, his 1951 piano work.[28] While innovative, Cage's use of chance was highly criticized: "When John Cage embraced compositional methods based on chance, his act was commonly interpreted as a rejection of history, a repudiation of all music—indeed, all culture—which had come before."[29] Indeterminacy provided a similar set of unknown variables. For example, a composer might provide a series of tones/pitches and time intervals with an instruction for the performer to establish rhythmic patterns for executing the sound details (these instructions might be arrived at by drawing from a deck of cards). Where the action of chance became fixed and irrevocable, indeterminacy was fluid and could, in essence, create vastly different performances of the same initial set of material depending on the performance instructions and the choice made by the performers.

Cage also developed a system for composing, with brackets of time (sounds mapped out over clock time) speeding up the process of writing music. He also came up with a system to help name the works, based on the number of players in the work.[30] "Chance and speed helped Cage achieve his goal . . . to make a musical composition the continuity of which is free of individual taste and memory (psychology) and also of the literature and 'traditions' of art."[31] He believed in adapting to the world around him, rather than trying to shape the world and, as an extension, wanted audiences to bring their own structure to his music. Thus, structure would not be inflicted but self-created in the mind of the listener.

In addition to compositional innovations, he was also at the forefront of electronic music. "Cage's pioneering use of electronic musical resources began in 1939, with his now-classic percussion ensemble composition *Imaginary Landscape #1*, in which he employed variable-speed phonograph turntables as performed musical instruments."[32] Cage's work with electronic sound continued through the 1940s, and in 1952 he created *Imaginary Landscape No. 5* on magnetic tape. The work consisted of sounds from forty-two gramophone recordings transferred to tape, then fragmented and reassembled according to chance. *Williams Mix* (1952) was created in a similar manner, but consisted of six hundred musical and nonmusical sounds, and took several months to complete.

Cunningham, Cage, and Collaboration

Cunningham once said, "Dance is movement, and its opposite, in time and space. It is this continuously changing fact that gives its structure—its permanence in fluidity—and provides a fascination that impels a good many people to be concerned with it: choreographers, performers, teachers, and spectators. It is its own necessity, not so much as a representation of the moving world, rather as a part of it, with inherent springs."[33]

During his second year in New York, Cunningham began to explore his own choreography, making solos for himself. Then, in 1944, he and Cage produced their first program together (Cunningham had six solos on the concert) and presented it at the Humphrey-Weidman Studio.

In his final year with Graham, he created a second concert with Cage, presented at the Hunter College Playhouse. From the beginning, Cunningham noted,

> I thought that any kind of movement could be used as dance movement, that there was no limit in that sense. Then I went on to the idea that each movement should be different from what you had used in previous dances. What I am trying to say by that is that in looking for movement, I would look for something I didn't know about instead of something I did know about.[34]

Even in these early works, Cunningham was beginning to turn away from what were then traditional ideas about form, content, and the dance-music relationship supported by the first wave of modern dance artists—ideas he had studied at the Cornish School and with Louis Horst, and was experiencing in Graham's work. Of his own choreography, he said that "the basis for the dances is movement, that is, the human body moving in time-space . . . the ideas of the dance come both from the movement, and are in the movement."[35]

While the first Cunningham-Cage works seem to have had a traditional dance-music relationship (see works like *Credo in Us* and *Totem Ancestor*, both 1942), the artists soon came to a common perspective that dance and music should be able to exist simultaneously, but independently. Cunningham eventually saw music as an aural production element that occurred during a specific time period, and dance occurred in a neighboring space. For Cage, melodic line was as irrelevant as theme was for Cunningham. Cage once said:

> . . .in working with Merce, the first thing we did was to liberate the music from the necessity for it go with the dance, and to liberate the dance from having to go with the music. . . . I established the rhythmic structure for the music . . . and then Merce would make a dance within that structure . . . . and then the two would come together without having forced each other in terms of details.[36]

Autonomy then became a cornerstone for their work together, and in the work they eventually began to do with other musicians and visual artists. (There were times when music and dance were so separate that Cunningham's dancers did not hear the music until the first performance of a new dance.)[37] Cunningham went so far as to say:

> This non-reference of the movement is extended into a relationship with music. It is essentially a non-relationship. The dance is not performed to the music . . . the music is composed and performed as a separate identity

of itself. It happened to take place at the same time as the dance. The two co-exist, as sight and sound do in our daily lives.[38]

This also meant that musical landmarks were never set, so that dance and music never coincided in identical patterns from performance to performance.[39]

Root of an Unfocus (1944) is traditionally seen as the piece where the "working methods of Cage and Cunningham began to coincide,"[40] particularly since Cunningham was now working with time structures in dancemaking as Cage had been doing in his musical compositions. Time structures then became the commonality in their works. In fact, time, as structure, led Cunningham to begin working with a stopwatch during rehearsals (which were conducted in silence, without music). He then began basing his dances on human rhythm, rather than musical rhythm: "You don't need a meter to walk down the street. . . . We all use the same mechanism [to walk], but we all walk differently. . . . Dancing is simply an extension, in a big way, of walking."[41] Longtime Cunningham dancer Carolyn Brown observed, "Merce worked with the stopwatch from the belief that rhythm comes out of the nature of the movement itself and the nature of the individual dancer."[42] Brown further indicated that Cunningham would choreograph a movement sequence and then figure out how much time it took to dance that sequence. The movement would be rehearsed that way until the timing was clear. She also commented that, "Group works, such as *Rune* (1959) and *Aeon* (1961), which had much unison dancing with constantly shifting tempi," often required weeks of intense rehearsal where phrases were counted and recounted to ensure that the integrity of time structures and space designs remained constant. Slight alterations in one could also shift any of the other elements.[43]

After leaving the Graham company in 1945, Cunningham spent several years at various workshops around the country, further developing his choreographic skill. In 1946, Kirstein commissioned Cunningham and Cage to create a new work for Ballet Society. (Although he had created Ballet Society as a vehicle for George Balanchine's work, Kirstein was also interested in "an opportunity to promote collaborations among young choreographers, composers, and painters.")[44] The work, *The Seasons*, also featured decor by longtime Graham collaborator Isamu Noguchi.

In 1948, Cunningham and Cage began working at Black Mountain College in North Carolina, considered "the birthplace of the aleatoric (chance structure) movement in avant-garde music and dance."[45] Black Mountain College was a leader in innovative educational methods at the time, and was dedicated to experimental arts as a core component of the curriculum.[46] This time at Black Mountain was crucial in several ways. Their interest in collaboration was truly fostered in that environment, and they had the opportunity to work with a number of developing avant-garde artists. The first year, Cunningham choreographed Black Mountain's production of Erik Satie's *The Ruse of Medusa*, designed by Willem and Elaine de Kooning. *Theatre Piece* (1952) marked the first time Cunningham and Cage worked with the artist Robert Rauschenberg; composer David Tudor and filmmaker Nicholas Cernovitch were also involved in the production. Further, the Merce Cunningham Dance Company emerged from the Black Mountain summer arts session (1953). The original company included Carolyn Brown, Remy Charlip, Jo Anne Melsher, Viola Farber, Marianne Preger, Paul Taylor, and Anita Dencks. Cage and Tudor were the resident composers, and Rauschenberg oversaw the visual elements of productions (lighting, decor, and costumes).

In the Merce Cunningham Dance Company's long history, numerous other musicians and visual artists would contribute a wide variety of work. Jasper Johns joined the company as artistic adviser after Rauschenberg departed. (Unlike Rauschenberg, though, Johns was not particularly interested in creating decor, preferring only to costume the works and frequently bringing in other visual artists to dress the stage when that was necessary.) Composers Earle Brown, Erik Satie, and Christian Wolff; artists Andy Warhol, Roy Lichtenstein, and Robert Morris; and filmmakers Charles Atlas, Elliot Caplan, and Stan VanDerBeek were just a few of the contributors to Cunningham's extensive repertory.

Cunningham treated chance much the way that Cage did, by using either the *I Ching* or other structures he established himself. In 1953, Cunningham created *Suite by Chance*, the first work where he used chance to structure the entire piece. In her memoir, Brown recalled that he had spent several hours a day for months establishing complex charts that contained possibilities for movement, stillness, and duration of action. The situating of each element was decided entirely by the flip of a coin.[47]

A master of entrances and exits, Cunningham used surprise to keep the audience guessing who or what would next appear, and from where it would arrive. He also questioned the use of meaning in movement and choreography: "I don't even want a dancer to start thinking that a movement means something. . . . That's what I really didn't like about working with Graham— the idea that was always being given to you that a particular movement meant something specific. I thought that it was nonsense."[48] For Cunningham, meaning should not be external, but must be intrinsic to the particular dancer's execution of the movement. This is not to say that Cunningham's work has no emotion, but that emotion comes from the fact that a human being is executing the movement. He contended that because human beings are not abstract, "everything that a human being does is expressive in some way of that person."[49] A correlation can be made here to Balanchine's idea that even in his own abstract ballets, putting a woman and a man together on stage creates plot, if not story. The disposal of narrative and character, however, often inspired Cunningham to costume his work in rehearsal clothes, bringing more attention to the work and the dancers. Cunningham further emphasized his views on meaning in the creation of "Events," where sections of older works were taken out of their original context and spliced together in a new context, illustrating his belief that "everything is subject to change."[50]

Technology and Cunningham's Repertory

In addition to all of these other innovations in choreography, Cunningham is also widely known for his embrace of technology over the years. As early as *Symphonie pour un homme seul* (1952), Cunningham began working with electronic music—a practice that remained a fixture in his work for most of his career. The score by Pierre Schaeffer and Pierre Henry, the founders of *musique concrète*, consisted of preexisting sounds that were "recorded on newly available magnetic tape, which was then elaborately edited in a cut-and-paste, collage-like fashion."[51] The idea of collage in the visual arts was such an influence in the development of *musique concrète* and in the choreography that Cunningham renamed the work *Collage* when it was added to his company's emerging repertory the next year. Roger Copeland, professor of theatre and dance at Oberlin College, noted both the dance *Collage* and the artistic practice of creating a collage were critical elements in Cunningham's work: "Cunningham's movement vocabulary in Collage was diverse: it juxtaposed his usual modifications of ballet with pedestrian movement (hair combing, nail filing) as well as steps drawn from ballroom and social dance. In other words, varieties of 'found' movement existed alongside varieties of 'found' sound."[52] Copeland then referred to Cunningham's process in creating his "Events" as a "splicing" process—material was extracted from existing work, manipulated, and pasted together in a new configuration. For Copeland, Cunningham worked like a film editor, "cutting, assembling, and re-assembling the fragments."[53] Dances like *Changing Steps* (1973), in which Cunningham employed indeterminacy to establish a new ordering of material for each performance, and his embrace of film strengthen Copeland's assertions about the place of collage in Cunningham's work. Furthermore, Copeland stated, this concept of collage in Cunningham's work certainly paved the way for his use of computer technology as a major component of much of his later choreography.

In the early 1990s, Cunningham began to explore computer software in the development of choreographic material. In her memoir, Brown discussed how chance operations could make movement sequences extremely difficult, and that they often pushed the endurance of the dancers. She added, "Of course, compared with the mind-bogglingly difficult and complex movement Merce devised through the *Life Forms* computer program in the 1990s, even the most difficult material in *Suite by Chance* now seems like child's play."[54] This computer animation program allowed Cunningham to continue choreographing even after crippling arthritis confined him to a wheelchair. "Seated at the computer," Copeland remarked, "Cunningham can dictate—and simultaneously notate—a wide variety of choreographic variables"[55] (an image reminiscent of Horton in the chair directing Cunningham and Lewitzky decades earlier). *Trackers* (1991) was the first work he created using *Life Forms*, followed by *Enter* (1992) and *CRWDSPCR* (1993). Copeland asserts that as early as *CRWDSPCR*, "the shapes and rhythms of *Life Forms* wire-frame figures" were directly influencing stage movement.[56] Just as had been the case when time was the driving force of the dancemaking and the slightest change to time affected the shape of the

Merce Cunningham's CRWDSPCR *with Daniel Madoff and Andrea Weber.*

spatial designs, changes in an element like rhythm in *Life Forms* "resulted from manipulating the spatial proportions between shapes."[57]

So, in essence, chance was still a significant element in Cunningham's work at its completion.

The Living Legacy Plan

Just weeks prior to Cunningham's death, the Cunningham Dance Foundation announced plans for the preservation of his work after his death. Development of the plan began in 2000 with the establishment of the Merce Cunningham Trust. Cunningham gave the Trust the rights to his repertory, but remained the sole trustee until his death. In an article in *The New York Times Magazine*, Arthur Lubow illustrated the incredibly complex series of events leading to the Trust's establishment and the development of the Legacy Plan. Informed by issues other dance companies have faced in the wake of the deaths of masters like Balanchine and Graham, and what he encountered himself as the sole heir of his partner Cage's estate, Cunningham eventually decided to make his wishes clear for his work's preservation.[58]

In accordance with the plan, The Merce Cunningham Dance Company began a two-year farewell tour in February 2010 to conclude with a final New York City performance on New Year's Eve 2011. At the terminus of the tour, the Merce Cunningham Dance Company and the Cunningham Foundation would close and transfer all assets to the Trust (including all artwork, production elements, archival materials, and Cunningham's choreographic notes). Additionally, at the time of this writing the Foundation is preparing a collection of "Dance Capsules" designed to preserve as much of Cunningham's work as possible. "These digital packages will assemble in uniform and stable digital form the array of creative elements that comprise each choreographic work, enabling works to be studied and performed in perpetuity with knowledge of how they originally came to life."[59] Performance video, sound recording, lighting plots, decor images, costume designs, and notes (production, rehearsal, and performance) will be included along with additional interview information from dancers and artistic staff.[60] The Plan also provides transition assistance for dancers, musicians, and staff upon the closure of the Company and the Foundation. "In establishing the Trust and endorsing the extinction of the Foundation," Lubow observed, "Cunningham seemed to be creating a structure as intelligent and farsighted as a Cunningham dance."[61]

Merce Cunningham: In the Studio

In his essay *The Function of a Technique for Dance* (1951), Cunningham said, "Technique is the disciplining of one's energies through physical action in order to free that energy at any desired instant in its highest possible physical and spiritual form."[62] Through an evolutionary exploration of movement, Cunningham created a training system that addresses the development of strong, flexible bodies and minds capable of meeting the demands his work exerts on the dancer's entire being. "You have to be alert and focused in class," said Robert Swinston, director of choreography for the Merce Cunningham Dance Company. Students definitely have to come to class with their "thinking caps on."[63]

Cunningham originally began evolving his technique for much the same practical reasons as other choreographers: as he began creating dances on other bodies, he discovered that he "didn't like the way they danced. It was not a kind of dancing that interested me.... In time, I began to teach in order to have dancers trained in the way I thought interesting."[64] In a panel discussion among some of Cunningham's early dancers, Brown recalled Cunningham's investigative process in establishing the technique:

> We have to determine just what vintage of Cunningham technique we are talking about, because the technique itself has changed. It's constantly if subtly changing, depending upon his specific interests at the time. There are basic things that get done generally . . . [but] in the early years . . . he was definitely exploring his technique—keeping things, tossing them out, finding out what worked and what didn't.[65]

Cunningham said that for this process, "You try something out and it does or doesn't work, and finally you keep what works."[66] The things Brown referred to that generally remained in the system were warm-ups for the back and legs, but the order in which those elements appeared in class was explored in the early days. The other element that always remained consistent was Cunningham's commitment to the energy he discussed in *The Function of a Technique for Dance*. Brown noted that, over time,

> Merce has remained devoted to "dance movement"—training the body to move with speed, flexibility, and control; to move with the sustained control of slow motion. . . . This devotion is perhaps most easily defined as a commitment to energy . . . to physical energy, expressed through the body moving (or still) in time and space.[67]

Generally, Cunningham technique is characterized by an upright physicality, a concentrated integration of the back and legs, rhythm, and movement experiences that prepare dancers for the ways time and space are addressed in Cunningham's choreography. Copeland points out that "nothing marks Cunningham's break with Graham and early modern dance quite so dramatically as the emphasis his choreography places on upright posture."[68] The upright nature of Cunningham technique is apparent from the first movements in the class. Unlike Graham before him, who began her class seated on the floor, Cunningham began standing "because that's mostly the way we move. We don't move sitting down much."[69] However, Copeland observed:

> Cunningham's verticality, the importance his technique places on the back rather than the torso, the speed and complexity of his footwork—all of these elements are more than just knee-jerk repudiations of that "love-affair-with-the-floor" which virtually defined modern dance at the time. Graham emphasized the tension between spine and pelvis; but Cunningham emphasizes the verticality of the spine.[70]

Cunningham described the relation between the spine and the legs, which points to the pedagogical ideas at the heart of the physical elements of his training system:

> The first exercises are usually for the back. You see the torso will only work certain ways. It doesn't do much, but you can extend those ways as much as possible. Starting with that idea of the legs and back working together, we alternate: legs firmly held, we work on the back, then we come to the legs and in order to isolate them, I keep the back still and do leg exercises. After that we put the legs and back together.[71]

Correlations are often made between Cunningham and classical ballet technique. Unlike ballet where a barre is employed during the beginning of class, the entire Cunningham class takes place in the center, requiring that "the dancers must learn how to use the back for support"[72] over the span of the entire class, rather than just the last third, as in ballet. Another important distinction from ballet is that Cunningham eliminated *épaulement*, which in turn eliminated the purely frontal orientation of classical ballet—[73] a front related to the audience and the proscenium that had dominated much of concert dance to that point. In Cunningham's work, the sense of front is related to whatever direction the dancer is facing at any given moment. Dancers need to develop an internal sense of direction changes, maintaining an awareness of the self in relation to the space around their own body and throughout the entire stage.

There are eight basic movements identified in the technique: bending, rising, extending, turning, sliding, skimming and brushing, jumping, and falling. In one of the few academic examinations of the technique, my colleague Mary Kate Campbell noted, "The Cunningham technique can be meditative, centering both the mind and the body. It emphasizes efficiency, clarity, strength, resiliency, individuality, rhythm, balance, and centering."[74] Generally, class structure moves from bounces that begin to warm up the back and legs, and to establish the back-leg connection; then rhythmic twists and tilts that emphasize flexibility. Exercises that establish balance and coordination follow. The accumulation of concepts builds to the end of the class, often in "a combination of spatial clarity, as well as a high level of difficulty for coordination, rhythmic challenges, design, and overall physicality."[75] At the end of class, there may be a combination incorporating falls, rising, and partnering.

While he gave workshops and broke down his exercises and explained their relevance and importance, Cunningham allowed his teachers to explore his technique and communicate it in their own way.[76] Mary Lisa Burns, education director at the Merce Cunningham Studio, pointed out that while the Cunningham technique is a progressive system, there is not a prescribed syllabus. "There is a flexibility in the way the technique is taught because it isn't written down—there is a video series available—but the teachers bring their own understanding to the class."[77]

Cunningham's is a "broad vocabulary," noted Swinston. "No one element is more important than another. Dancers have to constantly be aware of change and be ready to move to an unexpected place."[78] Because of the speed of the movement, and the unexpectedness of directional changes, Swinston continued, "There is very little time to think while doing the movement" so remaining observant is critical.[79] Burns said, "Merce encouraged students not to overthink, to not intellectualize, but to fulfill even the simplest movement so that dancing becomes an enlargement of everyday movement in its expansiveness and physical articulation."[80] There are no real preparations in the technique, yet each movement seems to prepare for the next, so that each movement must be equally, fully realized. Weight shifts should be clear, whether they are stable or are moving through space.

Swinston and Burns emphasized the need to leave habits behind when entering a Cunningham class for the first time. For example, while there are similarities to ballet, Cunningham is not ballet. Clarity is critical in the technique, so one of the most important things in approaching the experience is an ability to watch and listen in class, to see the things that aren't familiar. Leaving behind rhythmic habits is also important, because rhythm is a core component of the training, and of the choreography. "There are lots of steps and footwork. We talk a lot about 'frisky feet,'" Swinston noted. "The rhythms in the work aren't tied to musical rhythm, and there may be time changes within a given phrase."[81] Burns stressed the importance of the rhythm being physically clear because in the repertory, dancers "can't count on the sequence of movements to be expected or predictable, and those sequences may change in performance. That means the dancers can't count on a sequence of rhythms either. Movement and rhythm have to happen together in the body. Rhythm is internal, like a collective muscle memory, and the beginnings of that are rooted in the technique class."[82] As Cunningham himself said, "the dancer strives for complete and tempered body-skill, for complete identification with the movement in as devastatingly impersonal a fashion as possible. Not to show off, but to show; not to exhibit, but to transmit the tenderness of the human spirit through the disciplined action of a human body."[83]

Keep Cunningham's eloquent statement above in mind as you move through this encounter with rhythm. The simplicity and clarity of this sequence provide the foundation for a wealth of exploration and the possibilities for adaptation are quite broad—which is a useful lesson for developing choreographers and dance teachers alike. After you have spent time internalizing the accumulated rhythm and the foot pattern, be sure to fully examine each thematic variation. What other variations can you create based on this structure?

Begin with the Rhythm

Contributed by Mary Lisa Burns, Education Director, Merce Cunningham Studio

At a Cunningham Studio faculty meeting, longtime faculty member Meg Harper spoke to Merce, noting his skill in making combinations of movement for class that were both simple yet challenging and interesting. She asked him how he was able to accomplish this. His response was that he always "began with the rhythm."

The phrase described below is an example of this idea. The teacher begins with the rhythmic structure of the entire phrase, which is:

1, 2

1, 2, 3

1, 2, 3, 4

1, 2, 3, 4, 5

The steps are triplets, or versions thereof, which in a Cunningham class are always begun by sliding the heel along the floor prior to the relevé and by moving the body forward (or in whatever direction one is going) to the maximum extent possible. The dancer should also make the difference between the low level (in demi-plié) and the high level (relevé) as physically distinct and large as possible.

Start: In 1st position, facing front.

The steps are:

1: Slide R foot forward to 4th position
2: Close L foot to 1st position facing front

Tiplet front:

1: Slide R foot forward to 4th position
2: Step front L (through 1st to 4th position) on relevé
3: Step front R (through 1st to 4th position) on relevé

1: Slide L foot side to wide 2nd position, both legs in demi-plié
2: Hold
3: Cross R foot front in 5th position, relevé
4: Cross L foot front in 5th position, relevé

1: Slide R foot side to wide 2nd position demi-plié
2: Close L foot to the R foot in 1st position

Triplet front:

3: Slide R foot front, 4th position in demi-plié
4: Step front L (through 1st to 4th position) on relevé
5: Step front R (through 1st to 4th position) on relevé

Repeat entire pattern beginning with the L foot.

This can be varied by changing the torso to add tilts, twist, curve, arch; the whole phrase can be reversed, traveling backward; or changes of direction can be inserted at any point.

Alwin Nikolais (1910–1993) and
Murray Louis (1926–): Biographical Sketch

I do not hesitate to stress a sculptural form to the exclusion of motional excitement. Nor can I divorce myself from strong passions for sound and color, so I invade the fields of the composer and the painter as well. In truth, then, I am not a devoted husband to dance, for I choose to marry the lot of my inamorati rather than swearing fixed fidelity to one. I look upon this polygamy of motion, shape, color, and sound as the basic art of the theatre. To me, the art of drama is one thing; the art of theatre is another. In the latter, a magical panorama of things, sounds, colors, shapes, lights, illusions, and events happens before your eyes and your ears. I find my needs cannot be wholly satisfied by one art. I like to mix my magics.

—Alwin Nikolais, *No Man from Mars*

Murray Louis and Alwin Nikolais.

Murray Louis and Alwin Nikolais contributed much to modern dance through their individual artistic bodies of work. Nikolais received much critical attention during his lifetime (and historical consideration since his death) for his extraordinary achievement of total theater. Louis, too, earned a place in the modern dance cannon for his iconic virtuosity as a performer and the stunning purity of his choreography. Although it was relatively late in their relationship when they combined their individual dance companies, the couple spent much of their five decades together in artistic and educational collaboration. It is the fruits of that collaboration on which this section focuses.

Thus far, the stress has been on a largely American vision of this art form. Nikolais and Louis are the first link in this book to the German lineage in modern dance, as they studied with Hanya Holm. Certainly, there have been other European connections through the early training influences of Dalcroze and Delsarte on American dancers (and Duncan could be added to that list since much of her work and training ideas were generated in Europe). We also know that artists like Dunham were exposed to European ideas through her brief study with Harald Kreutzberg. It was Holm, however, who brought the German tradition to America in a major way. It is appropriate then to turn our attention momentarily to that lineage and give the Nikolais/Louis work the same developmental foundation given to the other artists thus far.

Dance Ancestors: Wigman and Laban

By the 1880s, there was a growing desire to rediscover the philosophies of Greek art (although not its forms) that had been an initial spark for artists like Duncan, and that led to the romanticism at the heart of early expressionist dance in America and parts of Europe. Unlike Duncan, however, the German Expressionists (Mary Wigman, Kurt Jooss, and Harald Kreutzberg) "were trying to devise dance forms to project the feelings arising out of the political and psychic struggle of the time."[84] While Duncan linked the power of motion to the "inner man," her work did not evolve its own form or vocabulary as fully as others who helped to shape the New Dance. In Germany though, ideas about dance would take a dramatically different direction and, by the end of World War I, an incredibly new shape. Mary Wigman revolutionized dance because "she abandoned the conventions of bodily harmony identified with art dancers such as Duncan and instead used distortion and dynamic extremes to awaken audiences to irrevocabilities of life."[85]

She had been a student at Dalcroze's school, the Rhythmische Bildungsanstalt (Rhythmic Educational Institute), where she sought refuge from ballet's "lovely storytelling in pantomime," but soon "felt the heavy shackles that bound the body to obey another art, and often I danced by myself without music. Then I happened to meet Rudolf von Laban, who in those days was the only and great experimenter in the dance."[86] After becoming Laban's student, Wigman eventually proved instrumental in helping her teacher shape much of his notation system. She called Laban the "initiator of the new dance," and said, "[h]e told me once that it was the vision of a great work of art, a combination of dance, music, and poetry, which started him on his way."[87] The problem, though, was that the instrument (a dancer with the proper facility) did not exist in the dancers of the period (at that point, ballet dancers), so Laban had to devise a system to create that dancer. "His gymnastic system, based on the natural organic movement of the human body and the principles of tension and relaxation, was born out his head for a new style of dancing and a new type of dancer."[88]

Wigman held Laban's ideas in such high esteem that she passed many of them on to her own students, even as she made her own tremendous contributions to training, choreography, and performance. Dance critic John Martin wrote, "With Wigman, dance ... touches for the first time in many centuries its common ground with theater."[89] Martin also noted:

> With Wigman the dance stands for the first time fully revealed in its own stature; it is not storytelling, pantomime or moving sculpture or design in space, acrobatic virtuosity or musical illustration, but dance alone, an autonomous art exemplifying fully the ideas of modernism in its attainment of abstraction and in its utilization of the resources of its materials efficiently and with authority.[90]

It was this already highly developed approach to dance that Alwin Nikolais inherited here in the United States when he began studying dance with two of Wigman's students.

Early in Nikolais' life, he began musical training in piano and organ, which eventually led to a job accompanying silent films—where he developed his vast skill in improvisation. When he encountered Wigman on her 1934 American tour, he was "profoundly impressed" and "Wigman's presence, choreography, and, most of all, the percussion accompaniment stimulated and challenged his imagination."[91] Following the concert, he made contact with Wigman's former dancer Truda Kaschmann, expressing interest in studying percussion. Kaschmann insisted that in order to learn the percussion accompaniment for dance, he must learn dance as well to fully understand what he would be doing with the percussion work. In short order, Nikolais had immersed himself in a world of music, drama, dance, and eventually puppetry (having taken on the role of directing Hartford, Connecticut's marionette theater). "This early training prepared him for his later multimedia excursions."[92] Nikolais received his first commission to create a modern dance piece in 1939, earning him a warm reception—and although he had started a dance company and school, his work was put on hold while he served in the army during World War II. When he was discharged, he began concentrated study with Hanya Holm, whom he had met in 1937 at Bennington College.

Teacher: Hanya Holm

Holm, one of Wigman's closet associates and lifelong friend, came to America in 1931 to establish a New York branch of Wigman's school. She, like her mentor, had received a eurythmics teaching certificate from Dalcroze's institute, but neither of them envisioned a lifetime of teaching his methods. Where Wigman had worked with Laban, Holm would later work with Joseph Pilates (and elements of his method can be seen in her floor barre). "Wigman's relationship to Laban had resulted in bitter competition at times, but Wigman and Holm developed a relationship marked by intense collaboration and friendship."[93] After arriving here, Holm quickly established herself as one of the leading modern dance artists in America. By 1936, concern was mounting in New York, however, regarding the Nazis' appropriation of Wigman's dance, and Holm was forced to rename the New York Wigman School of Dance the Hanya Holm Studio.[94] A few short years after Nikolais began his concentrated study with Holm, she recommended him for the directorship of the Henry Street Playhouse in New York. A year later, Nikolais and Murray Louis met and began their own lifelong collaboration.

Although Louis grew up in an orphanage, he had access to wonderful cultural outlets: the orphanage's substantial library provided a rich education in itself; his sisters often took him to museums, the Works Progress Administration's theater and dance programs, and to films. Although he saw modern dance companies at the time, his earliest influence was Fred Astaire—Louis often won talent shows, incorporating what he learned from watching Astaire, into his own dance improvisations. After a brief period in the navy during World War II, Louis began studying dance at San Francisco State College, then moved on to train briefly with Anna Halprin. In 1949, on his way to New York, Louis enrolled in Holm's Colorado Springs summer program. Since Holm had been delayed getting to Colorado, Nikolais taught the first two weeks of the program, and it was just enough time for Nikolais and Louis to establish their relationship. At the end of the session, Nikolais invited Louis to join him in New York and help him at the Henry Street Playhouse:

> For the first five years (1949–1954), the work at the Playhouse was arduous and often grueling. But the vision that lay ahead was so bright and promising that the labor to physically restore the building and develop a school, which peaked at five hundred students both young and professional, was its own reward.[95]

Nikolais' Background

When Nikolais began his dance company, it was called Playhouse Dance Company but was renamed Alwin Nikolais Dance Company in 1961, becoming Alwin Nikolais Dance Theatre in 1967, and finally for the start of the 1970 season, simply Nikolais Dance Theatre. With his broad artistic background, Nikolais forged a body of choreography that at once rankled and inspired both critics and audiences. His artistic "roots are reflected in his dances. In them the accoutrements of the theater—lights, props, costumes, sets—are so thoroughly integrated with the movement that the visual result is indeed kinetic art. His dances used mixed media before the term was invented."[96] Nikolais placed this integration of motion and media above psychodrama and narrative in his work. He was interested in motion, rather than movement, and he made the dancers components of the larger framework of a piece, rather than its central focal point.

> The new dance figure is significant more in its instrumental sensitivity and capacity to speak directly in terms of motion, shape, time, and space. . . . The choreographer of the new period of the modern dance is concerned with basic and legitimate elements, and is imbued with the urgency of pursuing the fleeting banshee of the moment of art according to the dictates of his individual vision.[97]

He said that, "Movement implies the displacement of matter. Motion implies the manner in which the action occurs. In this way, like music . . . the object is not the indiscriminate arrival of the first note, but the sense of the stuff as it transpires and culminates toward an end."[98] As a result of the attention to motion, decentralization, shape, and space, some dance scholars suggested a connection between Nikolais' work and that of Bauhaus theater director Oskar Schlemmer's excursions into choreography. According to Suzanne Lahusen, "Nikolais' main concern, however, has not been primarily with spatial aspects [as Schlemmer's was], but rather with the effects obtained by the media of film, costume, props and sound. Whereas Schlemmer was interested in the function of objects, Nikolais' aim [was] to create a 'theatre of illusion.'"[99]

The component clearly missing from Lahusen's list of Nikolais' interests is lighting, which was central to that illusion and was the unifying factor of many of his dances: "Unlike many other dance events in which setting is background for choreography, Nikolais dancers are immediately involved in a visual matrix. The relationship of dance motion to the total environment is established largely through the use of light."[100] In 1956, Nikolais was already experimenting with the use of light. In *Prism*, the lighting was as highly choreographed as the motion and was so integral to the work that the dance cannot be performed without it. By 1965, *Galaxy* employed black light in addition to conventional stage light and in *Vaudeville of the Elements*, the dancers both wore and carried lights on stage as part of their motional work—Nikolais himself had to design the lanterns used in the work, as no appropriate item was available on the market. With 1967's *Somniloquy*, Nikolais introduced the use of specially crafted slides projected onto both the stage and the dancers—an innovation that would become central to later works. That same drive for innovation led Nikolais to compose music and create sound scores for his dances (a recording of his music/sound work was released in 1993), to design costumes and puppets/ props, and to embrace new technologies as they developed. As early as 1959, he was making dance for television—a medium he clearly loved, making televised works for stations in eight countries.

Cultural Awareness

It should also be noted that, while Nikolais rejected narrative per se, his work was not devoid of social commentary. In 1977's *Guignol*, for example, he "commented on social relationships, violence, sexuality, self-deception, suspended disbelief, and confusion . . . we see Nikolais using puppet imagery to expose cultural distress. He ridiculed heterosexual hegemony and blind pleasure-seeking; and he exposed sadistic delight in a population numb to violence."[101] Of his decentralization idea, Nikolais said:

> Unfettering dance from its centralization not only allowed the smallest kernel of force to appear at any point in or on the body, it could also cause a force to arise from any source in the space surrounding the body. It was not a matter of eliminating the center but of relocating it to other parts of the body or other points in space. When one is released from centralization, one becomes more completely aware of an infinite environment."[102]

That statement helps us to understand the placement of the human in Nikolais' work. Rather than serving to dehumanize—as his critics asserted—it gives us a much larger framework in which to see the human self.

Murray Louis as Nik's Vessel

"Murray Louis was really Nik's vessel," noted Kim Gibilisco, former member of Murray Louis and Nikolais Dance and current lecturer for Mason Gross School of the Arts at Rutgers University and artistic director of Kim Gibilisco Dances. "At that time in dance, men didn't have Murray's facility. There may have been a sixteen-year difference in their ages, but Murray understood Nik from the beginning."[103] She also commented that as a result, the creation of the technique was a mutual project—as much as Murray was vital as the lead in many of Nikolais' dances, his own growing facility helped them both to discover what was possible within their shared technical philosophy.

Although Nikolais frequently receives more critical attention than his partner, Louis' contributions to dance are no less significant—either artistically or intellectually. Just a few short years after beginning work at the Playhouse and performing in Nikolais' dances, Louis began making his own dances with the premiere of *Journal* in 1957 He established Murray Louis Dance

Nikolais's Kaleidoscope.

Company in 1957, and within the decade, his work had gained such international respect that it became necessary for him to leave Nikolais' company. Over the years, his company toured all fifty states and five continents—the company was chosen for a 1968 U.S. State Department tour to India, among other honors. Critical recognition has followed many of his works, such as *Calligraph for Martyrs* (1961), *Facets* (1962), *Hoopla* (1972), *Four Brubeck Pieces* (1984), and *Sinners All* (1996). He has worked with and made pieces for major individual dancers and dance companies—of note are his tour with Rudolf Nureyev, and his dance *Isle* (2001) made for the José Limón Dance Company.

Louis also became highly respected as a teacher. In the early 1970s, he released a five-part video series, *Dance As an Art Form*, that immediately became a staple for university dance programs and civic libraries nationwide. Roughly at the same time, he instituted what became the Artist-in-Schools program. As a dance writer, Louis contributed numerous essays to *Dance Magazine*, which led to two collections of his writing: *Inside Dance* and *On Dance*. Other videos have followed, as well as numerous productions for television programming around the world. Louis' intellectual contributions to the arts in America were recognized when he was invited to participate in the 1997–1998 Phi Beta Kappa Visiting Scholars program.

The greatest strength of the Nikolais/Louis technique (from a choreographer's perspective) is likely the dramatically different choreographic choices it affords a dancemaker, as is evidenced in its progenitors' bodies of work. Both men were able to create an incredible range of work for their individual companies. Nikolais' own *Tensile Involvement* (1953) with its set created from stagewide elastic bands and attention to angles and straight lines could not be more different from *Blank on Blank* (1987), which is devoid of set pieces, but which borders on virtuosic gymnastics. Similarly, Louis used the powerbase in the technique to send dancers bounding through space with animalistic agility in *Figura* (1978), but had tapped the technique's grace and fluidity in *Proximities* (1969). When the two choreographers merged their companies in the early 1990s, audiences were exposed to vastly different, although quite complimentary, visions of our collective environment (the combined repertory comprised 250-plus dances). While the company was disbanded in 1999, the Ririe-Woodbury Dance Company now performs selections from Nikolais' repertory, and numerous other companies and university programs perform the works of both dancemakers the world over.

Alwin Nikolais and Murray Louis: In the Studio

The Nikolais/Louis technique is "really grounded in a philosophy that teaches the dancer to take control of the body. It gives us tools to develop as artists, and isn't just about creating a 'look' in the dancer's body," said Alberto del Saz, co-director of The Nikolais/Louis Foundation for Dance.[104] The technique was designed to create

Alberto del Saz teaching a master class at Shenandoah University.

individual dancers and choreographers, not copies of a rigid, singular approach. . . . Although it is called the Nikolais/Louis technique, it should be thought of as a basic technique, one that is applicable to any dance form. . . . [It] covers four areas with which dancers should be familiar because they relates to all facets of the profession: technical training, improvisation, choreography, and performance.[105]

Thus, the training emphasizes both the physical work of preparing the body for motion and the creative work of artist (and teacher).

Certain elements common to ballet and other modern systems were absent in Nikolais and Louis' classes: there were no mirrors on the walls, no accompanist (both Nikolais and Louis played drums in class, as had Holm and Laban before them, in order to avoid emotion overlaid on the motion), and traveling across the floor occurred in patterns that destabilized frontal facing, requiring students to focus on the action of dance rather than a superimposed egocentric presentation.[106] According to del Saz, "Nik's work is about the abstract, and how the dance and motion become one. That gets us to the idea of decentralization, and the removal of ego so we can get to that purity of motion. But that's not dehumanizing. You as the dancer are the movement without the ego."[107] Gibilisco agrees:

> The technique is meant to develop a sensitive human being. Nik and Murray wanted dancers to draw from their experiences and encounters with great art. When we were on tour, Murray used to plan stops in our itineraries so we could see an amazing cathedral in Greece, or visit the Hearst Castle. Then, when we were back in New York, he'd sit us down to discuss what we saw. Murray also reads with a voracious appetite. He would trade books with dancers on tour. Students should definitely look at lots of other art. They should develop their own appreciation for music, theater, and art.[108]

The four pillars of the technique are shape, space, time, and motion. Other fundamental ideas in the technique are decentralization, grain, gravity and verticality, movement range (locomotor, flexion and extension, peripheral action, rotary), and the three conditions of energy (tension, relaxation, and release), among others. In the broader context of the Nikolais/Louis body of work, decentralization is a complex consideration. For present purposes, in a technique class experience, decentralization seeks to "contrive methods of releasing the body from the limiting vortex of the ego, the self. . . . [It] releases the central ego's hold and allows the body and mind to freely shift the focus and movement center to any point in the body or surrounding space."[109] That decentralization "and the removal of ego help us reach a purity of movement. But, that's not dehumanizing. You as the dancer are the movement without the ego."[110] *Grain* is a critical element in that decentralization, as it colors and highlights direction through internal fluidity instead of rigidity, where a concentrated focus is employed. According to Nikolais, "When we speak of grain in wood, we refer to the various channels of force that visibly show the linear life direction of the wood's fiber. The human body can also produce directional grain, but in a much more complex way. By accentuating direction, grain adds aesthetic colorations to kinetics. Without grain, motion is somewhat bland."[111] A natural duality exists for the human body in motion—in the case of dance, this is expressed in the polarity of gravity and verticality. The physics of life in this dimension employs the immutable force of gravity, and for the dancer, that means a constant exertion of will in order to rise above that gravitational force. It is with the addition of movement range and the three conditions of energy (not to mention pedestrian movement in the class) to decentralization and grain that this training method comes into focus as a precursor to early postmodernism.

PRACTICAL LESSON PLAN

In the technique, as Nikolais and Louis taught it, a lesson plan always guided the classroom experience, spanning a twenty-five-week period. "When I was going through the school, you really had to commit to the movement for at least a semester. You were there at least six hours a day for six months in daily technique classes, improv, and composition classes. We also had music and percussion lessons and lighting classes,"[112] del Saz said. The technique class itself was two hours, five days a week. Del Saz went on to say:

> The warmup is set, but there is a different emphasis each week. For example, even though you are doing the same series of movements [in the warm-up], one week you might be looking at the impact of gravity as it plays out in the movement phrases. The next week, the concentration might be on finding a deeper understanding of abstraction within the same movements. . . . This work clarifies the intention—each step has intention and purpose. *Dancers have to develop that idea in their body and make decisions about what they bring to the movement.* The beauty for me as a teacher is to see that happening. Technique is beyond a series of steps. It's about moving toward performance. It's about how dancers, who by nature are quite pedestrian, bring artistry and sophistication to those steps in order to create that performance.[113]

The warm-up incorporated ideas that stem from Wigman's own *Gymnastic* training, which Holm modified and refined upon arriving in America. As Nikolais and Louis further refined and expanded the system, "gymnastic elements remained as the warm-up became streamlined and more extreme in its demands for unrestrained motional responsiveness. Careful attention to joints and muscles in the first exercises gave way to whorls of swings, rolls, coils, and stretches."[114] Elements of the floor barre contain clear relationships with Pilates (via Holm) and yoga, illustrating that bricolage (a conflation in the use of the body of disparate forms, such as bharata natyam and modern dance; also called "fusion") was occurring before the concept became popular in the post-Judson era. (For more information on somatic work, see Appendix C.) After the warm-up, the class plan was composed of three basic components: technique across the floor, improvisation, and composition. All of these directly flowed from the premise of the week's class plan. In addition to preparing the dancer for performance, the clear class outlines used in the Nikolais/Louis tradition served to introduce dance teachers to building their own dance classes in progression from a daily class lesson through an entire semester's syllabus.

"Generally, the instructor begins class with a locomotor pattern including directions and turns at a pulse that can be doubled or slowed. A simple way to begin a class is with a basic floor pattern. Then add the premise of the day to this form."[115] Varying the type of locomotion (walk, run, jump, etc.), changing levels, adding turns, and metric changes are just a few of the basic building blocks for the progress of a class.

For the purpose of this experience, we are working with ideas drawn from Week 14: SHAPE in the Nikolais/Louis lesson plan series.[116]

It will be helpful for both the instructor and the students in the class to maintain a keen spatial awareness during this experience. As dancers move across the floor, it is important to keep clear lines so that the design intention in each dancing body remains sharp. During the group improvisation work, each dancer should be aware of the positive and negative space around his or her own body, and how the body and its shape(s) fit into the larger picture being created. With regard to shape-oriented improvisations, Louis noted in his film *Dance As an Art Form* that the dancer is "called upon now to extend himself into a larger concept. The dancer must have the skill to sense sculptural design."[117]

SHAPE[i]

Introduction

Of all the principles of dance, shape is the easiest and most rewarding to explore. First, it is the most visible principle, and second, the body need not transform itself physically into something other than what it is, unless we extend it with other properties. Shaping varies considerably from amusing to disturbing and most of the time the principle of shape is rewarding in its creative presentation. Although shape may appear simple, we must deal with it imaginatively and clearly because it has the dancer's physical and pedestrian habits and mannerisms to contend with and overcome.

Shape is specific. What you see is what you get; therefore, the dancer needs a keen inner eye to recognize what the viewer is seeing. This is where the dancer's skill in conceptualizing what he looks like comes into play, when the ability to deal with

the many parts of the body at the same time becomes important. Designing where a toe and the shoulders might relate or how the placement of the head and the left knee are to look is intrinsic to sensing the totality of a shape.

In designing and performing shape, the ability to focus and to adjust a shape demands an internal eye to pull the entire body into focus like a camera lens. This focus is achieved by the body's sense of consonance: the desire to seek a totality or balance of design. When the dancer achieves this shape, he achieves this consonance and the shape will speak for itself. Once a shape is determined, then the ability to determine its mobility into another shape or into locomotion becomes its next challenge.

Shape awareness is an aesthetic skill. Designing three-dimensional forms with the body is another sensitivity. Developing the mobility of shapes is still another achievement.

Technique

Premise

- Learn to shape and sculpt the body inventively. Move shapes effectively.

- Imbue the center of the shape with an energy that radiates outward, enlivening the entire form. This involves using principles of decentralization.

- Shape the entire body. Use total body consciousness. Grain the body to its totality.

Monday

- Start with a simple locomotor floor pattern.

- Set a shape (dancers can set their own) and carry it across the floor. Let the shape influence the nature of the locomotion.

---

[i] This lesson plan is from Week 14: SHAPE in *The Nikolais/Louis Dance Technique: A Philosophy and Method of Modern Dance* by Alwin Nikolais and Murray Louis, 2005.

- Start with just arm variations to determine the shape. Then add chest and hips. Combine them.
- Change shapes every four counts.
- Change the shape from slow to fast as you move across the floor.
- Generate energy out from center to enliven the shape.
- Develop shape phrase with under- and over curves, and other locomotions.

Tuesday
- Develop shape phrases with levels, hops, turns, and so on. Shape is a totality, not a singular isolation of a body part. Shape speaks of itself.
- Shape is a total body involvement. Let shape influence the locomotion.
- A close tight shape won't have a large loose walk, change shape during patterns like run, run, leap. Let the shape dictate the time and space and motional quality necessary for it to achieve itself.

Wednesday
- Constant shape awareness during a lyric nonstop phase. Check for smooth transitions.
- The speed should be slow enough that you can see the shapes evolve. Dancers create their own phrases across the floor. Dancers begin after every twelve counts.

Thursday
- Contrasts: shape the space around you with volumes, then change to concentration on sculptural body shapes. Go from outside around the body to the total body itself.

- Call attention to a single body part, then change to the attention of the whole body.
- Let locomotion vary with every body change.

Friday
- Create a shape phrase using everything but always calling attention to the total body's shape.
- Do not move too fast or we shall see the movement.
- Small-based precariously balanced shapes have a more kinetic sensation than wide-based shapes.
- Releves and balances for kinetics.
- Stabiles have a large and secure base on the floor, like sitting or lying on the floor.
- Motional illumination of the form from the inside radiating out.
- Shape is torso-generated and three-dimensional. Design is peripheral.

Improvisation

Select the week's improvisations from this list of suggestions. Get rid of baggy or torso-obscuring clothing.

Divide the class in halves. Create four shapes. Evolve a transition between the shapes. Evolve a locomotion as transition, clearly arriving at each of the four shapes. Repeat the whole phrase three times, changing the time values of each variation.

Half of class at a time: group moves to general drumbeat. Drum slows when the dancers begin to arrive in a finale shape. Teacher directs: "Adjust the shape and bring it into focus and now enliven it from the inside." Counts 1 – 2 – 3 – 4 – Hold. The rest of the class watches this process to see the subtleties of correction. Like through a camera lens, the shape becomes clearer and focused. Repeat process and adjust new shape.

- Students pair off; one of each pair physically forms the other one into a series of shapes.

- Create three different shape transitions. I want you now to go from shape to shape, without any pausing at all. So, in effect, you are going through millions of shapes.

- Get in threes. The first person assumes a shape; the second tries to duplicate it exactly; the third makes corrections, trade roles.

- Get in twos. Improvise moving in relation to each other sculpturally; keep the sense of shape and don't let it get motional. Think, one body shape plus one body shape equals three, a new body shape. The dancers should sense the third shape they are making all the time.

- Walking: In groups, walk first with awareness and change of shape, then walk plainly. Alternate.

- Walk four counts, hit shape on fourth count. Repeat.

- Walk four counts with four different shapes. Repeat, changing shape order.

- Walk with a partner, sculpturally relating to each other.

- Walk four counts; add four shapes turning.

Free improvising in groups of four to six. Sense how to sculpturally relate to create an aesthetic totality. It seems this ability of sensing consonance is inherent in humans. Give this improvisation four or five minutes for each group. End it with "Bring to an end" and let the group sense the ending without sound accompaniment. This improvisation has almost never failed to produce some of the most memorable and successful studies.

Composition

A shape dance. Let us see the vividness of your shapes and the manner of the evolution and locomotion. Concentrate on calling attention to the entire physical form. You can either move evolving sculpturally or dart from shape to shape. This change of speed will contribute to the kinetic effect.

Play a two-way role: there is a shape-taker you, and a choreographer you. The first performs and the second watches. Develop in your mind's eye the skill to see what people will be looking at in your shapes. Make sure the vitality goes through all the extremities.

You can shape space, you can shape time, you can shape motion. But we're shaping the body's shape, which means we're shaping bulk. When you use what you feel is a distorted or ugly shape, don't think of it as distasteful, but fulfill it as you would any shape. Bring it to life as a total. By doing so, it will find its consonance and reveal the intrinsic beauty of whatever form it takes.

Sense how you look and pause when you've arrived at an interesting shape. When something handsome happens, pause. It takes time for shape to register, and it also helps you to know what wants to develop from it. You are not dealing with what the shape represents, but enlivening the shape itself. You're performers! Be concerned with shape. The message exists in the shape, so dig into that shape! Release its potency.

Final Questions

1. The artists in this chapter removed the concept of meaning from their choreography. They worked toward choreographic ideas that were nonrepresentational, nonliteral, and based solely on an idea for movement. How have those ideas informed your aesthetics? In what ways have your perceptions changed regarding content in dance?

2. Describe how your physical understandings of rhythm and time have changed based on this idea that dance and music don't have to be intricately tied to one another.

3. What is your perception of yourself in relationship to your gender? How does that identity influence your work in the dance studio/on stage, in the classroom, on the sports field, or out in public?

Works Cited

Anderson, J. (1992). *Ballet and Modern Dance: A concise history*. Princeton, NJ: Princeton Book Company.

Barnes, C. (1967, December 3). Genius on the Wrong Coast. *Los Angeles Herald Examiner*.

_____. (1991, July). Martha's dance immortal. *Dance Magazine*, p. 98.

_____. (1993, March). Cunningham and Tharp—originals. *Dance Magazine*, p. 122.

Blofeld, J. (1968). *I Ching (The Book of Change)*. New York: E. P. Dutton & Company, Inc.

Bodley, J. H. (1994). *Cultural Anthropology: Tribes, states and the global system*. Mountain View, CA: Mayfield Publishing Company.

Brooks, W. (1993). John Cage and History: "Hymns and variation." *Perspectives of New Music*, 31 (2), pp. 74–104.

Brown, C. (1986). In J. Klosty (Ed.), *Merce Cunningham* (pp. 19–31). New York: Limelight Editions.

_____. (2007). *Chance and Circumstance: Twenty years with Cage and Cunningham*. New York: Alfred A. Knopf.

Brown, C. et al. (1987). Cunningham and His Dancers. *Ballet Review*, 15 (3), pp. 19–40.

Brown, J. M. (1979). *The Vision of Modern Dance*. Princeton, NJ: Princeton Book Company.

Burns, M. L. (2009, June 16). Mary Lisa Burns on Cunningham Techinque. Interview by J. Legg.

Burt, R. (1995). *The Male Dancer: Bodies, spectacle, sexualities*. New York: Routledge.

Campbell, M. K. (2004, April 27). *A Pedagogical Study of the Merce Cunningham Dance Technique*. Winchester, VA: Shenandoah University.

Carbonneau, S. (2008, February 22). *Paul Taylor*. [Lecture]. Cambridge, MA: Harvard Dance Center, Harvard University.

Copeland, R. (1999). Cunningham, Collage, and the Computer. *PAJ: A Journal of Performance and Art*, 21 (3), pp. 42–54.

_____. (2004). *Merce Cunningham: The modernizing of modern dance*. New York: Routledge.

Cunningham, M. (1970). Choreography and the Dance. In S. Rosener & L. E. Abt (Eds.), *The Creative Experience*. New York: Grossman.

_____. (1985). *The Dancer and the Dance*. (J. Lesschaeve, Ed.) New York: Marion Books.

_____. (1992). Space, Time and Dance. In R. Kostelantez (Ed.), *Merce Cunningham: Dancing in space and time*. Pennington, NJ: a cappella books.

_____. (1997). The Function of a Technique for Dance. In D. Vaughan (Ed.), *Merce Cunningham: Fifty years* (p. 60). New York: Aperture.

_____. (1999). Choreography and the Dance. In G. Celant (Ed.), *Merce Cunningham* (pp. 42–49). Milano: Edizioni Charta.

DeFrantz, T. (2001). Simmering Passivity: The black male body in concert dance. In A. Dils and A. Cooper Albright (Eds). *Moving History/Dancing Cultures: A dance history reader*. (pp. 342–349). Madison: University of Wisconsin Press.

_____. (2004). *Dancing Revelations: Alvin Ailey's Embodiment of African American Culture*. New York: Oxford University Press.

del Saz, A. (2009, February 26). Nikolais/Louis Technique. Interview by J. Legg.

Dunn, D. (1986). In J. Klosty (Ed.), *Merce Cunningham* (p. 39). New York: Limelight Editions.

Foulkes, J. L. (2002). *Modern Bodies: Dance and American moderism from Martha Graham to Alvin Ailey*. Chapel Hill, NC: University of North Carolina Press.

Gibilisco, K. (2009, May 7). Nikolais/Louis Technique. Interview by J. Legg.

Gilbert, P. (1993). John Cage. *Dance Magazine*, 67 (3), pp. 46–48.

Gitelman, C. (2001, Spring). The Puppet Theater of Alwin Nikolais. *Ballet Review*, 29 (1), pp. 84–91.

_____. (2003). *Liebe Hanya: Mary Wigman's letters to Hanya Holm*. Madison: University of Wisconsin Press.

_____. (2007). Sense Your Mass Increasing with Your Velocity: Alwin Nikolais' pedagogy of unified decentralization. In C. Gitelman & R. Martin (Eds.), *The Returns of Alwin Nikolais: Bodies, boundaries and the dance canon* (pp. 26–45). Middletown, CT: Wesleyan University Press.

Hamm, C. (1980). John Cage. In *The New Grove Dictionary of Music and Musicians* (pp. 597–603). Washington: Grove's Dictionaries of Music, Inc.

Hanna, J. L. (1988). *Dance, Sex and Gender: Signs of identity, dominance, defiance, and desire*. Chicago: University of Chicago Press.

Hodgins, P. (1992). *Relationships Between Score and Choreography in Twentieth-Century Dance*. Lewiston, NY: Edwin Mellen Press.

Lahusen, S. (1986, Autumn). Oskar Schlemmer: Mechanical ballets. *Dance Research: The Journal of the Society for Dance Research*, 4 (2), pp. 65–77.

Lamhut, P. (n.d.). New and Uncharted Directions. *Alwin Nikolais' Henry Street Playhouse Legacy*. New York.

Legg, J. (2006, December 1). Cunningham Technique. *Dance Spirit*, pp. 96–98.

Louis, M. (1973). Film. *Dance as an Art Form*. Chimera Foundation for Dance, Inc.: New York.

Lubow, A. (2009, November 8). "Can Modern Dance Be Preserved?" *The New York Times Magazine*, pp. 38–43.

Martin, J. (1965). *Introduction to the Dance*. New York: Dance Horizons.

Martin, L. (1994, Spring). Black Mountain College and Merce Cunningham in the Fifties: New Perspectives. *Dance Research Journal*, Vol. 26, No. 1, pp. 46-48.

Martin, R. (2007). Nikolais Returns. In C. Gitelman & R. Martin, *The Returns of Alwin Nikolais: Bodies, boundaries and the dance canon* (pp. 1–25). Middletown, CT: Wesleyan University Press.

Merce Cunningham Dance Company (2010). *Merce Cunningham Dance Company: Dance Capsules*. Accessed May 9, 2010 from Merce Cunningham Dance Company: http://www.merce.org.

Mazo, J. (1977). *Prime Movers: The makers of modern dance in America*, 2nd Ed. Hightstown, NJ: Princeton Book Company.

Morris, G. (2006). *A Game for Dancers: Performing modernism in the postwar years, 1945–1960*. Middletown, CT: Wesleyan University Press.

Mumma, G. (1999). Electronic Music for the Merce Cunningham Dance Company. In G. Celant (Ed.), *Merce Cunningham* (pp. 202–206). Milano: Edizioni Charta.

Nickolich, B. E. (1973, June). The Nikolais Dance Theater's Uses of Light. *The Drama Review*, 17 (2), pp. 80–91.

Nikolais, A. (1965). No Man from Mars. In S. J. Cohen, *The Modern Dance: Seven statements of belief* (pp. 63–76). Middletown, CT: Wesleyan University Press.

Nikolais, A. & Louis, M. (2005). *The Nikolais/Louis Dance Technique*. New York: Routledge.

Richards, S. (1992, October 1). John Cage: 1912–1992. *Rolling Stone*, 23 (640), p. 21.

Rogosin, E. (1980). *The Dance Makers: Conversations with American choreographers*. New York: Walker and Company.

Sheets-Johnstone, M. (1966). *The Phenomenology of Dance*. London: Dance Books Ltd.

Siegel, M. B. (1985). *The Shapes of Change: Images of American dance*. Berkeley: University of California Press.

_____. (1993). *Days on Earth: The dance of Doris Humphrey*. Durham, NC: Duke University Press.

_____. (2007). Artisans of Space. In C. Gitelman & R. Martin (Eds.), *The Returns of Alwin Nikolais: Bodies, boundaries and the dance canon* (pp. 53–63). Middletown, CT: Wesleyan University Press.

Sorell, W. (1975). *The Mary Wigman Book*. Middletown, CT: Wesleyan University Press.

Stratyner, B. N. (1982). *Biographical Dictionary of Dance*. New York: Schirmer Books.

Swed, M. (1993, Summer). John Cage: September 5, 1912–August 12, 1992. *Musical Quarterly*, Vol. 77, No. 1, p. 132–144.

Swinston, R. (2009, June 18). Robert Swinston on Cunningham Technique. Interview by J. Legg.

Terry, W. (1956). *The Dance in America*. New York: Harper and Brothers Publishers.

Towers, D. (1984, February 1). Cunningham Dance Technique: Elementary level. *Dance Magazine*, 60 (2), pp. 82–83.

Vaughan, D. (1995). Merce Cunningham's "The Seasons." *Dance Chronicle*, 18 (2), 311–318.

Warren, L. (1977). *Lester Horton: Modern dance pioneer*. New York: Marcel Dekker.

CHAPTER 6

Transition to Postmodernism

Paul Taylor

Modern dance technique is often enshrouded in the myth of an individual creator, whose urge to be free of convention gives rise to new expressive forms. This trope of freedom through self-transformation is at the root of the claim that modern dance is one of the few distinctly "American" art forms . . . the establishment of modern dance is treated as evidence of the belated emergence of an authentic American character. The distinctiveness of modern dance from other dance forms can therefore come to stand for the freedom of Americans more broadly, a name for a national universal that grants equality as a birthright.

— Randy Martin, *Critical Moves*

In the history of concert dance, there are few clear moments of *diakritikos*—moments that tell us precisely that things have changed and that we no longer live in the same art form that we did yesterday. Much of the revolution of this art form was a process, and as was indicated in the introduction of this book, progressive development discourages attempts to say definitively that "on this date" we left one era and entered the next. After all, there are few moments in the general history of concert dance that speak as loudly as did the premiere of Nijinsky's *Rite of*

Paul Taylor's House of Cards *with Ruth Andrien, Christopher Gillis and Daniel Ezralow, 1981.*

Spring (1913). While he worked in the ballet idiom, there can be little doubt that Nijinsky found inspiration in the growing ideas of modernism in the arts (just as Balanchine would later). At the time, not only was Nijinsky highlighting ballet's sixth position (parallel) in *Rite*, but he also had already used two-dimensional movement in *Afternoon of a Faun* (1912). With *Rite*, Nijinsky also eschewed a certain amount of the geometrical stage space common in ballet at the time, and he also became one of the first major choreographers to use eurythmics in devising his dance material. Nijinsky's ideas though were infamously too radical for the times, and earned him riotous scorn.

More than forty years later, in 1957—the same year *West Side Story* and *On the Road* made headlines—George Balanchine produced *Agon*, the pinnacle of modern ballet,[1] while simultaneously Paul Taylor foretold the end of the modernist era in dance when he presented *7 New Dances*.

Let us consider the state of the union during the 1950s in order to place coming dance events in sociopolitical perspective. Post–World War II America was a nation trying to avoid the great strife and turmoil that was clearly on the horizon. Americans had been living under the excesses of McCarthyism since the late 1940s, and had supported United Nations efforts in the Korean War from 1950 to 1953. At the same time, tensions were mounting as the nation began to confront racism head-on. The civil rights movement gained its first major victory with the original desegregation decision in the United States Supreme Court's 1954 ruling in *Brown v. the Board of Education of Topeka, Kansas*. Finally, too, the threat of nuclear war was increasingly ever present in those years.

Rather than explore hyper-emotional responses to their national circumstances at this time (which might have been an understandable reaction), the avant-garde choreographers of the late modern period (and avant-garde artists in general) seemed to be reaching for greater rationality in their work as they retreated from controversial subjects and pressed for heightened clarity in abstractionism. As we saw in Chapter 5, it was an era marked by inquiry, innovation, and experimentation. We will see in this chapter that the epitome of experimentation occurred in 1957, and that the zenith of abstractionism arrived in 1962. Paul Taylor engineered both of those events, and also served as the conduit between the modernists who came before him and the Judsonists who followed.

On the structure and presentation of this chapter

This chapter marks a series of turning points in our story—a story that could now be considered a biography of modern dance techniques. The first turning point results from artistic changes already alluded to in the preceding paragraphs. The second regards the fact that Paul Taylor did not create a training methodology to prepare dancers for his work. There is no singular, codified Taylor technique, no syllabus. In fact, Taylor was not particularly interested in teaching at all. So, why include Taylor in this discussion?

Although Taylor did not establish a system, dancers have long found inspiration and ideation from training in the Taylor style(s). Members of Taylor's company have found their own ways of addressing technique classes, often employing ideas from his dances to prepare themselves, and students, for the work of dance. That brings us to the third turning point.

We will look at Paul Taylor's life and work as we did with the choreographers introduced thus far. After the biographical look at Taylor and his repertory, we will shift to a conversation with Ruth Andrien, director of Taylor 2. Andrien received critical acclaim as an artist in Taylor's works, has earned international respect as a répétiteur of his dances, and has spent much of the last two decades training dancers with a pedagogy inspired by the Taylor repertory. Because of the breadth of my discussion with Andrien, this material is presented in a journalistic interview format. Components of this interview span nearly three years of talks that I have had with Andrien, beginning when I served as her teaching assistant at Harvard University.

Core Ideas

Observations and Experiments

Journal I: Find a spot where you might be able to observe people's honest emotional reactions to a situation. Choose a place where the people are likely to have their guard down and are allowing themselves to react spontaneously. For example, you might watch the fans at a sporting event. Take note of how elation, anger, frustration, or anticipation affects any of the following: gesture, weight shift, the design of shapes in the body. Notice the difference in energy and sense of body weight if a fan stands up from his seat in frustration or in elation. Shift your attention to the athletes and try to isolate your observation in two ways. First, look for the same characteristics you did in the spectators while the team is between plays. Notice the difference between the energy and gesture of a runner on second base and that of the player who covers third base.

Second, look at the honesty and integrity of their labor (the real work of the sport, such as pitching or batting in baseball, blocking or punching in boxing).

Observe the range of energy exerted based on what you think the desired outcome was: the pitcher looking for a strike and the throw of an outfielder who just stopped a potential home run with a catch. Other examples of interesting places for this observation are a restaurant, a city street, and weddings. Ultimately, you are looking for moments that are honest reactions to a situation that could also read as a person dancing at the same time.

Journal II: Observe nature. In this observation, you are looking for form and power, and for facile bodies in moments of explosive motion. Study the ocean; the wind, from subtle breeze to thrashing violence. Watch the motion of animals. Look for the difference in weight shifts as the animal takes off in full sprint or propels itself leaping through the air. What is natural has profound organic qualities. Look for the dualities of thrust and retreat. Pay attention to rhythm and balance as well. Now, turn your attention again to athletes. See if the sense of weight shift, power/ force, and rhythm is similar or different in a runner exploding out of the starting block, a swimmer diving into the water for a race, a diver on the ten-meter platform, and a dog, racehorse, or large predatory cat hurtling forward at full speed and force.

Experiment I: Find two pieces of art: one that is abstract and one that deals with some kind of content. These might be paintings, sculptures, or photographs. Isolate an element of each piece and create one short dance phrase for each element. Keep the phrases brief, perhaps 64 counts or less. Prepare to perform them individually in a set structure (not an improv). Also prepare to perform them in a linked or integrated manner. (The order and organization of the latter sequence is up to the dancer.) Make a few notes about the original pieces *after* you have created your phrases. Don't think so much about *why* you originally picked that painting or photograph to work from. The "why" isn't as important as the "what" in this experiment. What you did with the information you saw in the art, and the choices you made in crafting your short phrases are more important than the meaning you may have interpreted in the original artworks.

Experiment II: Stop at five different locations, and select two gestures that you observe people doing at each, paying attention to the energy, honesty, and intent in each gesture. Later, in the studio, try the ten gestures you accumulated and cut them down to your five favorites. Pick gestures that are not commonly connected and that demonstrate a range of intentions, emotions, and goals. Create a phrase with your found movements so that (part a) the original introduction to the gestures incorporates stillness between each gesture and you may also use connecting movements between them, (part b) do the gestures using level changes, (part c) move as fast as possible through the series of gestures without stopping and without adding additional connecting movements, and finally (part d) construct a pattern based on your own sequencing ideas. Weave the sequence together in such a way that you can present the material as though playing a character in a dance. Try to create meaning out of this sequence. Keep in mind, though, that meaning does not require storyline. Make some notes about what you found about your own movement affinities in the choices you made regarding the gestures, the structure of the phrase, and your characterization.

· ·

Technical Genesis

Paul Taylor (1930–): Biographical Sketch

I get my energy I think from being afraid—being afraid to choreograph, being afraid to fail—because pieces turn out OK, and others stink. On the other hand, it's what I do. I probably couldn't do any other kind of job.

— Paul Taylor, *Paul Taylor: Dancemaker*

Paul Taylor is at once the ultimate avant-garde artist, and the defender of the American ideal of individual liberty. His story is one of dichotomy: creator of the quintessential abstract dance of the 1960s, and the blue-collar, working-class man ready to expose society's darkest secrets even as he celebrates humanity's most glorious qualities. Dance critic Deborah Jowitt noted, "He can make dances that are so beautiful in which the people all seem blessed like spirits in some kind of Eden —like *Aureole* (1962) or *Airs* (1978)—and then he can make dances that scare the daylights out of you like *Last Look* (1985)."[2] Fellow critic Marcia Siegel observed, "Paul Taylor is one of the most perplexing figures in modern dance. His work can be artful or instinctive, lyrical, funny, grotesque, or demonic—sometimes in the same dance."[3] Despite his openness about feeling vulnerable when it comes time to make a new piece, he does not seem to shy away from blazing a trail in whatever direction might interest him, and that directness has often isolated him from his contemporaries. The isolation, however, certainly had its rewards as indicated in dance critic Edwin Denby's observation that Taylor "is the first New York choreographer since Robbins who has taken the trouble to teach himself the continuous clarity of a well-made ballet."[4]

Paul Taylor, 1960.

Born in 1930, Taylor grew up largely in and near Washington, DC. His parents were divorced when he was a small child, and as a result, Taylor's early life was often desolate. As a single parent, his mother was forced to work long hours and to relocate her children many times. At one point, Taylor was sent to live on a farm in Bethesda, Maryland, in a foster-like situation with a couple for whom he developed a clear affection. The Buttses were a source of stability—if momentarily—and Mr. Butts seems to have been something of a surrogate father, since his own was largely absent. Taylor later learned that the situation had been one of financial benefit to the Buttses:

> Although missing the Buttses, I make no effort to stay in touch. I've found out that Mother was paying them to have me live at their farm, and since I'd thought they had taken me in to help with the chores, maybe even because they had become fond of me, I'm too disappointed and embarrassed to visit. It isn't easy to accept the fact that affection sometimes needs to be arranged for with hard cash.[5]

As a dancer and choreographer, Taylor has long been noted for exceptional, virtuosic athleticism—a trait he began to develop on his boarding school's football team. Then, as a freshman art student at Syracuse, he joined the swim team. Where he had found being a right tackle in football easy—"All you have to do is push on whoever's in front of you,"[6]—he found swimming more demanding:

> [I was] being trained for freestyle sprints as well as the longer distances; and to build strength and endurance, laps, starts, and flip turns are practiced for four or more hours a day.... I didn't know it then, but the swimming made a good introduction to the equally, if not more, demanding discipline of a dancer's never-ending training. The meets weren't unlike stage performances in that they called for delivery of goods at set and unavoidable times, and they also caused opening-night jitters.[7]

Although Taylor mentions in his autobiography that he was not certain early on what sparked his interest, he realized during his sophomore year that he was destined to dance. His first classes occurred at a summer dance school in Bar Harbor, Maine, and later, on the advice of Bessie Schönberg, he prepared to transfer to Juilliard. His initial immersion in dance began the summer following his departure from Syracuse at the American Dance Festival (then held at Connecticut College). Three daily classes in Graham technique as well as composition classes with Horst and Humphrey rounded out the training there. Even before that summer was completed, he had received offers from Graham and Limón to join their companies.

In his early years in New York, Taylor danced for Pearl Lang, Merce Cunningham, Jerome Robbins, and, of course, Graham. Almost from his arrival in New York, though, he started experimenting with his own dancemaking. Taylor's first choreographic work presented before an audience was *Jack and the Beanstalk* (1954). While no one in the audience applauded, there were no boos either. Taylor said, "This was not surprising to me, as I had assumed that the dance was neither good nor bad."[8] Such a noncommittal response would not, however, be the standard reaction to a Taylor concert for long.

Paul Taylor: In the Studio

Over the years, critics have tried diligently to pigeonhole or categorize Taylor's style(s), often focusing on the dark/light duality that frames large portions of his work. Dance scholar Angela Kane, presently director of dance at the University of Michigan, noted, however, that

> because Taylor's choreography is so diverse, any categorization of it can only be made according to certain types of works and/or certain patterns of progression. It is impossible to pigeonhole either his style overall or any one of his dances because his choreography presents multiple possibilities —sometimes even within a single work.[9]

Working from that clear perspective, Taylor's repertory may be viewed as multifaceted. It may also be viewed as fluid and mutable even as it is crystalline in its ability to shed insight on vastly diverse aspects of the human experience.

The repertory has been complex almost from the beginning: "In *3 Epitaphs* (1956), the larger idea seems to be the contrast between our poor, miserable, primitive apelike selves and that struggle to be human, to hold our backs up straight—and the spurts of energy and failure of being upright."[10] Robert Rauschenberg's costumes for *3 Epitaphs* included an abstract head covering that masked the face of the dancers, giving them an other-than-human appearance, highlighting the struggle in the choreography Taylor mentioned above. "Martha Graham had come to see it," Taylor recalled, "and she got me aside afterwards and she said, 'Naughty boy, we don't cover up their faces.'"[11] Taylor, however, was already eschewing the inner landscape of the human psyche so critical in Graham's work. Avant-garde artists like Rauschenberg and Jasper Johns provided a rich source of inspiration for the young dancemaker. Experimentation, abstractionism, and nonlinear narrative quickly became hallmarks of his repertory, as would a willingness to make bold, unexpected— and sometimes, unwelcomed—choices.

Furor

After attending Taylor's first evening-length concert, *7 New Dances* (1957), dance critic Walter Terry wrote:

> To disturb an audience, as I noted in these columns last week, is a perfectly valid function of the theatre. I did not, however, suggest the creator-

performer attempt to drive his captive audience insane. Paul Taylor, who presented a program called 7 *New Dances* (there were seven items, they were new but they weren't dances) last Sunday . . . seemed determined to drive his viewers right out of their minds (or out of the theatre). Before cracking up completely, several persons left but I managed to stick it out for five of the seven numbers.[12]

Louis Horst, too, in his *Dance Observer* review, made his feeling about the concert plain: four column inches of blank white space signed with his initials. It would seem that Taylor had raised questions in crafting the evening-long suite that his audience, and the critics, were not prepared to encounter, despite the seeming innocence of the queries. As Taylor went into the eight-month creative process for the concert, he examined his prior works, "and when I try to analyze what I've done, several confusing questions arise . . . what is dance in the first place? Could it be anything?"[13] He also looked to the work of other choreographers for leads, but found none that were particularly interesting to him, so he

decided to start over from scratch. Some kind of building blocks were needed, some clearly defined ABCs that could be ordered into a structure that would be antipersonality, unpyschological (no Greek goddesses), would achieve a specific effect (no Merce dice decisions), and would have a style free from the cobwebs of time (no ballet). So it is easy enough to know what not to do, and since it seems unlikely to find a solution in other people's work, I go out and look around in the streets.[14]

In his quest, Taylor began working with "found objects" as the "movement consisted of ordinary, pedestrian movement. I thought this was such a wonderful idea, to show people in the street walking, or running, or chasing a bus, or lying down drunk. Anything. You know, if you looked at it fresh, it was beautiful."[15] He noted that in the rehearsal process, the highly trained artists had to unlearn dancerly habits because

the natural movements, when done in a dancy way, look unnatural, and so we have to find a new, yet equally stylized, way to do them. We memorized vast amounts of uneven counts in order to give rhythmic variety and to keep from falling into monotony. . . . We find that each posture tends to get blurred when executed consecutively, and so it's necessary to surround each with stillness. The sequences take little physical exertion, making it impossible to rely on muscle memories, and are difficult to remember.[16]

Linda Hodes and Paul Taylor in his Insects and Heroes, *1961.*

7 New Dances then was a suite pared of dancerly movement, and sequenced by postures rather than steps, all accented by stillness—in fact, the stillness in the section titled *Duet* lasted exactly four minutes as Taylor stood near a seated Toby Glanternik, both motionless. In a lecture at Harvard University, Suzanne Carbonneau, professor of Performance at George Mason University, pointed out the conceptualism in the concert. She noted the distinction in his work from that of Cunningham, who "never rejected a highly specialized movement vocabulary" as Taylor had by using pure pedestrian movement delineated by stillness.[17] Carbonneau talked about the radical experimentation of the avant-garde artists: Cage's controversial composition *4' 33"* and Robert Rauschenberg's white-on-white paintings. Based on his inquiry, the nature and structuring of the material, and the stripping away of traditional virtuosic technique, it is difficult to simply label the suite as avant-garde experimentation. While Judson dancers would not ring in postmodernism in dance for five more years, Taylor had telegraphed the pending transition in dance. He was a soothsayer, standing in that moment as the singular early postmodernist.

Despite severe spectator and critical reaction to *7 New Dances*, the work did not spell the choreographer's downfall, as *Rite* almost had for Nijinsky four decades earlier. Instead, Taylor seemed to take the reaction in stride (at least eventually), and searched for new discoveries in his approach to composition. This constant quest led to an early, uncanny ability to develop strikingly unique dances that bore almost no resemblance to one another.

Aureole

Dance writers Allen Hughes and Angela Kane have both presented illustrations of this diversity in comparing *Junction* (1961), in which Taylor developed a choreographic tool he called "scribbling"; *Aureole* (1962), with its formal, lyric abstractionism; *Piece Period* (1962), which revealed his masterful humor; and *Scudorama* (1963), which as Kane stated "confirmed his interest in probing difficult subject matter—most particularly amoral behavior and social malaise—through non-linear, often multi-layered, narratives."[18] While each of these works is critical, let us focus on a standard-bearer of the Taylor canon: *Aureole*. In 1962, dance critic Walter Sorell wrote of Taylor,

> In my eyes, Paul Taylor is the prototype of the American dancer-choreographer. He has an athletic body—it is one of lyric masculinity—and a straightforward mind. You will rarely meet him without noticing an ironic twinkle in his eye . . . [he] is very much like a picture postcard image of everything American, outgoing in his conceits, in wit, and phrasing.[19]

Jowitt recalled that the first time she saw *Aureole*, "I'd never seen a man that large move so fluidly. The solo is like water . . . there are no positions."[20] Siegel noted that *Aureole* was one of the first dances I ever saw being born—I watched its first technical rehearsal. . . . Not until I was able to study a work film made of it that first summer did I realize its compositional depth and ingenuity. . . . Aureole is one of the most balanced yet off-balanced dances imaginable.[21]

The work, in all its beauty, stunned the avant-garde dance world at the time. Set to a Baroque score by George Frederick Handel, *Aureole* dared to be musical in its rhythmic structure—so much so that we see the musical rhythm not only when dancers are traveling through space, but often when they stand in place as well, the pulse maintained in the dancers' backs. That musicality, the formal Apollonian quality, and the balletic lyricism seemed an apostasy from Taylor's avant-garde foundation. It was dramatically different, certainly, from any component of 7 *New Dances*. It did, however, take the avant-garde's greatest ideal, abstractionism, to its pinnacle.[22] Siegel observed:

> *Aureole* has five main sections, but the dance is so constructed as to blur the divisions between them. In fact, many of the traditional ways of ordering a dance to help the audience find its way are disrupted. . . . Dances begin unexpectedly and end before they seem over: some dances seem almost to sneak into action; others begin importantly, only to go into suspension while something else takes over. All these devices work toward deemphasizing the individual dancer or part of the dance, throwing the audience's attention on the dance as a whole.[23]

The dance can be read, then, as a dance between centralization and decentralization of space, and of the dancing body. By working solidly in musical time and with musical rhythm in the work, Taylor further blurs our perceptions of those shifting emphatics. Finally, where *Aureole* is one of Taylor's light dances—even providing its own connection to the sun—it has a watery quality as well (recall Jowitt's comment about Taylor's fluidity). Carbonneau relates the sense of weight in the work to swimming and the gravity of water.[24]

Dance observers have long referred to Taylor's days as a swimmer and his athletic virtuosity as a significant factor in his performance and as an influence on his dancemaking. What does that mean? Well, as a dancer who is also a lifelong swimmer, I posit this: swimming can be treated as a somatic form for dancers. (See Appendix C for more on somatics.) The full set of stroke styles in competitive swimming are core-based, ballistic, full-bodied movement. You simply cannot swim with any degree of efficiency (or grace) without using the power of the core to initiate movement. As you work to streamline (decrease resistance) and "align your body and limbs to reduce the resistance of oncoming water throughout the stroke cycle,"[25] you are also lengthening the spine and striving for a balanced rotation between the sides of the body. (That sense of balance can be achieved only with deep core integrity.) At the same time, you strive for the longest stroke cycle possible. I propose that this attention to the core, spine length, and rotation, combined with the Graham spiral and Cunningham twists Taylor experienced in working with those choreographers, had a tremendous influence on his use of the back. It is likely, too, that the freestyle stroke was so mapped into his muscle memory that it made arm circles a natural movement affinity for his body, thus a frequent element in his choreography. All of this can be seen in the duration of the solo Taylor created for himself in *Aureole*.

Other Dances

At the time *Aureole* premiered, Lillian Moore said in her review for the *New York Herald Tribune*, "Taylor has at last created a work which gives full play to his fantastic virtuosity."[26] Then, just a year later in his review of *Scudorama* for *The New York Times* Allen Hughes stated, "Sometime in the past few years, perhaps while we were looking and not comprehending, Paul Taylor ceased being a promising choreographer and became a mature one."[27] Certainly a far cry from the critical response to *7 New Dances* six years earlier. The ride though, was just beginning.

From the abstractionist, Apollonian splendor of 1962, he has constantly shown audiences new aspects of himself at every turn, and revealed much about who we are in the process. *Churchyard* (1969) looked at "the horror and anguish of death that stalked the middle ages under the mask of the plague and all the disease that flesh is heir to."[28] Under the guise of a carnival setting for *Big Bertha* (1970), Taylor revealed society's moral decay by stripping bare a family's middle class veneer, exposing the incest and drug use destroying their world. Returning to his 1957 pre-Judson idea for creating dance strictly from pedestrian movement, Taylor's *Esplanade* (1975) invests tremendous virtuosity in the performance this time around—revealing, as critic Arlene Croce noted, that "[h]is invention, his gift for sheer rhythmic propulsion [had] never been more exciting."[29] Much later in his repertory, he returned again to the pedestrian, in *Eventide* (1997), this time building lyricism from patterns of couples walking. A decade later, Taylor would create another powerfully virtuosic work woven by gesture, *Lines of Loss* (2007)—an elegy created after the death of his lifelong partner. Numerous other dances stand out through the years: *Runes* (1975), *Cloven Kingdom* (1976), *Polaris* (1976), *Airs* (1978), *Le Sacre du Printemps (The Rehearsal)* (1980), *Musical Offering* (1986), *Speaking in Tongues* (1988), *Piazzolla Caldera* (1997), *Promethean Fire* (2002), *Le Grand Puppetier* (2004), *Banquet of Vultures* (2005), *De Sueños Que Se Repiten (Of Recurring Dreams)* (2007), and *Brief Encounters* (2009) are just a small selection of works that together demonstrate the vastness of Taylor's versatility.

Although Taylor had to stop dancing in 1973 owing to poor health, in 2011, at eighty-one, he is still making dances, still leading audiences into new worlds, and to the extent that the avant-garde exists he remains its standard-bearer. This from a man who once said of himself, "I came from a family that really wasn't terribly cultured, and I wasn't brought up in classical music. I can't read music—I've never bothered to learn. I'm a hick, basically, and proud of it."[30] It is this duality in Taylor that makes him an everyman . . . complete with all the complexities that implies.

Because Taylor's repertory is so extensive and spans such broad spectrums/categories in style, formalism, abstractionism, content, and extreme athleticism, those who approach teaching a Taylor-based system have their work cut out for them. In addition to preparing the body for the work of dance, class must also lead students to develop the magical, primal power of dance. In a lecture-demonstration that concluded the course Ruth Andrien taught at Harvard University in 2008—the first credit-course in the country to address Taylor's work—she noted that Taylor referred to a dancer's magical passion as "zunch." According to Andrien, Taylor said:

> Zunch is the quality that sets the adequate dancer apart from the exciting one. Zunch is fullness. It is being generous with your spirit. It is the magic that sticks with the audience after the dance is done. The dancer starts a circuit flowing, a kind of St. Elmo's fire, that radiates around the dancer, the defined space and the audience. Not technique, physical beauty, choreography, or anything short of zunch will click this circuit on.[31]

Ruth Andrien on Technique: An Interview

Joshua Legg: What observations can students bring from the mundane world into their first Taylor experience to enhance their understanding of the material?

Ruth Andrien: I love that you used the word *mundane.* Paul has a saying, "Beauty is all around us, just open your eyes." Most of us walk around in a mechanical stupor half the time, but when we really look, we can find meaning in the most common things. Paul's movement ideas come from nature, the animal kingdom, and human history with everyday bits and pieces thrown into the mix. He can turn a storm into a dance or study the sideways movement of a crab to create vocabulary. In the end, the rhythm, design, and energy of his movement forms and the content of his dance themes become a launching pad for dancers' imaginations. The mystery completes itself there. I love what Guy Davenport said in his book *The Geography of the Imagination: Forty Essays,* "The imagination is like a drunk man who has lost his keys and must get drunk again to find them." Each dancer must find confidence to work in that way.

JL: Unlike other dancemakers in this book, Paul Taylor was always intent on not making a technique. Former company members, however, have been quite successful in extrapolating technical ideas from his choreography in order to teach technique classes. Why wasn't Paul interested in creating his own technique? Also, even though he did not develop a technique, he did design three exercises that are still passed along. How did those exercises come about?

RA: Paul doesn't like two things: being pigeonholed or cloning himself. The fact is, he actually has created a technique but it's one that shall remain nameless. It is open for discussion, a work in progress, yet to be determined. However, you could describe it by what it's not: gratuitous arabesques, upper-crust affectations, ramrod verticality, or lackluster physicality.

As for the exercises, Paul had to create a lecture-demonstration for the modern dance touring program back in the 1960s. So his three exercises, the (drum roll) Back Exercise, the Arm Exercise, and the *Party Mix* Exercise were created to school the uninitiated in the ways of modern dance, seen through his eyes. I heard it this way: one day Bettie de Jong was warming up with some back movements and Paul saw her and said, "Everybody do like Bettie." The Arm Exercise is a series of arm swinging movements and under- and overcurve "S" movements for the back that came from *Aureole*. The *Party Mix* Exercise is from that work, which uses a two-dimensional movement vocabulary.

JL: I have been trying to differentiate the developmental processes that led to the establishment of the training systems in this book. I refer to the act of drawing training ideas from a body of choreography as retrogenerating a technique—extrapolating ideas from existing dances. It's sort of like reverse engineering. To a large extent, that was Graham's process for making her technique. Hawkins, in turn, worked on training ideas first, then started making dances with those theories in a creative context. Were you informed by anyone else's process for developing a training system?

RA: As a child I studied with an unforgettable teacher named Phyllis Dersh in Pottstown, Pennsylvania. Miss Dersh taught good behavior, Cecchetti technique, Horton technique, Labanotation, and improvisation. She was influenced by Antony Tudor, and also by the New Dance Group's approach to dance training, which emphasized the simultaneous development of technique and creativity. She believed in teaching the whole person—body, mind, and spirit— and that stays with me to this day. But yes, Paul's dances are what stimulate my teaching ideas.

One day when I shared them with Paul, he said, "Those are very beautiful ideas but they are yours and not mine, so believe in them, Ruthie." I spoke about emphasizing an undertow kind of polarity in the movement, building volume from the ground up, sensing energy or shape extending through space beyond one's body, and developing characterization by using images to help dancers visualize things never seen or experienced directly. Paul was interested in what I was saying but in his typical anti-authoritarian style, he cut the ribbon. He does not need to control how his work gets out there, as long as it's good. I guess you could call it good parenting, and he's especially proud when his dancers go on to choreograph, like David Parsons, Lila York, Karla Wolfangle, Patrick Corbin, Hernando Cortez, or Takehiro Ueyama.

Paul had to turn away from Martha Graham to find his way and expects others would do the same. Choreographers do teach and teachers do choreograph, but they are distinctly different drives and teaching turns more toward past experience than away. Experience becomes a creative platform, so I guess you could say I definitely fall in the retrogenerative category. That sounds so passé, but rebirthing dances produces similar labor pains and the rewards are delivery on everyone's part.

JL: How did you derive a successful training method from a style?

RA: After twenty-five years of teaching, I'm still not sure I have developed a successful training method, although I know I can teach people how to dance. Correct warmups are still a mystery to me. In any case, I began developing my class by borrowing a ballet format—plié, tendu, all the way through movements across the floor—while adding less tidy stylistic elements and gestures from Paul's choreography.

Of course, I use ideas from my good old-fashioned "modern" dance training—moving from the back, contract, release, lateral, falling off balance, and so forth. I studied Horton and Graham at the Ailey School in the 1970s, but my dancing was really forged by emulating Paul and the completely unique dancers in his early company, Bettie de Jong, Carolyn Adams, Eileen Cropley, and Nicholas Gunn. When I joined the company in 1974, you could even feel the spirit bodies of dancers like Liz Walton, Danny Grossman, Sharon Kinney, and Dan Wagoner, who were gone by that time. The Taylor technique is really a kind of stone soup in that way, because of Paul's ability to glean the corporeality of each beloved dancer. Most of my class material, though, comes from deconstructing the repertory. Each dance is like a magic carpet that takes the dancers to lands unknown.

JL: Tell me a little about your process for extrapolating ideas from Paul's choreography that went into the structure of your method. How did you analyze dances and decide, "Okay, this is an element of a particular dance I need to address in class"? How did you make those choices? How much of your ideation came from your own awareness as an artist living inside Paul's dances and how much came from staging his work on professional and student dancers? Did seeing non-Taylor dancers try to approach his work make you realize that certain ideas and information should be emphasized?

RA: The process of teaching is both intuitive and analytical. I plan my classes as a way of making room for spontaneity. There is so much material to be rifled: flat movement, round movement, angular movement, body designs, and spatial patterns that can be put into motion. Each dance has its own language, but there are also certain ABCs that are in most of the dances, ways of contracting or falling or turning or gesturing that are stylistically connected. They occur and reoccur, they stimulate variations or departures. It's a natural progression.

Yes, staging the works made it necessary to articulate these ideas because a dance can be so off that it's an aberration. It's not possible to have an *Esplanade* danced like *Swan Lake*, so the work of

Ruth Andrien's class at the American Dance Festival, 2009.

translation and inspiration begins. It's very exciting, working with ballet dancers especially. They are so grateful for artistic input, especially the corps members whom we usually love because they are the workhorses of any company.

JL: So far, we haven't really talked about the tremendous demand in Paul's repertory for dancers to be versatile. There aren't simply extreme ranges in character that must be approached, but extreme variation in stylistic material. How does one prepare a pedagogy that encompasses that complexity?

RA: Each dance has a signature vocabulary as well as a mood or atmosphere that charge the imagination. I revisit the pieces and create phrases or studies that bring the dances to mind. Dancers love to be challenged to go beyond technique to find expressive opportunities, and Paul's dances are layered with these. The dances are rich with puppet images, goddess or fool, wicked or Apollonian characterizations, classic forms and fractured forms. It's all right there. I try to construct a class that has integrity as a whole, like the dances, with a beginning, middle, and end.

JL: Has your work in developing a teaching method based on Paul's work enhanced your artistic understanding of the rep? Does it help you as you stage the rep on professional or student dancers?

RA: Yes, because deconstructing dances to teach them breaks them down into fathomable pieces, so I learned that anything could be understood with enough explanation. As a whole, dances are more of a mystery, but they are made tangible through the bricks and mortar of their construction —contraction 1, chassé 2, conniption 3, wait for the group to pass 4—these are elements that are arranged in a very particular fashion. The how and why of movement comes from the dancers and their intuition for bringing meaning to the movement.

I would say as well that dancing these dances has enhanced my understanding of teaching. They resonate inside anyone who has danced them and they inspire me to tell their stories.

JL: You mentioned earlier that Paul's work eschews ramrod verticality and lackluster physicality. I think about dances like *Aureole* (1962), *Private Domain* (1969), *Le Sacre du Printemps* (1980), *Arden Court* (1981), *Last Look* (1985), *Banquet of Vultures* (2005), *Lines of Loss* (2007), and *Brief Encounters* (2009). They all call to mind the psycho-emotional and physical risk in Paul's work. The movement is so off-balanced and demands such extreme athleticism that in the process, the dancers seem stripped bare of defenses and are left vulnerable, raw, exposed. How does your approach to training address that spectrum of risk in terms of your class material?

RA: Dancers offset the physical risk themselves by breaking down accumulated toxins and correcting alignment issues before they even get to class. They pay what little money they have to massage therapists, nutritionists, chiropractors, acupuncturists, ballet, yoga or Pilates teachers, you name it. In my classes, I try to have them break a sweat during the warm-up section of class, which we gradually lengthen to be about twenty minutes of nonstop movement to build endurance. Risky things like falls can be slowed way down to show how to fold the body softly to the floor, to avoid bruising or banging. I always hope to minimize any danger, but a great deal of the risk is ultimately diminished by the dancers' total commitment.

The body organizes in that way, from the psyche to the action, and it protects the dancer because of the organic connection between emotion and movement. For example, a whipping thrash is a reaction from a state of mind, and your body unconsciously anticipates the suddenness. I guess you could say dance shares some technical characteristics with Method acting but extended even deeper into the body and more subliminally directed.

About the psycho-emotional risk, that's a loaded issue. At times the dances ask too much of the dancer. This is when something remarkable happens, usually brought on by physical exhaustion. Dancers will produce something outside their conscious mind at that point, and go one toke [or inch] over the line. As a choreographer, Paul is a Pied Piper to be sure. But the children don't disappear into the mountain; they transform, so he's a bit of Merlin as well. I've heard Paul refer to dance as a kind of alchemy and he attributes that elemental shift to dancers' courage, loyalty, and imagination. He calls it talent. I always encourage dancers in my teaching, but they usually come with a predisposition for enchantment from childhood. Otherwise, they'd be computer technicians. They do that too, but as a backup for their dream schemes.

JL: Even though in your new role as director of Taylor 2 you don't have to teach a company class, how do you talk about technical ideas with the dancers as they approach learning new elements in the rep?

RA: Technique is an interesting word. I emphasize the special quality that a movement can have, its undeniable essence. I use metaphor shamelessly to encourage dancers to use their unique sensibilities to animate the movement with spirit, intellect, psyche—whatever they can muster that brings the dance to life. Sometimes we study the original cast on film or DVD to find the range of interpretation. Then we choose the most powerful performance and work from there. Dancers are inherently selective and recognize what they can use from past performances to launch their own performance. A dance can be both interpretive and unadulterated at the same time. Dancers make the truest choices they can.

JL: I think it's clear how the structure of your class reflects the sense of classicism found in many of Paul's dances, but you also talk about Paul as the father of postmodern dance. How does your class structure and material then reflect the postmodern elements of his work? For example, how do you approach the pedestrian in class or Paul's concept of "scribbling"?

RA: Paul has his postmodern instincts but without any agreed-upon formula whatsoever. In his works, the postmodern sense of rupturing conformist ideas happens more thematically than through a simplistic obsession with nonconformity. Suzanne Carbonneau speaks of this in her lecture on Paul's iconoclasm. She speaks of his use of Mozartean forms, or *claritas* [clearness to the mind, clarity], to describe moral order and his contrasting impulse to expose the gaps. My class material draws on a palette of symmetry and balance of forms in a similar way, to offset what is chaotic and Dionysian in my own self. Because the framework of pedestrian movement is throughout Paul's work in its use of gesture and locomotion, it's embedded in my class as well, but I don't tend to undress the movement in a postmodern sense. I'm mostly interested in the ritual and theatricality of movement.

Paul's use of scribbling is more of a choreographic approach for movement invention. He takes a series of skeletal shapes and whips through them to tease the eye. It's a great technique for improvisation, very whimsical.

JL: In addition to straightforward technique, I know you also incorporate other processes in your classes that help students to explore creative ideas. Tell me more about your scaffolding idea.

RA: This idea came to me while teaching at the American Dance Festival, where improvisation is a critical part of the dance training. I think of scaffolding as a way of using an existing dance as a supportive framework for movement exploration. In moving from emulation toward innovation, fixed points like a single movement or phrase could be used as themes either to vary or to destabilize and cast off. I believe that no choreography is so fixed as to deny the interpreter her own story. However, scaffolding, by using fixed points as a way to discover if forms themselves inhibit or inspire creative response, may open the possibilities between artists at opposite ends of the traditional dance/improvisational dance spectrum.

Take a dance and break it down to its fixed elements. Look at a variety of categories—theme may be a point of departure, the spatial patterns of how the dancer/dancers move from one formation to another, the defining shapes or how the choreography is counted. Decipher the elements and use one or more as a template to piece together your own movement. Challenge yourself to stay within the framework and work through the snags. You can decide to vary the course when you hit an impasse by inserting a new structural element, like putting a patch on a quilt. But, primarily work from the scaffold of the material.

PRACTICAL LESSON PLAN

Exploring Taylor Through Scaffolding

When Andrien was preparing to teach her course on Taylor at Harvard University, she walked me through a breakdown of how she would approach the technique, introduce the repertory the students would learn, address the discussion components of the course, and plan the final project/presentation. She also mentioned that she was considering an improvisational component, and began to talk about her idea of scaffolding. It struck a chord for me as a way to introduce improv while also helping the dancers to analyze the technical and choreographic devises in a specific dance. I saw it as a way to lead the student deeper into an encounter with an artist's work. As an artist, too, I was reminded of the process Limón had used in creating *A Choreographic Offering* based on Humphrey's dances.

I was inspired to try the scaffolding idea myself during the semester when Andrien began teaching Carolyn Adams' solo from Taylor's *Runes*. The section seemed perfect for this—it was captivating, rhythmically dynamic, and technically clear. What began as an improv evolved into a new piece of choreography that I staged on a colleague that semester. The experiment was so successful that Andrien has suggested I use it as an example for this experience. To that end, two approaches to scaffolding are presented below. The first is an introduction to the concept using an etude I created for the experiment. The second example is based on the process I used in examining the *Runes* solo. (*Runes* is available on video from the *Dance in America* series.)

SCAFFOLDING EXPLORATION I

We'll begin with a concrete example of the idea. Below is a phrase that can be repeated left and right. The phrase can be performed as a slow, sustained 3 or a quicker, staccato 5. Learn both variations of the phrase, and when you are comfortable, try the scaffolding adaptations. (Note that the material here is written for the 3/4 variation.)

Timing: 3/4 metre

Start: 5th position, R foot front, en face, arms in bras bas. Lightly accent each downbeat, and suspend the 2, 3.

Part 1

[cts. 1–3] R arm circles down and across the L side of your body, arcs up overhead, and back down the R side; the upper back may arch slightly through the circle.

[cts. 1–3] The back spirals, bringing the chest to the downstage R corner, causing the L foot to tendu to the downstage L corner, in an undercurve the arms scoop into a half-moon (but imagine you are holding the volume of the entire moon), the head looks L.

[cts. 1–3] Rotate back to en face as the L foot closes front 5th, demi-plié, arms inverting the half-moon then closing to bras bas as you straighten the knees.

[cts. 1–3] The back spirals, bringing the chest to the downstage L corner, causing the R foot to tendu to the downstage R corner, in an undercurve the arms scoop into a half-moon (but imagine you are holding the volume of the entire moon), the head looks R.

[cts. 1–3] Rotate back to en face as the R foot closes back 5th, demi-plié, arms inverting the half-moon then closing to bras bas as you straighten the knees.

Repeat, starting with L arm circle. L foot closes back following last tendu.

Part 2

[cts. 1–3] Spiral to the R as before, tendu L with the half-moon arms.

[cts. 1–3] Step on the L foot into a lunge, and spiral the back around so that the R hand is now on the same downstage L diagonal as the L foot (your back will be visible in the mirror).

[cts. 1–3] A slight contraction draws the R foot into 5th position to the back, the torso returns en face with the arms in bras bas, and the head is down.

[cts. 1–3] Relevé 5th sous-sus, head and arms shoot heavenward, wrists flex and fingertips point out to the sides.

[cts. 1–3] Demi-plié, arms to bras bas, straighten the knees.

Part 3

[cts. 1–3] L foot steps into relevé in 2nd, arms raise into a V with wrists and fingertips lengthened this time, palms facing outward.

[cts. 1–3] Grand plié in 2nd, break at the elbows and wrists so that the fingertips meet and touch the crown of the head, palms heavenward.

[cts. 1–3] Return to relevé in 2nd with arms in the V.

[cts. 1–3] Demi-plié as the arms circle out and down to bras bas.

[cts. 1–3] Rotate to the L, transferring the weight to the L foot as the R leg raises to arabesque with arms in 1st arabesque.

[5 threes] Using the back to initiate your movement, promenade L bringing the arms through

1st to 5th, and folding the R leg into attitude. Finish facing en face, R foot in passé.

[cts. 1–3] Rotate the back so that the torso faces downstage R diagonal, opening the arms to a V, développé the R leg forward to corner.

[cts. 1–3] Fondu on the L leg.

[cts. 1–3] Piqué on the R foot, L leg to low arabesque, arms remain in V.

[cts. 1–3] Close relevé 5th L foot front as you return en face, arms in V.

[cts. 1–3] Demi-plié and straighten.

Repeat parts 2 and 3 starting R.

Assignment 1: What are the primary thematic elements in the phrase? The obvious element is shape: the half-moon and V arms are common in the Taylor style(s). The use of the back is also Tayloresque in the way the back motivates movement. Decide if you want to work in the 3/4 or a 5/4 sequence, and then pick either 3 or 5 gestures that are driven by the back. You will insert these gestures at least twice into the basic phrase. The first time, strike a pose with your gestures on ct. 1, hold it cts. 2–3, so that there is stillness between each gesture. (Remember Taylor's work in *7 New Dances*?) The second time, strike the pose on ct. 1, then find a way to locomote on cts. 2–3. You might also insert the gestures another time so that you cycle through them quickly on cts. 1–3, breaking up the sustained pattern in a surprising way.

Assignment 2: The original sequence does not employ the full spectrum of levels. Without adding any additional steps or counts, increase the range of levels. Find a way to take a movement into the air and to the floor.

SCAFFOLDING EXPLORATION II—TAYLOR'S *RUNES*

In working with Carolyn Adams' solo, I began by learning the piece. (Even if you can learn only a few phrases for this experience from the video, you will be fine.) Then, I started breaking down as many elements as I could identify in it. I looked at rhythm, technical demands, gesture, use of the back, shape, locomotor movements, space, and time. I then explored each of these elements in improvisations, and next mixed some of the elements together in additional improvs. When I decided the experiment should be crafted into a dance, I obviously set the original choreography aside, but I kept some of the rhythms in Gerald Busby's score (even though my new dance was performed to an entirely different piece of music), and ideas about the space, gestures, and use of the back.

Here is my breakdown of Busby's musical structure to illustrate the way I approached his rhythms during my exploratory phase. Each line of numbers indicates the number of counts per dance phrase. The phrases are then broken down into counts per movement. Clearly, some phrases are long, others extremely short. You may find a different way to play with phrasing, and you may also completely eschew the need for counts in this experiment.

6/4/5/6/6/5/6/5/8/7/8/5/5
4/4
3/3/3/3/4
8/8
4/4/4/4
8/8
4/4/4/4
8/8
4/4/4/4

8/8

4/4/4/4

4/4/4/4

6/4/5/6/5/6

3/3/3/3

5/8/3/8/7/7/8/7/8

5/5

4/4/4/4/4/2/3/4

4/4/4/4/4/4

However you decide to approach this experience, make sure to look for the technical elements in the original phrase. Pay close attention to Taylor's use of the back. I know that I have mentioned that several times, but it is central to understanding his styles. One of the things I appreciate about Andrien's technique classes is that as she guides students through the building blocks of training, she also helps them to break apart movement and try to see it in a way that is meaningful for them as dancers. If a dancer finds inspiration in the movement in the

original solo, by all means that is what they should examine through scaffolding. If, however, they find the mystical nature of the work engaging, that is worth exploring. Try to stay within the framework of your original analysis of the solo, just as the assignments around the first scaffolding experiment remained connected to the etude. The final thought I suggest dancers keep in mind is this comment from Ruth Andrien:

"Moving from emulation to innovation is a natural creative process. I think we are taught that imitation inhibits creativity, but I see that choreographers borrow freely from one another because they are sensitive to beautiful or powerful ideas in the world, and they use that 'stuff' to grease the wheels of their own creativity. Imitation is so important to education. We live in a community of cultural ideas that connect us and distinguish us. If we think of imitation as an early stage of invention it can place the individual at the center of a highly creative and liberating process."[32]

Final Questions

1. Based on your sense of aesthetics, how do you perceive the difference between traditional "dancerly" movement and pedestrian movement? What is kinesthetically interesting or uninteresting to you about both concepts of movement?

2. How do you perceive the use of stillness in dance as you experience it in your own body? What import does the dynamism between motion and stillness seem to have in your dancing body, and

what do you think each idea might say to the spectator?

3. How aware of your own back were you prior to looking at the concepts in this book, and in this chapter? Think about that question in an everyday, pedestrian way and with regard to your dancing body as well. How has your awareness of your back and the back's influence on motion changed?

Works Cited

Andrien, R. (2008, May 6). *Paul Taylor*. [Lecture-demonstration]. Cambridge, MA: Harvard Dance Center, Harvard University.

Carbonneau, S. (2008, February 22). *Paul Taylor*. [Lecture]. Cambridge, MA: Harvard Dance Center, Harvard University.

Crisp, C. (1970, July 3). Paul Taylor. *The Financial Times*.

Croce, A. (1965, June 30). *Esplanade*. *The New York Times*.

Denby, E. (1964, June). Paul Taylor. *Seventh Spoleto Festival of Two Worlds*.

Diamond, M. (Producer/Director). (1998). *Paul Taylor: Dancemaker* [Motion Picture]. United States: Docurama.

Hughes, A. (1963, December 21). Dance: from Paul Taylor. *The New York Times*.

Kane, A. (2003, Winter). Through a Glass Darkly: The Many Sides of Paul Taylor's Choreography. *Dance Research: The Journal of the Society for Dance Research*, 21 (2), pp. 90-129.

Macaulay, A. (2007, November 25). 50 Years Ago, Modernism Was Given a Name: *Agon*. Accessed 5 November 2008, from *The New York Times*: http://nytimes.com/2007/11/25/arts/dance/25maca.html?_r=1&pagewanted=print

Martin, R. (1998). *Critical Moves: Dance Studies in Theory and Politics*. Durham, NC: Duke University Press.

Montgomery, J. & Chambers, M. (2009). *Mastering Swimming: Your guide for fitness, training, and competition*. Champaign, IL: Human Kinetics.

Moore, L. (1962, August 6). Dancers Litz & Taylor: Emotion and discipline. *New York Herald Tribune*.

Siegel, M. B. (1985). *The Shape of Change: Images of American dance*. Berkeley: University of California Press.

Sorell, W. (1986). *Looking Back in Wonder: Diary of a dance critic*. New York: Columbia University Press.

Taylor, P. (1988). *Private Domain*. San Francisco: North Point Press.

Terry, W. (1957, October 27). Experiment? Joke? Or War of Nerves? *New York Herald Tribune*.

CHAPTER 7

Post-Judson Training Practices

Choreographers are no longer training dancers, at least not in the traditional sense of giving technique classes that train the dancers in their personal movement style separate from the rehearsal process. The rehearsal replaces training for many.

—Melanie Bales and Rebecca Nettl-Fiol,
The Body Eclectic

Although the techniques introduced in this book are still taught worldwide, and the choreography of the dancemakers discussed is widely sought after by dancers and audiences alike, we no longer train in the era that inspired their genesis. We presently dance in the post-Judson era—an extraordinarily broad region of dance experience mapped out by one hundred years of ideas and approaches, where modern, postmodern, ballet, and somatics meet new ideologies almost daily.

In this chapter, we'll briefly examine how dancers reached this new landscape of eclecticism, and what our opportunities for training are. Part I provides a quick view of the bridge from early postmodernism discussed in Chapter 6 to our current era, and a look at some of the economic causes for prevailing company trends in contemporary dance that have an impact on training. In Part II, we'll look at a contemporary choreographer's efforts to generate a new technique for the post-Judson age and talk about general approaches individual dancers are taking to their training practices.

Choreographer Ting-Yu Chen in a solo performance.

Part I: Bridging the Gap—Evolution and Economics

If the statement at the beginning of this chapter accurately describes the current American modern dance landscape, how did we get to this place? How is the dance environment so different from the days when modernist like Graham and Humphrey were molding their dancers to specific aesthetic ideals? The answers to these questions are multilayered—layers shaped by dance practices of the Judson Movement (1962–1964), and construction of a dancing life during economic hard times.

The Judson Movement

Let us briefly shift attention to events between 1957 and 1964 to better understand the terrain of dancemaking—and therefore dance training—in the post-Judson era. As we saw in the last two chapters, by the late 1950s a new generation of avant-garde choreographers was planting the seeds for the next evolution of American dance. In *7 New Dances* (1957), Paul Taylor was several years ahead of the curve when he stunned an audience with a simple question: is the absence of motion still dance? By that point, too, Merce Cunningham had already discarded traditional concepts of choreography through his use of chance operations. Aside from Cunningham, two major influences on the next group of dance rebels were James Waring and Anna Halprin. In New York, "Waring taught his protégés a great deal about collage techniques, music, theater, and art."[1] In San Francisco, Halprin offered "freedom to follow intuition and impulse in improvisation . . . [and she] also encouraged an analytic approach to anatomy and kinesiology; students were asked to understand and analyze the physical changes they experienced during the course of their improvisations."[2] Then, in 1960, John Cage invited Robert Dunn to teach a dance composition course at Merce Cunningham's studio.

Dunn, a dance musician with a broad knowledge of contemporary art, eschewed the traditional ideas about choreography fostered by Louis Horst and Doris Humphrey in their composition courses (see Chapter 2). Instead of working inside musical structures or using theatricality, Dunn suggested that his students consider more contemporary musical ideas like time determined by the duration of motion, rather than by musical time signatures or bar lines. While Dunn offered ideas for assignments, workshop participants also offered ideas for exploration. They questioned standardized dance aesthetics and, to a large extent, rejected the reigning ideas about technique in favor of a more pedestrian motion. (Pedestrian motion refers to movement one might encounter in the everyday world.) By 1962, workshop participants were ready for a professional showing of their work, and secured performance space at the Judson Memorial Church in Greenwich Village, which had hosted a vital arts program since the mid-1950s. From its beginnings, noted dance historian Sally Banes, participants in Judson Dance Theater sought a "cooperative method for producing dance concerts." Banes also observed:

> The Judson aesthetic ... was never monolithic. Rather, the Judson situation was deliberately undefined, unrestricted. Styles of choreography grew out of the groundwork done at Judson, but the wealth of dances created by Judson Dance Theater show, above all, a remarkable diversity. Still, within the group a few specific themes and interests arose. ... Within the Judson workshop, a commitment to democratic or collective process led on the one hand to methods that metaphorically seemed to stand for freedom (like improvisation, spontaneous determination, chance), and on the other hand to a refined consciousness of the process of choreographic choice.[3]

After producing sixteen concerts, the original Judson Dance Theater project ended in April 1964. Of the numerous choreographers and dancers who participated in the project, the most famous are Trisha Brown, Lucinda Childs, Judith Dunn, David Gordon, Steve Paxton, and Yvonne Rainer. It was Rainer, in fact, who a year after the project disbanded gave voice to many of the era's overarching themes in her manifesto, in which she said, "... NO to virtuosity ... no to involvement of performer or spectator ... no to moving or being moved."[4]

More than fifty years after Taylor's 7 *New Dances* and the movement exploration that began in the Cunningham studio and moved to Judson Church, modern and postmodern perspectives now thrive together as a mélange of motional ideas. The genesis of choreography comes from an increasingly broad range of concepts, and training is radically different today than it was even thirty years ago.

It should be noted here that while numerous ideas about dance training were explored during the Judson period, and while new technical ideas have emerged as a result of that exploration, no singular technique or style was created by the Judson collective. Certain ideas have developed from the era, however, that still have a profound impact on current training. A little later in this chapter, we will look at the differences between classic and eclectic training ideas, deconstructing or debriefing the body of dancerly movement and bricolage (the layering of ideas) in training practices. There is one additional layer to examine first.

Economics and the Rise of the Independents

It could easily be stated that there have never been economic good times for dancers or dance companies in this country. For the most part, that statement would be accurate. Successful dancers, like other successful artists, rarely become millionaires. Throughout Western concert dance history, even the most talented, most successful dance artists almost always have had a benefactor or patron in order to produce their work and keep their companies afloat. In many ways, the most important American dance benefactor was the federal government itself from the 1930s into the early 1990s. From the Works Progress Administration in the 1930s through the

State Department tours, and the establishment of the National Endowment for the Arts (NEA, 1965), the federal government was once the major source of funding for dance companies in the United States. (See Chapter 4 for further discussion of these funding bodies.)

For much of this history, the funding agencies and the artists they supported have been shrouded in controversy. During the State Department years, for example, dancers themselves were concerned about the exclusion of certain artists from the program—Katherine Dunham and Pearl Primus, for example, were never funded, and their exclusion was read as racially motivated.[5] Conversely, support for Alvin Ailey in 1962 was read as an attempt by the federal government to offset international concerns about America's growing Civil Rights struggle. (The contradiction in those statements illustrates the complexity of the situation.) Additionally, by the late 1970s, concern in the dance world was mounting that the same small handful of choreographers and companies were regularly receiving grants from the National Endowment, a charge still leveled against that organization.

Beginning in 1980, the NEA faced a tidal wave of attacks by prominent conservative social groups and politicians that lasted nearly two decades. Originally, the disputes surrounded the concept of public arts funding in general, but those arguments never gained enough steam to generate significant cuts to federal arts spending. In 1989–90, the situation erupted, however, with a major controversy surrounding the specific content of work created by NEA grant recipients— particularly the work of artists Andres Serrano and Robert Mapplethorpe, and later Annie Sprinkle. For much of the next decade, the resulting cultural war threatened to destroy both the NEA and the National Endowment for the Humanities as well.[6] In the end, both agencies survived the battle, but severe cuts in appropriations for the NEA had a devastating effect on arts organizations nationwide, including dance companies. (Additionally, Congress initiated a regulation that placed content restrictions on work created with NEA funding. Although a legal challenge was brought against the regulation, the United States Supreme Court upheld it in 1998.)

To illustrate the impact of the battle in dollar figures, consider this: Congress appropriated $2,898,308 for the agency's first budget in 1966. In 1992, the NEA appropriations totaled $175,954,680. Just six short years later, the cultural war on public arts funding led to a catastrophic slashing of appropriations to $98,000,000 in 1998.[7] It took a full decade to begin any serious recovery of those public funds. In 2008, appropriations totaled $119,604,600. Now, when nonfederal grants and other monies were added to the Congressional allocation, the NEA's total funds available for 2008 reached $157,737,258[8]—a figure still far below the Congressional allocation in 1992.

As public funding plummeted for American arts, the structure of dance changed dramatically. Gone were the days when up-and-coming choreographers could really expect to gather enough backing to form long-term sustainable companies. They either succeeded in forming pick-up companies, or became independent artists making work for the handful of modern and ballet companies that could afford guest artists. Dancers, too, faced a similar situation. By 2002, there were

> barely ten modern dance companies in the city of New York that offer their dancers forty-eight weeks of work with a salary you can live on and health insurance; that's steady, viable employment for perhaps two hundred modern dancers. Below that very narrow top tier, dancers are all working for more than one choreographer and/or holding down outside jobs to fill in the gaps financially.[9]

Part II: Training Dance in a New Era

Some of the developmental and economic realities behind the quotation at the start of the chapter are now clear. Whatever the reasons though, the situation is in stark contrast to the work of choreographers introduced in this book. Even Erick Hawkins and Lester Horton, although they were interested in training versatile performers, saw the importance of their company members training in their own movement systems. The techniques we call modern (Humphrey, Dunham, Hawkins, etc.) are considered *classic* techniques. "These techniques have become classics for a reason. They stem from a clear philosophical point of view and they are brilliant in their design."[10] In contrast, contemporary dancers often approach dance training through an *eclectic* system they usually piece together themselves based upon both need (in order to address the work they are performing) and availability of classes. Some, though, are merging a wealth of ideas to form new systems.

Kinetic Intellect

Typical of current training is the exploration dancer/choreographer Ting-Yu Chen has been doing for more than a decade. Both in developing material for her company, Ting-Yu Chen and Flying Lions Dance Company, and in training her students at Shenandoah University (Winchester, Virginia), Chen keeps a check on

> how much pain, or unnecessary tension is imposed on the dancer's body. I look at how much effort it takes to do a tendu—which is just an extension of the leg in order to accomplish a length of line without the color of emotion—and I ask why that tendu has to be done in such a way that it creates tension. Then, I have to ask what is the technique serving? Is it just serving one choreographer's artistic vision, or is it helping to fine-tune the body, the instrument, in order to play all kinds of songs, all kinds of

melodies? I want dancers to go into any audition and to have them feel that they can be eloquent, and to recognize the difference between technique and style . . . to recognize the appropriate use of weight and effort for the work they are encountering.[11]

In an interview for this book, Chen went on to say that she is examining language cues to help students to move more comfortably from classic to post-Judson movement. The concepts of centralizing and decentralizing energy/tension are key in this process, where initiating energies can be moved from the core to an extremity. "In many classic modern techniques, and in classical ballet," Chen noted, "there is tremendous use of opposition. This creates dramatic tension. Techniques that create tension build musculature. In the kinds of postmodern work that I've done, in the release techniques I've encountered, opposition is not engaged. Because when you engage opposition, it requires maximum effort to execute a simple task."[12]

• •

Release Techniques: Since the 1960s, a variety of movement-training ideas have developed that are commonly referred to as release technique. While some of these training approaches have been developed into progressive systems like Skinner Releasing and Safety Release, the general concept is that the dancer will let go of old movement habits so that tension and holding patterns can be diminished throughout the body. There is a focus on "movement efficiency: doing more with less, using momentum rather than force."[13]

• •

Chen acknowledges that her training certainly affects her choreography. "I try," she said, "to avoid using terminology in class that might trigger too much familiarity with movement when students later come in to learn my work. I don't want them to have preconceived notions with regard to what a particular movement is, or what it might mean."[14]

The fusion of classic modern ideas, ballet, Chinese opera dance, and somatic work in Chen's technique makes it difficult for dancers to bring preconceived notions to her repertory.

Chen continued, "My artistic vision is less about form, and more about something organic, free, and abstract. Dancers who train in my technique class know that while there is vocabulary, I focus on pathways and that the vocabulary [experienced in class] might be manipulated in rehearsal. The intention of the movement is more important than a step with a name. The intention behind the movement is what is going to affect the movement. The entry points are often intellectual so that anyone can find their way into the movement, and physicalize the ideas. That's

Shenandoah University students in Chen's Betrayed.

more accessible for a wider range of dancers, and it leaves some room for autonomy for the dancers. There are opportunities for improvisation so that the dancers can make some decisions, and express their intellect."[15]

The Eclectic Dancer/Teacher: The Author's Experience

The exploration of the kinetic intellect is one of the elements I have long appreciated about the post-Judson mindset. The somatic work I started with Melissa Hayden in the late 1980s as a student at North Carolina School of the Arts, my Ashtanga flow practice (a form of yoga), release technique, Klein technique (see Appendix C), the Bartenieff Fundamentals (see below), running, lifting weights, and swimming all informed my body-mind-spirit as a dancer.

. . . .

Bartenieff Fundamentals[SM] consists of a set of concepts, principles, and exercises developed by Irmgard Bartenieff in applying Rudolf Laban's movement theory to the physical/kinesiological functioning of the human body. Some of the concepts studied are dynamic alignment, breath support, core support, rotary factor, initiation and sequencing, spatial intent, center of weight/weight transference, effort intent, and developmental patterning and its support for level change.[16]

. . . .

Release, somatics, and swimming inform my kinetic intellect, helping me to find freedom and efficiency—highlighting the fluidity of the dynamism I want in my movement. Swimming in particular informs my spine as it decompresses the discs between each vertebra. These approaches though never replaced my own training in classic techniques, however, because opposition and dynamic tension resonate with my body-mind-spirit.

The dynamic tension in the Balanchine Style®, Dunham, Horton, Humphrey, Graham, and Cunningham techniques and the Taylor style were organic to my physicality and informed the basis of my movement aesthetic. Certainly as a young, developing dancer, I never thought of my experience as eclectic. I was just training to be the most versatile dancer I could be. I also knew and was able to articulate my body's preferences and needs alongside my artistic aesthetics as a performer and choreographer, and this approach seemed to be facilitating my needs. When bricolage *(see below) came into my consciousness as a theoretical structure for training practice, I knew instantly that it was the perfect description for how I was training.*

For me, oppositional energy and dynamic tension allow for a critical, political statement that is subversive. We can be explosive and radical even as we seek democracy in our own body. It has to be efficient though, and it has to be organic. As a dancemaker, I may opt for a purely classic or pure post-Judsonist approach to the choreography, or I may embrace fusion, incorporating whatever will bring to tension, shape, speed, and power to the dance.

The author in his solo Of Future Space.

Deconstruction in dance is a "repatterning, stripping down, getting back to basics, debriefing the body of unwanted habits of movement. **Bricolage** is the layering of disparate practices upon one another within the body, such as a classic Western form (ballet) with an ancient Eastern practice (yoga), reflecting postmodern "radical juxtaposition" through a training agenda styled and structured by the interests of the independent dancer.[17]

Working in pick-up companies (mine or those of other choreographers), I grew accustomed to the contemporary idea that choreographers generally have to focus on coaching stylistic elements during rehearsals. Save for the rare company class, I have never had the luxury of making any real training contributions to the development of my dancers (outside of the academy). To a certain extent, contemporary dancemakers have had to acclimate ourselves to working with a group of dancers that likely will not have a unified physical vocabulary or look. Coaching the style of each individual piece has to be our focus. That's certainly true when I've worked with professional dancers, and it is becoming increasingly true when working with student dancers. Of the four dances I created at Northwestern State University of Louisiana while writing this book, two of them were a fusion of technical ideas—with one incorporating classical ballet and Horton. While all of the fourteen dancers had studied some form of technique with me during the year, only three of them had studied both ballet and Horton in my studio. The other eleven dancers had gaps in their training and in their vocabulary that we did not have time to address in rehearsal, except for issues of weight shift. I had to focus my coaching time on sculpting and clarifying shape and fine-tuning effort to develop the movement qualities necessary for the dance. Would the experience have been easier for everyone had they all had the same training background? Yes, certainly. The experience though was typical of so much contemporary dance practice today. Perhaps the most important factor in our work these days is the ability to adapt—an ability fostered by versatility and an open body-mind-spirit.

Evaluating Your Own Training Needs

So, how do you find a system of training that helps to meet your own dance goals? Well, there is not a single, straightforward answer to that question. Obviously, if you are a university student, you have to follow the curricular direction of your department. *There are things you can do while still in school to investigate your own training needs and interests.*

1. Talk with your faculty or studio teachers about your dance goals and see if they have ideas about other things you could do/ought to do that will help you toward those goals beyond your regular class schedule. Even within the framework of a curriculum, you can still explore other options

and begin to experiment with bricolage. If, for example, your program does not offer a somatics course, check the university's athletics facility or local gyms and dance studios for their offerings.

2. Talk with dancers whose work you appreciate, find out how they train, and try the dance classes or fitness tools they like.

3. Journaling and making observations and taking notes has been a regular assignment in this book for a reason. Even if you are doing nothing more than keeping a log of bullet points in order to express your aesthetics as a dancer, you have to analyze your reactions to what you see and what you feel. That truth only grows stronger as you begin to choreograph and teach. Keeping a journal is the simplest way to track your observations, analyses, and experiences. Colleagues of mine frequently say they go back to notes they made decades ago about technical questions they had as dancers, and how those notes help them as teachers or choreographers. Refer to the textbox below for ideas about what you should be considering.

4. Explore and evaluate as you experiment. Trying different techniques and somatics practices requires dancers to constantly be aware of the progress we are making toward our particular dance goals. If you want to be cast in the Graham Company, you have to be in Graham technique daily—go to that Limón class you like as a treat but not instead of the Graham class you need. If you like the way that Graham feels in your body, but you know that you really want to dance for Bill T. Jones, then you may need to blend that training with ballet, release work, and somatics material (or a different combination altogether). Also, keep in mind that eclectic training like this is a form of athletic cross-training and can confuse your muscles. Be aware of that and try to ensure that your overall training is well rounded. Try not to overtrain one muscle group or overuse one concept. Look for a sense of balance in your training. (See Appendix A for more on efficient training and issues of cross-training.)

Most of all, be honest in evaluating your training needs/practices measured against your goals. That kind of self-awareness and self-examination is the only way dancers ever really progress and achieve their goals in this art form. That was true during the classic era of modern dance, and it's true now in this eclectic era. Do what feels right in your body, but do what will help you safely, effectively, and efficiently become the dancer you were born to become.

Final Questions

1. What training supports your performance goals—both current and long range?

2. What training supports your own choreographic interests?

3. How do you ensure continued technical growth?

4. What internal and external measures are in place to help you track your progress?

Works Cited

Bales, M. (2008). Falling, Releasing and post-Judson Dance. In M. Bales & R. Nettl-Fiol (Eds.). *The Body Eclectic: Evolving practices in dance training* (pp. 153–164). Urbana: University of Illinois Press.

Bales, M. & Nettl-Fiol, R. (Eds.). (2008). *The Body Eclectic: Evolving practices in dance training.* Urbana: University of Illinois Press.

Banes, S. (1980). *Democracy's Body: Judson Dance Theatre 1962–1964.* Ann Arbor, MI: UMI Research Press.

Chen, T.Y. (2009, August 12). Ting-Yu Chen on Post-Judson Training. Interview by J. Legg.

Dittman, V. (2008). A New York Dancer. In M. Bales & R. Nettl-Fiol (Eds.). *The Body Eclectic: Evovling practices in dance training* (pp. 22–27). Chicago: University of Illinois Press.

Erkert, J. (2003). *Harnessing the Wind: The art of teaching modern dance.* Champaign, IL: Human Kinetics.

Koch, C. (1998). "The Contest for American Culture: A Leadership Case Study on the NEA and NEH Funding Crisis." Penn National Commission [Report].

Prevots, N. (2001). *Dance for Export: Cultural diplomacy and the Cold War.* Middletown, CT: Wesleyan University Press.

Laban/Bartenieff Institute for Movement Studies (2009). *What are Bartenieff Fundamentals?* Accessed May 22, 2010, from Laban/Bartenieff Institute for Movement Studies: http://www.limsonline.org/what-are-bartenieff-fundamentals-bf.

National Endowment for the Arts Annual Report 2008. Accessed 21 May 2010, from the National Endowment for the Arts: http://nea.gov/about/08Annual/index.php#

National Endowment for the Arts Appropriation History. Accessed 31 May 2011, from the National Endowment for the Arts: http://nea.gov/about/facts/appropriationshistory.html

Tharp, T. (1992). *Push Comes to Shove: An autobiography.* New York: Bantam Books.

Economy of Movement

Tips for Effortless Dancing

"The three most critical elements to economy of movement are intelligent feet, proper hip alignment and coordination."

— Sara Neece

I n the first attempts at a skill, young dancers often rely on the wrong muscles or too many muscles. What is correct in one class/form doesn't always serve you well in another.

Have you ever wondered how professionals make dancing look so easy? It's because their bodies are like well-oiled machines tuned to dance with an economy of movement—in other words, to dance efficiently. Understanding this concept is key in being able to handle the physical demands of a life in dance.

Efficiency is doing the least work (using the fewest muscles) to perform accurately (dancing with good technique). Misalignment, weakness of the prime movers in a movement, and inelasticity of the muscles that oppose the prime movers can all contribute to movement inefficiency. [We] talked to two experts to find out how best to begin moving efficiently—to not only increase the facility of your body, but also to prevent injury and extend your dance life.

This article by the author originally appeared in DanceSpirit *magazine (February 2007).*

Balanced Alignment

Proper alignment is the foundation of good dance technique. In fact, it isn't possible to dance efficiently if your alignment is askew. For example, "If you dance with your hips aligned over the back of your heels [for an extended period of time], you'll run into problems down the line," says Sara Neece, ballet instructor at Ballet Arts in NYC and former ballet mistress for such choreographers as William Forsythe. With that kind of misalignment, your quads will work overtime pulling you forward, which is, "a great way to develop thunder thighs," Neece explains.

Moreover, some misalignment issues pave the way for injuries. For instance, if you consistently train without your knees tracking properly over your feet, you increase the risk of damaging cartilage or tearing tendons (particularly in landing jumps).

If you can master "intelligent feet [no "rolling in" on the arches or toes "crunched," and weight well balanced over the foot] proper hip alignment and coordination," you'll be on your way to moving efficiently, she says.

Try Neece's alignment check: Stand with your feet in parallel, demi plié, then roll up to demi-pointe (with knees still bent), straighten your legs, and then lower your feet back to the floor without going through demi plié on the way back down.

Ask your dance teacher or an advanced dancer to watch as you do this exercise. They should observe your feet, hip alignment, knee structure, and how your upper body is seated on your hips. You shouldn't roll in on your arches, and toes should never curl; knees should track over the balls of feet; hips need to be well balanced over your feet (not resting on your heels, and not tipped back or tucked under), and your torso must follow a plumb line over your hips.

If any alignment deviations are revealed, your teacher can help you correct them—but realize that problems are rarely fixed overnight. You may have to learn to utilize muscle groups in new ways, develop more flexibility in certain areas and remain diligent in changing habitual patterns. It may seem like once you've started working on retraining your body, your technique will suffer. As with most rehabilitation programs, the situation will likely get worse before it gets better. Keep this mind, and try not to get frustrated. Conduct this alignment check periodically to track your progress.

Balanced Effort

A more balanced alignment will eventually enable you to work with less effort. "The goal is for the movement to feel easy," says Sally Fitt, former professor in modern dance at the University of

Utah and author of *Dance Kinesiology.*

Finding the "prime movers"—the muscles that are most efficient at the desired action—is often a matter of trial and error. In the first attempts at a skill, young dancers often rely on the wrong muscles or use too many muscles. For example, when doing a plié with an outwardly rotated hip, young dancers often activate all of the outward rotators to maximize rotation. However, the most efficient muscles (the prime movers) for going down into a plié or coming up from that plié are the lower fibers of the buttocks muscles, which Fitt calls the "swing seat" muscles. When a young dancer "finds" these muscles, he or she often exclaims, "Wow! That was easy!" Actually, that was efficient.

Strength and Flexibility in Efficiency
Repeating the same movements over a period of years sometimes leads to overdeveloping the strength of one muscle group at the expense of other muscles—and this muscular imbalance is a major cause, not only of inefficient dancing, but also of injury.

Pitfalls of Cross-Training

It's possible for your body to get confused when cross-training, which can mean studying a variety of dance forms, or training in dance while at the same time participating on a sports team.

"If you're training in ballet and a contemporary form like Graham, you're asking your body to do conflicting or contradictory activities, and it's important to be aware of that," says Neece. For instance, if you've spent time working on a Graham contraction standing in parallel, you've had your hips aligned over the heels rather than toward the front of the feet. When you get back to ballet, do the alignment check for yourself and see if you need to readjust before ballet class—you might ask another dancers to observe this for you, but you should also start to make your own observations both visually in the mirror, and through the physical sensations.

Good habits are as easy to develop as bad ones! You might find it useful to stretch out the hip flexors to counter the stress placed on them while they were contracted in parallel. In order to be efficient in a variety of dance forms, you must assess and adapt to the unique physical demands of each form, and remember that what is correct in one class/form doesn't always serve you well in another.

Neece urges dancers who are active in dance and sports to make sure they do an appropriate warm up for each activity (what your body needs prior to ballet is different than what it needs prior to soccer for instance) and that they cool down and stretch afterward. When going from practice to rehearsal, check your alignment, adequately warm up, engage your rotators, or do some other appropriate work in opposition to the sports training.

"If you do a movement in one direction," says Fitt, "be sure to do it the other way. What you flex, be sure to extend. What you contract, be sure to stretch. In so doing, you're more likely to maintain balanced flexibility and strength."

A common goal for young dancers is to increase the height of their extensions. (What dancers refer to as extensions are actually flexions of the hip while maintaining knee extension.) Two factors are necessary for a high extension: the strength of the hip flexors and the elasticity of the hip extensors (hamstrings). But no matter how strong your hip flexors are, if you lack flexibility in your hamstrings, you'll never have a high dance "extension" to the front.

Fitt points out that not all movements of hip flexion stretch the hamstrings equally. "Just because you can bend forward while standing in parallel, and touch the floor, doesn't necessarily mean that you're maximally stretching your hamstrings. It might simply mean that you have a supple, flexible back." To focus the stretch exclusively on the hamstrings, do that stretch using a flat back, while trying to press your naval between your thighs, instead of imagining head-to-knees, which localizes the stretch to the spine. This will focus the stretch more directly into the hamstrings and will likely begin to make a visible difference in the height of your front extension. Fitt also emphasizes the importance of demanding straight knees when stretching the hamstrings, even if it means you have to work from a more limited range of motion at the hip. She says, "You simply can't stretch the hamstrings with a bent knee." The goal is to create a more elastic hamstring, allowing a greater range of hip flexion in grand battement. It's not about getting your nose to your knee.

The Buddy System

When working toward increasing your efficiency, it's often necessary to change habitual movement patterns. Fitt recommends the buddy system. "Pair up with a fellow dancer in class who's changing the same habit. Agree to watch each other, give feedback to one another, and adapt your observations to your own process," she says.

Tip of the Iceberg

If you work with proper alignment, identify/utilize the prime movers to execute a movement, and develop good overall strength and flexibility (avoiding imbalances), you'll be on the road to easier, more efficient dancing. This article, however, is just an introduction to the concept of economy of movement. There's a great deal more to explore on the topic as you develop as a dancer, but the earlier you begin working efficiently, the more likely it is that you'll avoid bad habits and chronic injury along the way. For those who've picked up bad habits or had some faulty training, Neece offers these words of encouragement: "As long as you still love to dance, your teachers did something right. Even if you've trained your body incorrectly, [most] everything can be fixed."

What to Read:

Sally Sevey Fitt's *Dance Kinesiology*, from Schirmer Books, 1996 (second edition)

Eric Fanklin's *Conditioning for Dance*, from Human Kinetics Publishers, 2003

Improving Your Improv

How to Move in the Moment

"Don't judge or self-edit as you go through these explorations..." [g]ive the unexpected room to emerge by allowing each movement to evolve from the one before and lead naturally into the one that follows.

—Brenda Divelbliss

Improvisation—generating spontaneous movement in the moment—can be a daunting and agonizing prospect for dancers who are used to being told precisely what to perform. What if you can't think of anything cool to do and end up just standing there? What if you mess up? Will people laugh at your movement?

It may be scary at first, but improv is a tool that can alter your relationship to dance completely. You'll begin to identify your natural movement patterns and become more comfortable moving in unusual ways—and maybe even come up with ideas for choreography. Whether you've never done improv in your life or loved it for years, here are some ideas to help you hone your craft.

Improv's Practical Side

Improv devotees love the practice because it's fun, unpredictable and challenging. But even if the idea of creating movement on the spot makes you uncomfortable, mastering the craft can take

This article by the author originally appeared in DanceSpirit *magazine (March 2007).*

your dancing—in any genre—to new levels. "You're not worrying about the sequence of steps, so you can explore who you really are as a mover," says Brenda Divelbliss, who teaches modern and choreography at Cambridge Rindge & Latin High School in Cambridge, Massachusetts, and has taught at Bates Dance Festival and Harvard University's dance program. Improv can help you understand what types of movement resonate with you and what interests you artistically—which can help you decide which professional companies you're best suited for.

For choreographers, improv can be an efficient use of time when you're looking to create new material. Additionally, you might discover certain "signature moves" that you will want to repeat—you can embrace these steps as part of your movement style, but be aware of overusing them. And even if you're not a choreographer, you may be asked to contribute to the choreographic process. "Many choreographers in both modern and ballet companies look to their dancers for new ideas," says Divelbliss. You could be given a few steps or a complete phrase and be asked to manipulate the movement, pushing the dance in a new and personal direction. Taking an improv class will give you the tools to do this.

· ·

Five Tools to Try

1. Start with a structure. In an improv class, you're likely to be assigned a topic to explore, such as weight, space, a particular movement quality (fluid or airy) or even an emotion. To practice, go into the studio and give yourself such an assignment. You can use music or create your dance in silence. Move with your structure in mind, and if you find yourself drifting away from your original idea, return to it.

2. Watch improv. Your teachers may divide you into groups and have you watch each other improvise. Observing someone else's practice will help you gain a keener eye for the things that make an improv interesting. You may also pick up new ways of moving by watching others. Take turns improvising with a group of friends, maybe even videotaping your movement. Watch each other

or the tape and make notes about what worked and what didn't, and have friends give you constructive feedback.

3. Push for contrast in your tempo, levels and other aspects of the movement you create. Teachers and choreographers will give you notes as you move, but be aware of your tendencies when you're practicing on your own. Developing contrast—and trying things that are new or unfamiliar to you—will make your dancing stronger and your choreography more engaging.

4. Stay in the moment and the movement. If you're given a set amount of time to improvise in class, stay focused the whole time. "Don't judge or self-edit as you go through these explorations," says Divelbliss. Give the unexpected room to

emerge by allowing each movement to evolve from the one before and lead naturally into the one that follows. Shadowing and mirroring can be a great way to create movement when working with a partner or a group, but don't spend time copying your neighbors—even if it's embarrassing at first, you'll learn more from taking risks on your own.

5. Layer an improvisation by creating your own experience, even if you're working on an assigned structure that a teacher or fellow dancer has given you. For instance, if the assignment is to work on timing and direction in space, but you know you have a problem transitioning through level changes, try exploring different levels as you work.

Try It

Create an improv around one of these prompts—or combine several ideas for an extra challenge. Remember, you're just moving in response to these words, so there's no wrong answer.

Movement Qualities	Time and Space	Body Parts
Airy	Direction	Fingers
Fluid	Level	Head
Heavy	Tempo	Knees
Sharp	Weight shift	Pelvis

Keys to Success

The two most important components of a successful improv are staying true to the structure you set up, and staying open to how the dance can evolve. Within your chosen or assigned framework, allow the unexpected shape or movement to emerge from your creative center. You might just find yourself moving in a whole new way.

Somatics and the Dance Technique Class

Soma is a Greek word that . . . has meant "living body." This living, self-sensing, internalized perception of oneself is radically different from the externalized perception of what we call a "body," which could just as well be a human, a statue, a dummy, or a cadaver—from an objective viewpoint, all of these are "bodies." . . . The uniqueness of human beings is in being, simultaneously, subjects and objects. Humans are self-sensing and self-moving subjects while, at the same time, they are observable and manipulable objects. To yourself, you are a soma. To others, you are a body. Only you can perceive yourself as a soma—no one else can do so.

—Thomas Hanna, *Somatics*

While the focus of this text has been on classic modern dance techniques, dancers train in the context of their own eras. At present, we work in an era in which we dancers, regardless of our primary genre, regularly incorporate somatic work into their overall approach to dance training. It is appropriate then to briefly address somatic methodologies and examine their incorporation into our systems of training. To that end, brief descriptions of three popular somatic forms follow (including Feldenkrais, Klein, and Pilates). Other forms such as Alexander Technique are not covered here, nor are yoga and newer forms of aquatic training (designed to build flexibility and muscular/cardiovascular endurance while reducing joint strain). An interview with Kim Gibilisco, a dance educator who infuses Pilates in to her classes, is included to address questions students and university departments often have.

· ·

To a large extent, the forms introduced in this section are a reflection of Amer-Eurocentric viewpoints of somatic studies, and Asian or African ideas are not incorporated here. Students should be aware, however, that broader global influences/ideas do exist within the somatics field.[1] A deeper exami- nation of the somatic/holistic body-mind (and spirit) training field should also include the major contributions of the following women: Bonnie Bainbridge Cohen, Emilie Conrad, Anna Halprin, and Irmgard Bartenieff.

· ·

Examples of Somatic Systems

The Feldenkrais Method was created by Moshe Feldenkrais and seeks to increase range of motion, flexibility, and coordination. It is "based on principles of physics, biomechanics, and an empirical understanding of learning and human development."[2] Sequential movements bring attention to habitual neuromuscular patterns, and focus on improved posture and fluid movement pathways. There is a concerted body–mind connection that attends to the imagination as well as personal awareness within the self and in spatial relationship to the external environment.[3]

Dancer Susan Klein began to develop the Klein Technique as an effort to deal with her own knee injury. In the end, what emerged is a "process through which the body is analyzed and understood to improve and to further movement potential. . . . [It works] to align the bones using the muscles of deep postural support: the psoas, the hamstrings, the external rotators, and the pelvic floor . . . to become conscious of their role in the support and movement of the body."[4]

Originally called "Contrology" by its creator, Joseph Pilates, the Pilates Method is commonly referred to simply as Pilates. It is likely the most popular somatic method (next to yoga) in America. Pilates believed that "physical fitness is the first requisite to happiness." He described Contrology as the "complete coordination of body, mind, and spirit. Through Contrology you first purposefully acquire complete control of your own body and then through proper repetition of its exercise you gradually and progressively acquire that natural rhythm and coordination associated with all your subconscious activities."[5] Although Pilates wanted everyone eventually be able to complete his entire system at home, production of the apparatus was cost-prohibitive. His mat exercises, however, can be used anywhere and are the portion of the system most dancers encounter. The series of movements strengthens the core, builds muscular endurance, and encourages core integration into simple movements of the limbs.

Kim Gibilisco on Pilates Certification

Kim Gibilisco is a Gold Certified Pilates Trainer through the Pilates Method Alliance, and presently serves as Vice Chair/Secretary of the Pilates Method Alliance Certification Commission. She is also a former member of Murray Louis and Nikolais Dance, and was an assistant professor of dance at Shenanodah University (2005 to 2009) where she established the school's Pilates Mat Teacher Training Program—one of only a handful of such programs in the nation. In this interview, she briefly discusses her own introductions to somatic forms as a dancer, and provides insight on selecting a Pilates teacher.

Kim Gibilisco is a lecturer at Mason Gross School of the Arts at Rutgers University, and is teaching a Pilates Mat class at the university in this photo.

Joshua Legg: With so many options out there now for somatics work, how should a young dancer determine which one to dive into? What, for example, led you to Pilates?

Kim Gibilisco: It's much the same as choosing a dance technique. Something about the work should resonate with you. For me, I first came into yoga because Alberto del Saz, artistic director of Murray Louis and Nikolais Dance, infused it into his technique class for the company. His best friend is the president of the Iyengar Association in New York, so the information that was coming through was really refined and thorough. I found yoga rejuvenating, and started taking full-on yoga classes nine years ago. It deepened my dance practice, my understanding of Pilates, and my spirituality. In fact, Joe Pilates was a yogi.

JL: So then, how did you come to Pilates?

KG: Again, it was in the company. Somatic work heightens your kinesthetic awareness and facilitates movement analysis, and Pilates is a major core of the Nikolais/Louis floor barre. The technique comes from the German lineage: Laban–Wigman–Holm (see pages 174–176). Hanya Holm had worked with Joseph Pilates, and she had incorporated Pilates mat work into her floor barre. The importance of that in our work in the company was really clear to me as I moved deeper into technique.

Then, in addition to the exposure to Pilates in the company, I really started working with it in a more concerted way after a back injury. My husband is a physical therapist, and he suggested I move into a deeper exploration of the apparatus work. From there, I went on to become certified in Pilates.

JL: Let's talk about certification for a moment. What major criteria should be considered when selecting a certification program?

KG: While the Pilates profession does have the Pilates Method Alliance (PMA) to bring us together and support industry standards through the PMA Board Certification Exam, in the Pilates community, we are self-regulated. We do not have a licensing board. Our PMA Board Certification is not required in order to set up shop and offer classes and private lessons. You want to make sure that the person doing the training is themselves certified by a reputable organization. The trainer should also be participating in continuing education courses so that they are staying current on the latest information and techniques. It's also a good idea to take class with that person before you enter a Teacher Training Program of study with them. A good Pilates class is a lot like a good dance class. You know five minutes into a class if someone's teaching is sound. You know if the students will grow and learn something new in the experience. You can see if a teacher has prepared for the class. Students who want to get certified can look on the Pilates Method Alliance website to find certified teacher trainers in their area. [See the note below for more information on the PMA and basic requirements for certification.]

JL: If a college program wants to hire a new faculty member to teach Pilates, what qualifications should that program seek?

KG: I sit on the certification steering committee for the Pilates Method Alliance and we're hoping that sometime in the future there will be community standards for teacher training certification programs. For now, though, the requirements for PMA certification are solidly rooted and comprehensive. It's a rigorous process. The PMA Board Certification Exam is offered by a third party, Castle Worldwide. If a college dance program wants to bring someone in to teach Pilates, I recommend finding someone who is PMA certified.

JL: In the mat certification program that you offered at Shenandoah University, what did you do differently from other programs?

KG: Because I was working in the college setting, I was able to increase the hours for the training program. The structure of the university class schedule and curriculum requirements supported my sixty-hour design, which would be a "tough sell" in the private sector. I worked with students on teaching methods and helping them to build lesson plans. They had to incorporate props like the foam roller and the magic circle into their teaching, and they had to design their own exercises based on the fundamentals of Pilates.

· ·

About the Pilates Method Alliance and Certification

In addition to fostering an understanding of the teachings of Joseph H. and Clara Pilates, the primary mission of the Pilates Method Alliance is to protect the public through certification and continuing education standards for Pilates professionals. This international nonprofit organization promotes unity among Pilates teachers and advocates for educational standards in teacher training methodologies. While PMA itself does not offer training programs, it does recognize programs currently offering courses that prepare a practitioner to sit for the PMA certification exam, or that count toward recertification. In order to sit for the certification exam, candidates must either complete 450 hours in a teacher training program or have spent 720 hours of full-time employment as a Pilates teacher in the twelve months leading up to the examination.

· ·

Works Cited

Eddy, M. (2002, Winter). Somatic Practices and Dance: Global influence. *Dance Research Journal*, 34 (2), 46–62.

Feldenkrais, M. (1972). *Awareness Through Movement*. New York: Harper/SanFrancisco.

Fitt, S. (1988). *Dance Kinesiology*. New York: Schirmer Books.

Franklin, E. (2004). *Conditioning for the Dancer: Training for peak performance in all dance forms*. Champaign, IL: Human Kinetics.

Hanna, T. (1988). *Somatics: Reawakening the mind's control of movement, flexibility, and health*. Cambridge, MA: Da Capo Press.

Isacowitz, R. (2006). *Pilates*. Champaign, IL: Human Kinetics.

Klein, S. (1998). *A Movement Technique—A Healing Technique*. Accessed 21 June 2009, from http://kleintechnique.com/articles.html.

Nikolais, N. and M. Louis. (2005). *The Nikolais/Louis Dance Technique: A philosophy and method for modern dance*. New York: Routledge.

Pilates, J. H. and W. J. Miller. (1998). *A Pilates Primer: The millennium edition*. Ashland, OR: Presentation Dynamics.

Pilates Method Alliance (2009). Welcome, About, CEC Workshops, Certification pages. Accessed 6 September 2009, from http://pilatesmethodalliance.org/index.html.

NOTES
....

Introduction

1 Clark and Johnson, p. 332
2 Fischer, p. 7
3 Bales & Nettl Fiol, p. 30
4 deMille, p.446
5 Martin, p.13

Chapter 1: The Expressionists

1 Kurth, pp. 28–29
2 Anderson, p. 8
3 McPherson, p. 5
4 Gallemore, p. 52
5 Rath, pp.v–vi
6 Anderson, p. 13
7 Stebbins, pp. 400–401
8 Anderson, p. 14
9 Jaques-Dalcroze, p. v
10 Ibid., p. 7
11 Pennington, p. 6
12 Jaques-Dalcroze, p. 52
13 Spector, p. 56
14 Ibid., p. 118
15 Jaques-Dalcroze, pp. 232–231
16 Pennington, pp. 14–15
17 Spector, p. 162
18 Kurth, p. 30
19 Lloyd, p. 3
20 Martin, p. 225
21 Ibid., p. 227
22 Levien, p. xi
23 Gold, 1984, p. 7
24 Duncan, pp. 1–35
25 Ibid., p. 7
26 Kurth, p. 367
27 Lloyd, p. 24
28 Ibid., pp. 23–24
29 Rogosin
30 Shawn, 1948, pp. 5–8
31 Sherman, 1976, p. 15
32 Mumaw & Sherman, p. 91
33 Ibid., p. 92
34 Sherman, 1983, p. 18
35 Sherman & Mumaw, pp. 315–316
36 Mumaw & Sherman, p. 92
37 Ibid., p. 94
38 Ibid.
39 Sherman, 1976, p. 24
40 Houseal
41 Mumaw & Sherman, p. 95
42 Sherman, 1983, p. 11
43 Sherman, 1976, p. 23
44 Sherman, 1998
45 McPherson, p. 6
46 Ibid.

Chapter 2: The Originators

1 Martin., p. 1
2 Kriegsman, p. 232
3 Sherman, pp. 179–193
4 Smith
5 Brown, pp. 43–44
6 Martin, 1975, p. 254
7 Fischer, p. 2
8 Ibid.
9 McDonagh
10 Graham, 1991, pp. 55–56
11 McDonagh, p. 22
12 Ibid., p. 23
13 Terry, p. 82
14 Tracy, p. 9
15 Tobias, p. 62
16 Ibid.
17 Soares, p. 1
18 Armitage, p. 93
19 de Mille, 1950, p. 29
20 Kirstein, pp. 230–231
21 Siegel, 1985
22 Tobias, p. 67
23 Kennicott
24 Horosko, p. 8
25 Eilber
26 Helpern, pp. 1, 5
27 Eilber
28 The Kennedy Center for the Performing Arts
29 Ibid.

30 de Mille, 1991, p. 84
31 Ibid., p. 99
32 Helpern, p. 9
33 de Mille, 1991, pp. 132–133
34 Helpern, p. 8
35 Ibid., p. 17
36 Eilber
37 Ibid.
38 Eilber
39 The Kennedy Center for the Performing Arts
40 Helpern, p. 1
41 Humphrey, p. 19
42 Cohen, 1995, p. 11
43 Siegel, 1993, p. 29
44 Sherman, p. 181
45 Ibid., p. 187
46 Ibid., p. 191
47 Cohen, 1995, p. 61
48 Ibid., p. 70
49 Cohen, 1992, p. 144.
50 Johnston, pp. 146–149
51 Humphrey, p. 40
52 Schurman, p. 63
53 Ibid.
54 Humphrey, p. 9
55 Ibid., p. 13
56 Stodelle, p. 5
57 Ibid., p. 6
58 Ibid.

Chapter 3: The Mavericks

1   Manning, p. 257
2   Holmes.
3   Martin, 1931
4   Martin, 1940
5   Graff, pp. 36 37
6   Manning, p. 256
7   Franko, pp. 91–92
8   Manning, p. 256
9   Gottschild, 2001, pp. 32 335
10 Gottschild, 1996, pp. 11–12
11 Gottschild, 2001, pp. 338–339
12 Osumare, p. 12
13 Barnes, 1967
14 Pierre, p. 248
15 Ibid., p. 249
16 Ibid.
17 Barzel, Turbyfill, & Page, p. 187
18 Dunham, Video #38
19 Pierre, p. 249
20 Legg, 7 November 2008
21 Dunham Pratt, 2009
22 Barzel, Turbyfill, & Page, p. 178
23 Dunham, 2005, p. 131
24 Lloyd, p. 247
25 Martin, 1946

26 Hill, p. 1
27 Ibid., p. 6
28 Aschenbrenner, p. 115
29 Ibid., p. 116
30 Barzel, Turbyfill, & Page, p. 178
31 Dunham, 1964, p. 479
32 Rose, 1990
33 Legg, May/June 2008, p. 77
34 Aschenbrenner, p. 173
35 Dunham, 2005, p. 551
36 Dunham Pratt, 2009
37 Aschenbrenner, p. 98
38 Rose, 2008.
39 Clark, 1994, p. 321
40 Legg, May/June 2008, p. 74
41 Rose, 1990, p. 15
42 Rose, 1990, pp. 16–17
43 Rose, 2009.
44 Legg, May/June 2008, p. 74
45 Rose, p. 93
46 Lee, 2009, part 2
47 Warren, p. 6
48 Lloyd, p. 279
49 Warren, p. 8
50 Lloyd, p. 279
51 Warren, p. 10
52 Ibid.
53 Lloyd, p. 280
54 Warren, pp. 60–61
55 Ailey & Bailey, p. 59
56 Ibid., p. 65
57 Anderson, p. 180
58 Warren, p. 70
59 Ibid., p. 71
60 Ibid., p. 79
61 Ailey & Bailey, p. 60
62 Lloyd, p. 287
63 Warren, p. 84
64 Bizot, p. 35
65 Warren, p. 66
66 Lee, 2009, part 1
67 Legg, 2007, p. 95
68 Gibson, 2009
69 Forsythe & Perces, 2002
70 Ibid.
71 Lee, 2009, part 1
72 Perces, Forsythe, & Bell, p. 28
73 Forsythe & Perces, 1990

Chapter 4: The Next Generation

1   Larson, p. 492
2   Lewis, 2000, p. 79
3   Ibid., p. 80
4   Ibid.
5   Foulkes, p. 1
6   Ibid., p. 130

7   Graff, p. 3
8   Franko, p. 21
9   Graff, p. 5
10 Ibid., p. 55
11 Ibid., p. 3
12 Beckh, p. 3
13 Ibid., p. 2
14 The National Archives.
15 Federal Theatre Project, p. 1
16 Graff, p. 77
17 Cooper, p. 27
18 Graff, p. 87
19 Guilbaut, p. 18
20 Graff, p. 117
21 Guilbaut, pp. 49–50
22 Ibid., p. 187
23 Garafola, p. 26
24 Carr, p. 598
25 Guilbaut, p. 187
26 Prevots, p. 11
27 Ibid., p. 24
28 Ibid., p. 45
29 Sorell, p. 84
30 Vachon, 2010
31 Limón, 2001, p. vii
32 Limón, 1966, p. 24
33 Owen, p. 3
34 Limón, 2001, p. 6
35 Ibid., p. 8
36 Ibid., p. 15
37 Ibid.
38 Ibid., p. 16
39 Ibid.
40 Humphrey, 1995, p. 93
41 Limón, 2001, p. 19
42 Ibid., p. 20
43 Ibid., p. 28
44 Ibid., p. 33
45 Ibid.
46 King, pp. 29–30
47 Lewis, 1984, p. 19
48 Limón, 2001, p. 56
49 Ibid., p. 57
50 Ibid., p. 81
51 Ibid., p. 87
52 Lewis, 1984, p. 21
53 Siegel, 1985, p. 163
54 Ibid., p. 164
55 Sorell, p. 61
56 Vachon.
57 Lewis, 1984, p. 22
58 Limón, 2001, Spring, pp. 2–3
59 Siegel, 1985, p. 169
60 Sorell, p. 84
61 Vachon
62 Ibid.
63 Lancos, p. 19

64 Ibid., p. 21
65 Ibid., p. 141
66 Limón, 2001, p. 36
67 Vachon
68 Lancos, p. 180
69 Limón, 2001, p. 37
70 Taliaferro
71 Lewis, 1984, p. 35
72 Ibid.
73 Lancos, p. 155
74 Ibid., p. 236
75 Ibid.
76 Lewis, 1984, p. 27
77 Vachon
78 Dalzell
79 Vachon
80 Taliaferro
81 Ibid.
82 Legg, p. 123
83 Taliaferro
84 Ibid.
85 Vachon
86 Legg, p. 125
87 Taliaferro
88 Ibid.
89 Ibid.
90 Vachon
91 Ibid.
92 Celichowska, 2000, p. 1
93 Popkin, p. 4
94 Ibid., p. 5
95 Ibid., p. 6
96 Sorell, p. 216
97 Kriegsman, 1972
98 Celichowska, 2000, p. xvii
99 Brown, p. 8
100 Kriegsman, 1994
101 Celichowska, 2000, p. 6
102 Hawkins, 1966, p. 39
103 Hawkins, 1992, p. 31
104 Hawkins, 1966, p. 41
105 Ibid., p. 43
106 Hawkins, 1992, p. 55
107 Siegel, 1985, p. 317
108 Hawkins, 1992, p. 56
109 Celichowska, 2000, pp. xxv–xxvi
110 Siegel, 1993, p. 183
111 Needham Costonis, p. 298
112 Celichowska, 2000, p. 6
113 Ibid., p. 8
114 Hawkins, 1992, p. 6
115 Ibid., pp. 41–42
116 Celichowska, 2000, p. 9
117 Hawkins, 1992, p. 63
118 Ibid., p. 89
119 Ibid.
120 Ibid., p. 10

121 Celichowska, 2000, p. 143
122 Hawkins, 1992, p. 78
123 Ibid., p. 80
124 New Music Box
125 Celichowska, 2000, pp. 144–145
126 Hawkins, 1992, p. 78-79
127 Celichowska, 2000, p. 147
128 Brown., p. 10
129 Hawkins, 1992, p. 89
130 Ibid., pp. 91–92
131 Diachenko
132 Duke
133 Celichowska, 2009
134 Duke
135 Brown, p. 13
136 Diachenko
137 Brown, pp. 13–14
138 Diachenko
139 Celichowska, 2000, pp. 2–3
140 Matt
141 Celichowska, 2000, p. 17
142 Ibid., pp. 20–21
143 Ibid., p. 21
144 Ibid., pp. 23–77
145 Brown, p. 19
146 Hawkins, 1992, p. 94
147 Ibid.
148 Celichowska, 2000, p. 65
149 Ibid., pp. 69–70
150 Ibid., pp. 74–75
151 Ibid., p. 24
152 Diachenko
153 Celichowska, 2000, p. 55
154 Ibid., pp. 51–52
155 Ibid.
156 Duke
157 Celichowska, 2000, p. xvii
158 Ibid., film
159 Ibid.

Chapter 5: The Avant-garde

1 Foulkes, p. 3
2 Hanna, p. xiii
3 Ibid.
4 Bodley, p. 7
5 Siegel, 1985, p. 305
6 Burt, p. 28
7 Siegel, 1985, p. 307
8 Morris, pp. 34–35
9 Copeland, p. 213
10 Carbonneau
11 DeFrantz, 2001, p. 345
12 Ibid., 2004, p. 28
13 Ibid., 2001, p. 348
14 Brown, C., 1986, p. 23
15 Ibid., p. 19

16 Anderson, pp. 184–185
17 Cunningham, 1999, p. 49
18 Ibid., 1985, p. 33
19 Ibid., p. 34
20 Ibid., p. 37
21 Warren, p. 87
22 Ibid., p. 88
23 Cunningham, 1985, p. 37
24 Ibid., p. 38
25 Hamm, p. 598
26 Swed, p. 132
27 Blofeld, front matter
28 Ibid.
29 Brooks, p. 74
30 Swed, p. 133
31 Hamm, p. 589
32 Mumma, p. 202
33 Sheets Johnstone, p. 1
34 Cunningham, 1985, pp. 39–40
35 Cunningham, 1999, p. 42
36 Hodgins, p. 17
37 Mazo, p. 203
38 Cunningham, 1999, p. 42
39 Ibid., p. 48
40 Jordan, p. 61
41 Mazo, p. 204
42 Brown, C., 1986, p. 24
43 Ibid.
44 Vaughan, p. 311
45 Stratyner
46 Martin, L., p. 46
47 Brown, C., 2007, p. 38
48 Ibid., p. 204
49 Ibid.
50 Anderson, p. 186
51 Copeland, 1999, p. 45
52 Ibid.
53 Ibid., p. 47
54 Brown, C., 2007, p. 39
55 Copeland, 1999, p. 42
56 Ibid., p. 52
57 Ibid.
58 Lubow, pp. 38–43
59 Merce.org/p/dance capsules.php
60 Ibid.
61 Lubow, p. 43
62 Cunningham, 1997, p. 60
63 Legg, 2006, p. 96
64 Cunningham, 1999, p. 46
65 Brown, C., 1987, p. 39
66 Cunningham, 1985, p. 59
67 Brown, C., 1986, p. 23
68 Copeland, 2004, p. 212
69 Cunningham, 1985, p. 60
70 Copeland, 2004, p. 212
71 Cunningham, 1985, p. 60
72 Campbell, p. 10

73 Ibid., p. 13
74 Ibid., p. 27
75 Ibid., p. 31
76 Ibid., p. 16
77 Burns
78 Swinston
79 Ibid.
80 Burns
81 Ibid.
82 Burns
83 Cunningham, 1997, p. 60
84 Siegel, 2007, p. 53
85 Gitelman, 2003, p. ix
86 Sorell, p. 30
87 Ibid., p. 32
88 Ibid.
89 Martin, J., p. 232
90 Ibid., p. 235
91 Nikolais & Louis, p. ix
92 Ibid.
93 Gitelman, 2003, p. xxi
94 Ibid., p. 35
95 Nikolais & Louis, p. xiv
96 Brown, J. M., p. 111
97 Nikolais, 1965, pp. 64–65
98 Lamhut, p. 4
99 Lahusen, pp. 74–75
100 Nickolich, p. 80
101 Gitelman, 2001, pp. 88, 90
102 Nikolais & Louis, p. 11
103 Gibilisco
104 del Saz
105 Nikolais & Louis, p. 1
106 Gitelman, 2007, p. 31
107 del Saz
108 Gibilisco
109 Nikolais & Louis, pp. 9–12
110 del Saz
111 Nikolais & Louis, p. 13
112 Ibid.
113 Ibid.
114 Gitelman, 2007, p. 32
115 Nikolais & Louis, p. 95
116 Nikolais & Louis, pp. 181–190
117 Louis, 1973

Chapter 6: Transition to Postmodernism

1 Macaulay
2 Diamond
3 Siegel, p. 299
4 Denby
5 Taylor, p. 16
6 Ibid., p. 21
7 Ibid., p. 25
8 Ibid., p. 54
9 Kane, p. 92

10 Diamond
11 Ibid.
12 Terry
13 Taylor, p. 76
14 Ibid.
15 Diamond
16 Taylor, p. 77
17 Carbonneau
18 Kane p. 92
19 Sorell, pp. 43–44
20 Diamond
21 Siegel, pp. 334–335
22 Carbonneau
23 Siegel, pp. 334–336
24 Carbonneau
25 Montgomery & Chambers, p. 24
26 Moore
27 Hughes
28 Crisp
29 Croce
30 Diamond
31 Andrien
32 Ibid.

Chapter 7: Post-Judson Training Practices

1 Banes, p. xvii
2 Ibid.
3 Ibid., p. xii
4 Tharp, p. 88
5 Prevots, pp. 101–110
6 Koch, pp. 12–15
7 National Endowment for the Arts, 2011
8 National Endowment for the Arts, 2008, p. 3
9 Dittman, p. 23
10 Erkert, p. 5
11 Chen.
12 Ibid.
12 Bales, p. 157
13 Chen.
14 Ibid.
15 Ibid.
16 Laban/Bartenieff Institute for Movement Studies
17 Bales, pp. 2–3.

Appendix C

1 Eddy, Winter 2002
2 http://www.feldenkrais.com
3 Feldenkrais
4 Klein
5 Pilates & Miller, p. 9

PHOTOGRAPH CREDITS

Photographs ©

Cover photograph by Joshua Legg
Marcus Blechman, Courtesy Dance Horizons: 35, 113
Tom Caravaglia: 173, 179, 192
Tony Cenicola, Courtesy Erick Hawkins Dance: 98, 133, 137, 141
Elizabeth Sprague Coolidege Collection, Music Division, Library of Congress: 26
Dance Horizons: 79
Courtesy of Marie-Christine Dunham-Pratt and the Katherine Dunham Estate: 59, 62, 66
Anna Finke, Courtesy the Merce Cunningham Dance Company: 167
Rick Foster: 181, 216, 225
Daniel Kramer: 125
Photo from Keith Lee's personal collection: 85
Joshua Legg: 32, 42, 43, 45. 46, 69, 70, 72, 87, 91, 208
Constantine. Courtesy of Jacob's Pillow Dance Festival Archives: 50, 80
Robert C. Lopert. Courtesy of Jacob's Pillow Dance Festival Archives: 76
Eric M. Sanford. Courtesy of Jacob's Pillow Dance Festival Archives: 15, 109
Courtesy of Jacob's Pillow Dance Festival Archives: xx, 10
Josiah Kennedy: 88
Courtesy of the José Limón Institute: 115
Tony Miller: 223
New York World-Telegram and the Sun Newspaper Photograph Collection, Library of Congress: 23
Photograph by Myssi Robinson: 243
Richard Rutledge, courtesy the Merce Cunningham Dance Company: 152
William Schipp: 201
Carl Van Vechten. Library of Congress, Prints & Photographs Division, Carl Van Vechten Collection: 197